INEQUALITY
AND VIOLENCE
IN THE UNITED STATES

INEQUALITY AND VIOLENCE IN THE UNITED STATES

Casualties of Capitalism

BARBARA H. CHASIN

HUMANITIES PRESS
NEW JERSEY

First published in 1997 by
Humanities Press International, Inc.
165 First Avenue, Atlantic Highlands, New Jersey 07716

© 1997 by Barbara H. Chasin

Library of Congress Cataloging-in-Publication Data
Chasin, Barbara H.
Inequality and Violence in the United States : casualties of
capitalism / Barbara H. Chasin.
p. cm.
Includes bibliographical references and index.
ISBN 0-391-04046-4 — ISBN 0-391-04047-2 (pbk.)
1. Violence—United States. 2. Equality—United States.
3. Capitalism—United States. 4. United States—Economic policy.
5. United States—Social policy. I. Title.
HN90.V5C48 1997
306.6'0973—dc21   97-7901
                                                            CIP

All rights reserved. No part of this publication may be reproduced
or transmitted, in any form or by any means, without written permission.

Printed in the United States of America

10 9 8 7 6 5 4 3 2 1

To the students:
Their indignation against injustice and
their desire to have a better world
continue to give me hope.

Contents

Preface	ix
Acknowledgments	xi
1 An Epidemic of Violence?	1
2 Inequality in the United States	13
3 Interpersonal Violence: Street Crime	45
4 Interpersonal Violence and Race and Gender	76
5 Structural Violence for Workers and the Unemployed	104
6 Structural Violence Outside the Workplace	124
7 Militarism: The Circle of Violence, Interpersonal and Structural	151
8 Reducing the Casualties	178
Bibliography	193
Index	207

Preface

I first started thinking about the nature of violence at the start of my teaching career in the late 1960s. The violence that was on people's minds then was the war in Vietnam and what came to be called "the war at home." The same military forces that were operating in Vietnam were being called to inner cities, college campuses, and Native American reservations. Attention inside and outside of academia turned to the problem of violence. Many questions were raised as people tried to understand these seemingly disparate events.

As the issues were hotly debated, it became apparent that there were competing conceptions of why there was violence, who was violent, and how violence should be dealt with. There were even different ideas of what violence was.

The most conservative point of view blamed violence, whether in Southeast Asia or the United States, on outside agitators of one kind or another who succeeded in stirring up naive people. Violence was seen as the illegal or immoral behavior of those who did not have a respect for law and for democratic values. A more liberal point of view spoke of the need for social reforms but did not make much of an attempt to connect events at home with those abroad, nor did liberals have satisfactory explanations for the persistence of the injustices that they felt needed addressing.

Scholars with a more radical perspective reexamined the history of the United States to understand better what was happening in the 1960s. They discovered that much of the violence of our past, nationally and internationally, was perpetuated by those who were economically and politically more powerful than their victims.

By drawing parallels between the conditions that produced liberation movements in the Third World and those which fueled protests in the United States, the radical perspective led to an expanded conception of the definition of violence. Important for my own thinking was the insight that systems, as well as individuals, can be violent. Violence can be part of the everyday life of a society, with people suffering and sometimes dying, because they do not have access to the resources needed for a healthy life.

I wanted to help students understand the events of the time, not just as an academic exercise but so that they could make more rational choices about their lives. I first developed a course on the sociology of violence in 1970. Since then I have been trying to deepen my understanding of how class forces in the United States play a major role in perpetuating violence as defined in this book.

Today people are again thinking about violence, but now attention is focused more on violence in the streets. Although the specific examples of violence may have changed, the causes are similar. Mainstream analysts pay little attention to how our social system continues to produce violence. The violence that results from the decisions of the powerful is ignored or minimized while the violence of ordinary people is emphasized. A first step toward reducing violence is to understand what has produced it. I hope this book contributes to that understanding.

Acknowledgments

I would like to acknowledge the support of Montclair State University in granting me a sabbatical in 1994–95 to work on this project and the librarians at Montclair's Sprague Library who did their best to get me needed materials. I would like to thank the people who gave me advice and encouragement on various parts of the manuscript, especially David Dodd, Peter Freund, Jerry Kloby, Jay Livingston, Susan Lowes, and Evelyn Shalom. I would also like to thank the staff at Humanities Press, especially Melanie Hawley, Sheri Kubasek, and Diane Burke. Most of all, I want to express my thanks to Dick Franke, computer expert, advisor, and all-round support system.

1 / An Epidemic of Violence?

St. Mary's Episcopal Church in Harlem celebrates Christmas midnight mass at 7:00 P.M. "People are concerned about their well-being and you never know when you're going to run into someone high on drugs," explained Rev. Robert Castle. In Brooklyn, St. Rita's Catholic Church still has a midnight mass, but the priest encourages the congregation to come in groups, while patrols guard celebrants' cars.[1]

In 1989, Kyle and Kevin Scherzer, Christopher Archer, and Bryant Gorber, friends and high school athletes, sexually assaulted a retarded girl with a broom handle and a baseball bat. Ten other high school football players watched. The defense argued they were just "pranksters," explaining, "Boys will be boys."[2]

Television talk show host Jenny Jones promised twenty-four-year-old Jonathan Schmitz that she would present him with a secret admirer if he would appear on a March 1995 show. She didn't tell him his admirer was a man, Scott Amedure. Three days after the taping, Schmitz shot and killed Amedure. He told the police that the humiliation he had experienced had "eaten away" at him.[3]

In 1989, Patrick E. Purdy, wearing army fatigues and armed with an AK47 assault rifle, walked into a Stockton, California, schoolyard and began firing. When he stopped, five children, ages six to nine, were dead, and twenty-nine other children and adults were injured. Purdy then committed suicide. The student body was mostly Southeast Asian, and after an investigation, the state attorney general concluded that the attack had resulted from Purdy's "festering sense of racial resentment and hatred."[4]

On 7 December 1993, evening rush-hour passengers on the Long Island Railroad—reading, daydreaming, dozing—suddenly heard gunshots from Colin Ferguson's 9mm handgun. Seventeen people were injured and six died. In his weekly radio address, President Clinton described these shootings as "part of the epidemic of violence that has left Americans insecure on our streets, in our schools, even in our homes."[5]

Public officials are increasingly identifying violence as a threat to the quality of life in the United States. The director of the federal government's Centers for Disease Control and Prevention (CDC), David Satcher, said, "Violence is the leading cause of lost life in this country today. If it's not a public health problem why are all those people dying from it?"[6] The CDC's National Center for Injury Prevention and Control under the direction of Dr. Mark Rosenberg is taking responsibility both for analyzing the causes of interpersonal violence and for suggesting policies to combat this.[7]

In response to the violence in this country, the CDC and two other federal agencies, The National Science Foundation and The National Institute of Justice, sponsored a project, carried out by the National Research Council, on understanding and controlling violent behavior. The authors of the study stated that "the nation's anxiety on the subject of violence is not unfounded":

> In cities, suburban areas, and even small towns, Americans are fearful and concerned that violence has permeated the fabric and degraded the quality of their lives. The diminished quality of life ranges from an inability to sit on the front porch in neighborhoods where gang warfare has made gunfire a common event to the installation of elaborate security systems in suburban homes where back doors once were left open. Children in urban schools experience violence on the way to school and in the school building itself. Surveys show that large percentages of the population fear even walking in their neighborhoods at nights.[8]

Professional organizations are also calling attention to the seriousness of violence in this country. The authors of a special report for the American Sociological Association begin by saying, "American society is engulfed in a world of violence." In their view,

> The pervasiveness of violence, its spiraling negative impacts, and the emergence of what appears to be an ingrained pattern of violence are all manifestations of a crisis at the most fundamental levels of our social order.... No aspect of social life, whether in households, schools, health care facilities, recreation centers, workplaces, or businesses, and no geographic location, whether neighborhoods, cities, suburbs, or rural areas, are immune to violence.[9]

In very similar words, Phil B. Fontanarosa, the senior editor of the *Journal of the American Medical Association*, wrote of the "pervasiveness of violence in US society and the potential vulnerability of all US citizens to acts of violence." The American Psychological Association created a special Commission on Violence and Youth.[10]

THE LESS PUBLICIZED EPIDEMIC

The alarm is being sounded about interpersonal violence, but to appreciate how dangerous life in the United States is more fully, we need to have a broader conception. We will, therefore, look at some additional examples. These examples are not part of the usual conception of violence, but they do fit the definition of violence we will give below.

In March 1994, a man hunting for bricks in an abandoned New York City building was crushed to death when the structure collapsed. According to officials, scavenging for bricks in poor neighborhoods is a common practice. Companies are able to sell the bricks for twenty-five to thirty cents each to builders who want them for city fireplaces and suburban patios. In this case, a construction company had been paying the scavengers fifteen cents a brick.[11]

Between 1991 and 1992, three workers were crushed to death by improperly locked machines at the Stone Container paper mill in Louisiana. The same company operates a facility in Montana where a boiler explosion in 1991 killed one employee and injured two others. The company was fined $56,075 for the three Louisiana fatalities. Stone Container also released over 23 million pounds of toxic chemicals into the environment in 1989.[12]

In June 1994, as temperatures soared to over 90 degrees, children in East Harlem opened a fire hydrant to cool off. A truck ran over a three-year-old girl, who was pushed in its path by the hydrant's powerful stream. Rick Bragg, a *New York Times* reporter, pointed out that the little girl "was not the first person to be killed because of a hydrant," which discharges about *1,000 gallons of water a minute*. Bragg noted that many "hydrants are in neighborhoods where children have little access to decent parks or pools."[13]

The weather can be life-threatening to lower-income elderly persons. A July 1996 heat wave killed twenty people in Texas and Oklahoma. Dr. James Farris, director of the Dallas County Health Department, explained that "many elderly are reluctant to use air-conditioning because it drives up their utility bills and they're unable to make the payments." The previous year, at least 466 people died in a Chicago heat wave, 80 percent of them were living in lower income neighborhoods, 74 percent were 60 or over.[14]

People die from the cold as well as from the heat. In one week in January 1988, with temperatures falling below 5 degrees, at least three homeless people perished in New York City.[15] This was not the first winter that the cold had killed people. In 1988, the CDC reported that 1,010 deaths from exposure occurred. This was a 137 percent increase since 1976. Doctors at the Center attributed this increase to a rise in homelessness.[16]

Defining Violence

A useful definition of violence needs to include all the examples given above. If babies are murdered, we are horrified, and we want the killer caught and punished. But what if babies are dying from a lack of medical attention? The result in either case is the same: dead infants. People die as a result of shootings connected with the illegal narcotics traffic. But what of the approximately four hundred thousand people who die each year from the effects of tobacco, a currently legal commodity? In either case, death is the result of selling dangerous commodities.

In this book, we will use a definition of violence that focuses our attention on the basic forces that make our lives less healthy and more dangerous: *Violence refers to acts, intentional or not, that result in physical harm to another person or persons.*[17]

There are two major types of violence: interpersonal and structural. Interpersonal violence is what many experts and most of us mean when we use the word—identifiable persons injure others and are usually aware that they have done so. Structural violence, on the other hand, is a consequence of the routine workings of a society, especially of its stratification system. Structural violence occurs when peoples' lives are made demonstrably worse by their lack of access to resources. If identifiable groups are suffering physically from conditions that could be changed given the existing state of knowledge, while other groups are not, then there is structural violence.[18] One way we learn that a condition is not inevitable is to make comparisons between groups in the same country. We will do this below and in later chapters.

Victims of structural violence do not see and generally are unaware of those responsible for their injuries, while those responsible rarely see the suffering their actions have caused. No one pushed the building down on the man who was trying to earn some cash collecting bricks. But why was he doing such dangerous work? Why can a company operate when its employees are dying because of their working conditions? Why didn't the little girl, who was run over in East Harlem have a safer place to play? Why do some people live healthier, less dangerous lives than others?

Interpersonal violence occurs most often among people of the same economic group and often between members of the same community or household. Structural violence, on the other hand, is a direct or indirect result of decisions made at the elite level of society—those who suffer are from less privileged groups. Mainstream media and politicians regularly focus attention on interpersonal violence; they do not analyze structural violence or make the connections that would enable us to understand the forces that are leading to a less healthy and safe life for many people in this country.

There are several reasons to broaden our conception of violence to include structural violence.

1. Structural violence accounts for more deaths and injuries each year than interpersonal violence.
2. We need to understand structural violence to gain a fuller understanding of the dangers that many people in our society face.
3. We need to analyze structural violence to overcome stereotypes about who are the violent people in our society.
4. We need to understand the nature and causes of structural violence to learn what we have to do to create a more humane and less violent society.

How Violent is the United States?

There seems to be a sense that life is more dangerous than it used to be. Susan Shepherd, aged thirty-seven, from Salt Lake City, Utah, remembers as a child, "playing in the neighborhood at night and sleeping out in the backyard. I don't think you can do that anymore." Jeff Carr, who is only twenty-six, remarked, "I never used to worry about gangs or violence.... Now I'm aware of it all the time."[19] Their sense that the level of violence has increased in this country is shared by many other Americans. Pollsters have been asking people if there are places in their neighborhoods where they would be afraid to walk at night. In 1967, 31 percent of the respondents said yes; but since 1973, between 40 and 47 percent have been answering affirmatively.[20]

Fearful they may be victims of interpersonal violence, people adjust their behaviors. If they can afford it, some move to walled communities, with gates and security guards. The manager of Canyon Lake, a private community in southern California, noted, "It's too bad we need gates to protect ourselves from each other but on the other hand, it's really nice to know that you can go for a walk at night and not get hurt."[21] Others seek protection by arming themselves, forming neighborhood watch organizations, and being careful about where they go. Some of the elderly who have died in heat waves were afraid to keep their windows open, worried that an intruder would enter and harm them.

Does this mean that life in the United States is more dangerous than it was thirty or forty years ago? Yes, but the major increase has not occurred recently. On this point, homicide rates are the most reliable indicators: almost all homicides are known to the police, and they are also the only type of violence for which there are easily comparable data over a long period of time. Homicides are also the most dramatic type of violence—one that media and political figures focus on.

Table 1.1 lists homicide rates at selected points in the last thirty years.

Table 1.1 Homicide Rate, per 100,000, Selected Years, 1960–93

Year	Rate
1960	5
1965	5
1970	8
1980	10
1984	8
1990	10
1993	11
1994	10

Sources: 1960–90, U.S. Department of Justice, *SourceBook of Criminal Justice Statistics—1994*, Table 3.94, p. 305; 1993, 1994, "Murder Rate Fell in 1994 for 3rd Consecutive Year Agency Says," *New York Times*, 10 October 1995, p. A19.

Not all segments of the population are at equal risk of becoming a murder victim. Homicide rates have especially increased among teenagers. Between 1985 and 1991, homicide deaths among males aged fifteen to nineteen increased by 154 percent, but for adults the rate is actually declining.[22] In addition, some segments within the population are in greater danger from criminal violence than others, that is, African-Americans, males, and those living in urban areas. Combinations of these characteristics affect the likelihood of being a violent crime victim.

THE UNITED STATES IS MORE VIOLENT THAN OTHER COUNTRIES

The United States is a more dangerous place to live than any other advanced capitalist country, whether we look at interpersonal criminal violence or structural violence. Comparative data for criminal violence are presented in Table 1.2.

As the table shows, the United States has more murders and rapes than countries at a similar level of economic development, as well as the highest rate of imprisonment, which suggests that there is also a higher incidence of many other crimes.

As shown in Table 1.3, the United States also has higher rates of structural violence in the form of pollution, auto accidents, and illnesses than the ten richest capitalist nations.

For the six indicators in Table 1.3, the United States has the worst rates on four and is close to the worst on the other two.

Table 1.2 Comparisons of Interpersonal Violence in Advanced Capitalist Nations

NATION	PER CAPITA GNP[a]	HOMICIDE RATE[b]	REPORTED RAPES[c]	IMPRISONMENT RATE[d]
1. Switzerland	$36,080	1	23	54
2. Japan	$28,190	1	18	NA
3. Sweden	$27,010	2	43	NA
4. Denmark	$26,000	1	35	47
5. Norway	$25,820	2	20	NA
6. United States	$23,240	12	118	426
7. Germany	$23,030	1	26	77
8. Austria	$22,280	1	17	87
9. France	$22,260	1	17	40
10. Finland	$21,970	4	19	75
11. Canada	$20,710	3	23	94
United States Ranking	6	1	1	1

Notes: NA = data not available. Per capita GNP (gross national product) is the total value of goods and services produced in a given country in a year, divided by the population of that country. It is an often used measure of the relative economic standing of a nation. Data are for 1992.
[a] I have placed Canada where Belgium would be in the ranking, so that a comparison can be made between the United States and the only other industrially advanced country in North America. Excluding Belgium does not affect the U.S. ranking on any indicator. Canada is actually twelfth in per capita GNP ranking.
[b] Homicide committed by men, per 100,000 population, 1985–90. Dates are the range of years used in collecting the data. The U.S. rate here is higher than in the U.S. government sources cited in Table 1.1.[23]
[c] Per 100,000 women aged fifteen–fifty-nine, for 1987–89.[24]
[d] Prisoners per 100,000 people, for 1980–86.

Sources: [a] The World Bank, *World Development Report, 1994*, Table 1, p. 163; [b,c,d] United Nations Development Program (UNDP), *Human Development Report, 1994*, Table 29, p. 186.

PERSPECTIVES ON VIOLENCE

As with any social problem, our analysis of violence will be closely connected to how we think this problem can be solved. Should we focus on the individual, the family, the larger social structure? The approach we take will have political implications. What is it that needs to be changed? Do we make our streets safer by locking up criminals for longer periods of time or by having a policy that provides decent paying jobs to people so they can support their households? Or is some combination best?

We might not like the political implications of a theory, but the issue must be what are the facts, that is, the scientific evidence for or against a particular view. Being scientific means observing relationships and developing explanations to account for these, being able to explain counterexamples, and demonstrating the linkages between alleged causes and presumed effects.

Table 1.3 Indicators of Structural Violence in the Richest Capitalist Countries

	Infant Mortality Rate[a]	AIDS Rate[b]	Road Accident Rate[c]	Pesticide Consumption Rate[d]	Sulfur and Nitrogen Emissions[e]	Hazardous Waste Production[f]
1. Switzerland	6	7.0	436	0.4	39	13.0
2. Japan	5	0.2	640	1.0	NA	1.8
3. Sweden	5	1.0	263	0.2	61	1.2
4. Denmark	7	4.0	207	1.0	100	2.5
5. Norway	6	1.0	280	0.3	68	0.7
6. United States	9	20.0	1,398	2.0	160	19.6
7. Germany	6	2.0	660	0.4	60	17.2
8. Austria	7	2.0	786	1.0	NA	7.4
9. France	7	7.0	361	2.0	56	7.2
10. Finland	6	0.5	256	0.3	115	1.0
11. Canada	7	3.0	988	1.0	209	0.7
United States Ranking	1	1	1	1	2	1

Notes:
[a] The infant mortality rate is the number of infants per 1,000 who die before reaching their first birthday, 1992.
[b] Cases per 100,000 people, 1992.
[c] Injuries from road accidents per 100,000 people, 1990–91. The figure for the United States is from 1985.
[d] Metric tons per 1,000 people, 1985–91. The United States is tied with France for highest rate here.
[e] Kilograms of these gases per capita, 1989.
[f] Metric tons per square kilometer, 1987.

Sources: [a] The World Bank, *World Development Report, 1994*, Table 27, p. 214. [b,c,d,e,f] United Nations Development Program, *Human Development Report, 1994*, Table 35, p. 191; Table 29, p. 185; Table 48, p. 204.

For example, will we be able to show unemployment is correlated with crime and give plausible reasons why this is the case? Being rational is our best intellectual resource in developing solutions to our problems.

The causes of violence are usually discussed in one of three ways, from the least sociological to the most.

IT IS HUMAN NATURE TO BE VIOLENT: BIOLOGICAL DETERMINISM

The biological approach tries to find some aspect of our physical makeup that can explain why violence occurs. In the words of anthropologists Lionel Tiger and Robin Fox, "We are a naturally aggressive species easily aroused to violence."[25] According to this view, we have evolved in such a way that violence, for males at least, is a readily available response, not something that is learned. Female violence is not discussed by biological determinists.

Since the 1970s, biological determinism has taken the form of *sociobiology*, stressing the role of genes in human conduct. This approach would reduce most social science to a branch of biology.[26]

Our biological makeup obviously influences our behavior. We are a particular type of animal, and, in a general way, this explains some things about us: our sociability, our capacity for learning, our ability to have a language that is different from that of any other animal. Biology, however, cannot explain how we will treat each other. The range of human behavior is too wide to be explained by hormones or genes. We are all members of a single species, but some groups are very violent, and some are very peaceful. A common genetic heritage cannot explain diversity of behavior. Biological determinism cannot account for structural violence where there is no direct confrontation between the people involved.

To lessen violence, as this approach implies and some of its proponents explicitly state, we need to control those who are biologically disposed to violence. We do not need to change social conditions. The determinists, furthermore, are only interested in controlling the violence of ordinary people; the violence caused by elite behavior is ignored.

IT IS THE FAMILY'S FAULT: THE CULTURE OF POVERTY APPROACH

A second perspective is the culture of poverty approach, which also ignores structural violence. This viewpoint emphasizes finding some characteristics of a group that purportedly explain why its members engage in violence. It is often used to explain why African-American communities have higher rates of violence, seeing the roots of this in the large percentage of female-headed, single-parent households.

This approach, although acknowledging the role of some social variables, is too narrow in its scope. The implication of this view is that changes need to occur in relatively small areas of society, but we need not look at the larger social structure. This theory fails to recognize that families and communities are strongly influenced by outside political and economic forces.

VIOLENCE RESULTS FROM INEQUALITY: THE STRUCTURAL APPROACH

The structural approach to violence, taken throughout this book, stresses the ways in which the distribution of wealth and power influence behavior. It attempts to explain *both* interpersonal and structural violence by looking at the way decisions are made and social resources used, and it considers the impact these decisions have on communities and individuals. This approach further maintains that to understand violence it is necessary to look at patterns of inequality.

This perspective is supported, in part, by data from anthropology. The most egalitarian societies are bands of hunters and gatherers. Hunters and gatherers generally have low levels of violence internally and between themselves and other societies. Because we had this kind of society for most of our thousands of years as a species, the cross-cultural data show we are not inherently violent animals, though we are certainly capable of violence. Anthropologist Leslie R. Sponsel explains:

> Human nature may be seen as inherently violent if looked at from a perspective limited mostly to Western societies in recent history. However, this is not necessarily the conclusion if human nature is viewed through the anthropological lens, which brings breadth and diversity of perspective.... Cross-cultural studies reveal that relatively nonviolent and peaceful societies exist like the Inuit, Hutterites, Mbuti, San, and Semai among others.[27]

According to the structural approach, violence can best be explained by looking at the way social resources are used and decisions are made; it considers the impact these decisions have on individuals and their communities.

As we saw from Tables 1.2 and 1.3, the United States has higher levels of certain kinds of interpersonal violence and structural violence than societies at comparable economic levels. We also have higher levels of inequality as measured by the share of the national income received by those at the top of the income ladder compared with those at the bottom. The poorest 40 percent of the U.S. population receives only 16 percent of the national income, which is less than the bottom 40 percent in nine other wealthy capitalist countries.[28]

HOW ARE INEQUALITY AND VIOLENCE RELATED?

In following chapters, we shall show that inequality is associated with violence in a number of ways:

1. Inequality leads to structural violence by denying part of the population the needed resources for a healthy life and environment.
2. Interpersonal violence may become a way in which the less privileged react to their situation, for instance, by engaging in street crime; or, they may direct their anger at an unjust social order against scapegoats, the weaker and more vulnerable members of society.
3. Violence, especially repressive violence, is used to maintain inequality, for example, quelling public protest. This repression is another form of interpersonal violence.

The next chapter will examine in more detail the three major types of inequality in the United States: class, race, and gender.

Notes

1. Quoted in David Gonzalez, "Midnight Mass Comes Early as Urban Fear Battles Faith," *New York Times*, 24 December 1993, pp. A1, B12.
2. Quoted in Robert Lipsyte, "Must Boys Always Be Boys?" *New York Times*, 12 March 1993, p. B7.
3. Quoted in Janice Kaplan, "Are Talk Shows Out of Control?" *TV Guide*, 1 April 1995, p. 10.
4. Howard J. Ehrlich, "Reporting Ethnoviolence," *Z Magazine* (June 1994), p. 57.
5. Quoted in "Clinton Cites L.I.R.R. Shootings," *New York Times*, 12 December 1993, p. 57.
6. Quoted in Peter Applebome, "C.D.C's New Chief Worries as Much about Bullets as about Bacteria," *New York Times*, 26 September 1993, Section 4.
7. Mark L. Rosenberg, "Violence Is a Public Health Problem," in *UnNatural Causes: The Three Leading Killer Diseases in America*, ed. Russell C. Maulitz (New Brunswick, N.J.: Rutgers University Press, 1988), pp. 147–68.
8. Albert J. Reiss, and Jeffrey A. Roth, *Understanding and Preventing Violence* (Washington, D.C.: National Academy Press, 1993), p. 1.
9. Felice J. Levine, and Katherine J. Rosich, *Social Causes of Violence: Crafting a Science Agenda* (Washington, D.C.: American Sociological Association, 1996), pp. 1–2.
10. "The Unrelenting Epidemic of Violence in America," *JAMA* 273, no. 22 (14 June 1995), pp. 1792–93; American Psychological Association, *Violence & Youth: Psychology's Response* (Washington, D.C.: American Psychological Association, 1993).
11. Ronald Sullivan, "Brick Scavenger Is Killed When a Wall Collapses," *New York Times*, 18 March 1994, p. B3. The man is not named nor are other details of his life given in this account.
12. Russell Mokhiber, Julie Gozan, and Holley Knaus, "The Corporate Rap Sheet: The 10 Worst Corporations of 1992," *Multinational Monitor* (December 1992), p. 15.
13. Rick Bragg, "Three Killed in a Day Spent Escaping Record Heat," *New York Times*, 20 June 1994, pp. B1, B3; N. R. Kleinfield, "The Beach on the Street," *New York Times*, 24 August 1994, pp. B1, B3.
14. Farris quoted in "8 Day Heat Wave Claims 20 Victims in Texas and Oklahoma," *New York Times*, 14 July 1996, p. 24; Chicago figures from Debbie Howlett, "Heat victims' profile: Old, poor," *USA Today*, 24 July 1995, p. 3A.
15. Mark A. Uhlig, "At Least 6 Freeze to Death in Cold Snap, Officials Say," *New York Times*, 16 January 1988, pp. 29, 30.
16. "Deaths from Cold Soar as Homeless Increase," *New York Times*, 25 December 1988, p. 26.
17. Psychological violence also damages people's lives, but the complexities of defining, measuring, and analyzing that kind of violence are beyond the scope of this book.
18. Somewhat similar conceptions are found in Jamil Salmi, *Violence and Democratic Society: New Approaches to Human Rights* (Atlantic Highlands, N.J.: Zed Books, 1993), p. 19; David Leviton, ed., *Horrendous Death: Health and Well-Being* (New York: Hemisphere Publishing, 1991), p. xvii. Salmi speaks of "mediating violence" and Leviton of "horrendous death." John Galtung uses the term "structural violence" but in a somewhat different way in *The True Worlds* (New York: The Free Press, 1980), pp. 67–68.

19. Quoted in Isabel Wilkerson, "After 2 Weeks of Mayhem, The Nation Is Asking Why," *New York Times*, 14 December 1991, p. B7.
20. Jay Livingston, *Crime and Criminology* (Englewood Cliffs, N.J.: Prentice-Hall, 1992), p. 14; U.S. Department of Justice, *SourceBook of Criminal Justice Statistics—1994*, Table 2.34, pp. 168–69.
21. Quoted in Timothy Egan, "Many Seek Security in Private Communities," *New York Times*, 3 September 1995, pp. 1, 22.
22. Fox Butterfield, "Teen-Age Homicide Rate Has Soared," *New York Times*, 14 October 1994, p. A10; Butterfield, "Many Cities in U.S. Show Sharp Drops in Homicide Rates," *New York Times*, 13 August 1995, pp. 1, 18.
23. Even if we use the lowest rate for any year between 1985 and 1990, the U.S. rate remains the highest of all the countries listed.
24. Rape statistics are underreported in the United States and very likely in other countries as well. It is unlikely, however, that the relative differences between countries would be substantially altered if all countries had equally complete reporting of rapes.
25. Lionel Tiger, and Robin Fox, *The Imperial Animal* (New York: Delta, 1971), p. 220; Fox's latest formulation is found in *The Challenge of Anthropology: Old Encounters and New Excursions* (New Brunswick, N.J.: Transaction Publishers, 1994). Although this quote is from anthropologists, it is not at all typical of most anthropological thinking on violence.
26. See, for example, Edward O. Wilson, *Sociobiology: The New Synthesis* (Cambridge: Harvard University Press), pp. 547–75.
27. Leslie E. Sponsel, "The Mutual Relevance of Anthropology and Peace Studies," in *The Anthropology of Peace and Nonviolence*, eds. Leslie E. Sponsel and Thomas Gregor (Boulder, Colo.: Lynne Rienner, 1994), pp. 7–8. The Inuit are more commonly known as the Eskimos, whereas the Mbuti are Central African pygmies and the San, in Southern Africa, are often called Bushmen.
28. The World Bank, *World Development Report, 1994*, Table 30, p. 221.

2 / Inequality in the United States

Class, racial/ethnic, and gender inequality are the three major types of inequality we shall be discussing, and they are intertwined. American ideology emphasizes that individuals are each responsible for their own fate. In reality, however, a person is born into a family that has a given income level, and we do not choose either our gender or our ethnic heritage. Yet each of these factors has a profound impact on the opportunities available to us, our susceptibility to violence, and the quality of our lives.

CLASS INEQUALITY IN THE UNITED STATES

Inequalities in economic status are the most important type of inequality in society, affecting virtually every aspect of life. It is probably clear to readers of this book that there are differences in income, material possessions, in who has power, and in the ability to make important decisions. We shall use the term *class* to describe groups of people who have a similar relationship to the economic resources of society and who, because of that, share a similar lifestyle.

Economic resources come in two forms, income and wealth. Income means payments received regularly, such as wages, social security, welfare, and so on. Wealth refers to assets possessed, that is, what you own that can be bought and sold. Stocks, bonds, and real estate would be important forms of wealth in a capitalist society. Wealth produces income in the form of dividends, interest, and rents. The higher your income, the more wealth you can accumulate; the more wealth you have, the higher your income is likely to be. Households differ in their amount of income but even more dramatically in their wealth.

For most people, occupation is the principle determinant of income. Sociologists often use the occupation of the chief earner in the household to

Table 2.1 Class Composition of the United States

CLASS	TYPICAL OCCUPATIONS	PERCENT OF HOUSEHOLDS	TYPICAL INCOMES
Capitalist	Top-level executives	1%	$750,000 and up
Upper–middle	Professionals Managers Owners of medium-sized businesses	14%	$70,000 to $200,000
Middle and working	Lower-level professionals; white collar, craft, and semiskilled workers; small business owners	60%	$25,000 to $40,000
Working poor and underclass	Laborers Service workers	25%	$13,000 and lower

Sources: Based on Dennis Gilbert, and Joseph A. Kahl, *The American Class Structure: A New Synthesis*, 4th ed. (Belmont, Calif.: Wadsworth, 1993), p. 311; and Stephen J. Rose, *Social Stratification in the United States: The American Profile Poster* (New York: New Books, 1992).

assign that household a position in the class structure. Occupations are the sources not only of earners' incomes but also of their position in the economic authority structure, a measure of their power; and occupations are the sources of prestige or social esteem, which is also unequally distributed in class societies. People may have similar incomes, but the conditions under which they work and the esteem they receive may be different. A well-paid factory worker and an assistant professor at a university, for example, might have similar yearly incomes, but the professor will have much more autonomy and control over her/his daily work life, more prestige, and, most likely, greater job satisfaction.

Using the source of income and authority position, we can identify the classes shown in Table 2.1.

The capitalist class owns the economic resources in the form of stocks, bonds, and real estate. Many executives are capitalists but not all capitalists are executives: it is the ownership, not management, of the means of production that puts a family or individual in this class. Over 80 percent of the population is in the bottom two categories—middle/working and working poor/underclass. Even the 14 percent in the upper middle class depends on wages. Differences in wages and lifestyles can mask the fact that most of us rely on paychecks to support ourselves and our households. The exception is the very small capitalist class, which has a large amount of wealth as well as income. Table 2.2 shows the unequal distribution of assets.

If you have enough assets, you can be rich without working. On the other hand, if you do work, you may be in any of the other classes, including the poorest. According to a 1994 census report, since 1981 there has

Table 2.2 Ownership of Wealth by Households

	STOCKS	BONDS	REAL ESTATE (EXCLUDING OWN RESIDENCE)
Top 10%	81%	88%	82%
Other 90%	19%	12%	18%

Source: Adapted from *Global Exchanges* 27 (Summer 1996), special insert, "Globalization and the Downsizing of the American Dream," p. 3.

been a 50 percent increase in the percent of Americans who, in spite of working full time year round, are making less than a poverty level wage.[1]

The working poor have the least job security. When they lose their jobs, they often become part of what is now sometimes termed the underclass.[2] The term has become controversial, because it is sometimes used to refer mainly to blacks, with the implication that their problems are a result of a unique pathology.[3] There is a need, however, for a word that refers to the people Karl Marx called the *lumpenproletariat*, those whose work lives are very insecure in comparison to other workers.

The underclass are people whose connection to the labor force is the most tenuous of all. Their work, if they have any, is sporadic, temporary. They may be paid off the books and usually receive no benefits. Government transfer payments are an important part of their household resources. Used in this way, the term points to our need to understand what puts African-Americans disproportionately into this category, while recognizing that whites can also be members of the underclass. There is no need to assume that the underclass is created by personal flaws or community pathologies or that only persons of color can be in this class.

MORE CLASS INEQUALITY

Since the 1970s, those at the top have increased their share of the national income and their ownership of assets. This trend toward greater inequality was accelerated during the 1980s when Ronald Reagan acted like a reverse Robin Hood. As a union tune put it, "Take it from the needy and give it to the greedy. That's what Ronald Reagan says." Of course, no president makes policies on his own; the rest of Reagan's administration and Congress were his merry men (mostly), creating and enacting the legislation that allowed inequality to increase.

One way to get a picture of this increase in economic inequality is to divide the population into income fifths or quintiles and to examine what percent of the national income each fifth is receiving. If there were complete equality, each 20 percent of the population would be receiving 20

Table 2.3 Money Income of Families, by Quintile and Richest 5%

	1973	1980	1992	1993
Top 5%	16%	15%	18%	19%
Highest fifth	41%	42%	45%	46%
Fourth fifth	24%	24%	24%	24%
Middle fifth	18%	18%	17%	16%
Second fifth	12%	12%	11%	10%
Bottom fifth	5%	5%	4%	4%

Sources: For 1973, Jerry Kloby, "Increasing Class Polarization in the United States: The Growth of Wealth and Income Inequality," in *Critical Perspectives in Sociology*, ed. Berch Berberoglu, pp. 39–53 (Dubuque, Iowa: Kendell/Hunt Publishing Co.). For 1980 and 1992, U.S. Bureau of the Census, *Statistical Abstract of the United States, 1994*, Table 716, p. 470. For 1993, U.S. Bureau of the Census, *Statistical Abstract of the United States, 1995*, Table 733, p. 475.

percent of the national income, and ranking could not occur. There are also data that tell us what share the top 5 percent has. Table 2.3 gives us this information.

Most working people have seen a real decline in their wages, that is, prices have risen faster than the average paychecks. The wages of those at the top, however, have been increasing, and wages are not their only source of compensation. From 1947 to 1973, many wage earners experienced a real increase in their earnings, about 2 percent each year.[4] This trend has been reversed. Between the early 1970s and the 1990s, real wages fell by a total of about 19 percent.[5]

Wealth inequality also increased since the 1970s. According to a study done for the Twentieth Century Fund,

> The rise in wealth inequality from 1983 to 1989 (a period for which there is comparable detailed household survey information) is particularly striking. The share of the top 1 percent of wealth holders rose by 5 percentage points. The wealth of the bottom 40 percent showed an absolute decline.[6]

EXECUTIVES DO BETTER THAN EVER

Executives are one of the very few groups that have seen substantial increases between 1970 and 1990. In 1976, a CEO's compensation was about 35 times the pay of an average worker; twenty years later, it was nearly 190 times greater.[7] Of seven major industrialized countries, the United States has the greatest disparity between the compensation of production workers and executives' salaries, as the data from 1989 indicate (see Table 2.4).

The executives who head the Fortune 500 companies average, in salary

Table 2.4 Ratio of Executive to Production Worker Pay for Selected Capitalist Countries

Germany	6.5:1
Italy	7.6:1
France	8.9:1
Canada	9.5:1
Japan	11.6:1
United Kingdom	12.4:1
United States	17.5:1

Source: "the short run [sic]," *Dollars and Sense* (September/October 1994), p. 4.

alone, $1.4 million a year.[8] This works out to $26,923.08 a week, or, on the basis of a forty-hour work week, $673.07 an hour. For nonexecutives, the average hourly wage in early 1994 was $11.12.

Below are the yearly wages, and their monthly and hourly equivalents, for some Fortune 500 CEOs. (Hourly based on a forty-hour week).[9]

Cigna, Wilson H. Taylor, $1,039,000 = $19,980.77 a week = $499.52 an hour.

Johnson & Johnson, Ralph S. Larsen, $1,741,000 = $33,480.77 a week = $837.01 an hour.

Merck, P. Roy Vagelos, $2,525,000 = $48,557.69 a week = $1,213.94 an hour.

Pepsico, Wayne Calloway, $2,369,000 = $45,557.69 a week = $1,138.94 an hour.

Pfizer, William C. Steere Jr., $1,500,000 = $28,846.15 a week = $721.15 an hour.

Philip Morris, Michael A. Miles, $1,850,000 = $35,576.92 a week = $889.42 an hour

UNION MEMBERSHIP DECLINES; TAXES RISE FOR WORKING PEOPLE

The rise in economic inequality reflects another kind of inequality, that of power, the ability to make decisions that affect people's living conditions, actions, and beliefs. In a capitalist society, where employers control the economic resources and decide how these shall be used, workers need strong organizations to protect them. Part of the explanation for the increase in inequality is the decline in union membership. With a decreasing proportion of the workforce in unions, workers are weaker relative to their employers, especially as unemployment has increased.[10] In 1989, total compensation—wages, insurance, pensions—for all unionized workers was about 34 percent higher than for their nonunionized counterparts; for blue collar workers, it was 68 percent higher.[11]

Table 2.5 demonstrates the decline in union membership.

Table 2.5 Percent of Labor Force Who Are Union Members

1946	1960	1970	1980	1983	1994
36%	24%	23%	23%	20%	16%

Sources: For 1946, Murray Chass, "As Trade Unions Struggle, Their Sports Cousins Thrive," *New York Times*, 5 September 1994, p. 1; 1960, 1970, U.S. Bureau of the Census, *Statistical Abstract of the United States, 1980*, Table 714, p. 429; 1980, *Statistical Abstract of the United States, 1987*, Table 692, p. 408; 1983, 1994, *Statistical Abstract of the United States, 1995*, Table 695, p. 443.

One reason for this decline is that many of the jobs held by blue collar union members have been moved overseas, a result of corporate relocation of manufacturing. One example will illustrate the point. Thousands of jobs in the garment trades have been transferred to low-wage countries such as South Korea and Taiwan. Between 1970 and 1990, this industry lost 335,000 jobs in the United States.[12] Concomitantly, membership in the principle organizations that represented these workers, the International Ladies Garment Workers' Union and the American Clothing and Textile Workers' Union, has gone from having 967,000 members in 1972 to 276,000 in 1993, more than a two-thirds decline.[13]

Taxation policies also influence the distribution of income. Since the late 1970s, and especially during the Reagan years, the richest 1 percent of the population greatly benefited from changes in the tax laws. Corporations have used their considerable resources to make certain there are lots of favorable loopholes in the tax laws.[14] Although corporate profits rose from 1980–86, taxes on these profits fell.[15] In 1945, corporations provided 50 percent of federal tax revenues; by 1980, they provided 13 percent and by 1994, only 8 percent.[16] One result is that less money is available for social programs, which, in turn, affects the amount of violence in the United States, as we shall show throughout this book.

Some Are More Unequal Than Others

ETHNIC AND RACIAL INEQUALITY

In the United States, people are still treated differently based on their "race" or ethnicity. Although their social significance is great, the physical differences used to group people into "races" are, in fact, superficial. Furthermore, these differences are also so overlapping that clear categorization is impossible. Ethnicity refers to groups with common ancestries and does not carry the same connotations of biological differences. Popular perception and government statistical tables use both the concepts of race and of

Table 2.6 Percent of Occupation
African-American—1983, 1994

	1983	1994
Percent of Labor Force	9%	10%
Managerial/professional	6	7
Natural scientists	3	4
Architects	2	1
Engineers	3	4
Lawyers/judges	3	3
Doctors	3	4
Dentists	2	4
Nurses	7	9
Dental hygienists	2	1
College teachers	4	5
Elementary school teachers	11	10
Social workers	18	24
Athletes	9	11
Sales occupations	5	7
Office machine operators	16	17
Bank tellers	8	10
Craft jobs	7	18
Firefighters	7	9
Police/detectives	16	18
Kitchen work/food preparation	14	10
Janitors and building cleaners	23	21

Source: U.S. Bureau of the Census, *Statistical Abstract of the United States, 1995*, Table 649, p. 411.

ethnicity, therefore, we will use both terms here.

Polls conducted to determine people's perceptions of racial inequality show a consistent result: most whites think racial discrimination has been largely overcome, whereas most African-Americans believe it persists. Can we tell which answer is more accurate? There have been significant changes since the 1950s and the days of legal segregation. Antidiscrimination laws have been passed and to some extent enforced. African-Americans are more visibly present in the media and in certain occupations, as bank tellers, clerks, and so on. Occupational inequality, however, persists in affecting levels and types of violence. By 1983, affirmative action efforts had been in effect for over ten years, and there was emerging talk of "reverse discrimination." Yet African-Americans were then, as they are now, underrepresented in better paying positions, as shown in Table 2.6.

Because occupation and income are closely linked, it is not surprising that there are sharp income differences between whites, blacks, and Hispanics, as shown in Table 2.7. The table also shows income inequalities are increasing, not decreasing. The first year for which income data for Hispanics are available is 1975, so we will take that as a starting point.

These data do not take into consideration differences in educational background. Yet even where years of schooling are the same, inequalities as

Table 2.7 Median Income of Families and Ethnicity

	1975	1980	1993
White	$14,268	$21,904	$39,300
Black	8,779	12,674	21,542
Hispanic	9,551	14,716	23,654
Black/white ratio	62%	58%	55%
Hispanic/white ratio	67%	67%	60%

Source: U.S. Bureau of the Census, *Statistical Abstract of the United States, 1995*, Table 732, p. 474. Median income is in current dollars. Ratios are author's calculations.

Table 2.8 Education, Ethnicity, and Mean Monthly Income: 1993

	NOT A HIGH SCHOOL GRADUATE	HIGH SCHOOL	SOME COLLEGE	BACHELOR'S DEGREE	DOCTORATE DEGREE
White	$951	$1,422	$1,649	$2,682	$4,449
Black	713	1,071	1,222	2,333	3,778
Hispanic	786	1,106	1,239	2,186	2,677

Source: U.S. Bureau of the Census, *Statistical Abstract of the United States, 1995*, Table 241, p. 158.

measured by median monthly income, and unemployment rates persist, as shown in Table 2.8. In addition, African-American high school graduates have an unemployment rate that is nearly twice that of white high school graduates.

Furthermore, education itself is not equal. The schooling that African-American students receive is of much lower quality than that received by their white counterparts. What Jonathan Kozol has called the "savage inequalities" of the education system puts African-Americans at a further disadvantage in the labor market.[17] The relationship of this fact to some forms of violence will be discussed in chapter 3.

In the political arena as well, African-Americans and Latinos are not represented in proportion to their numbers in the population.[18] The U.S. population consists of about 12 percent African-Americans and about 10 percent Latinos (Hispanics). As of January 1996, there were thirty-nine African-Americans in the House of Representatives—9 percent of that body. In the Senate in 1996 there was only one African-American out of one hundred senators. The eighteen Latino representatives make up 4 percent of the House, and Latinos are currently totally absent from the Senate.[19]

GENDER INEQUALITY

Gender is the third important basis of inequality. White women have been the principle beneficiaries of affirmative-action legislation, and as a group,

Table 2.9 Percent of Occupation Female—1983, 1994

	1983	1994
Percent of Labor Force	44%	46%
Managerial/professional	41	48
Natural scientists	21	31
Architects	13	17
Engineers	6	8
Lawyers/judges	16	25
Doctors	16	22
Dentists	7	13
Nurses	96	94
Dental hygienists	99	100
College teachers	36	43
Elementary school teachers	83	86
Social workers	64	69
Secretaries	99	99
Bank tellers	94	84
Sales occupations	48	49
Athletes	18	22
Craft jobs	8	9
Firefighters	1	2
Police/detectives	6	13
Kitchen work/food preparation	77	74
Private household workers	96	96

Source: U.S. Bureau of the Census, *Statistical Abstract of the United States, 1995*, Table 649, p. 411.

they have improved their occupational representation more than African-Americans. But dramatic gender-based occupational differences still remain, as shown in Table 2.9.

Ethnicity and gender interact to affect a household's income levels. Table 2.10 shows that in each racial/ethnic category, women are earning less than men.

Gender inequality extends into political life, where women are greatly underrepresented. In January 1996, there were forty-seven women in the House, only 11 percent of that congressional branch. Women comprise only 8 percent of the Senate. By comparison, in most Scandinavian nations, between 30 and 40 percent of the legislative bodies are made up of women.

Because many working women are in lower-paying occupations or find it difficult to work full time because of child-care responsibilities, households that are dependent on women's wages are lower-income households. In chapter 4, we shall discuss additional forms of gender inequality and how these relate to gender violence.

CLASS AND POWER: THE COMMAND POSTS

Economic resources are a primary basis for exercising power. Having power should be distinguished from having money, however. If some lucky reader

Table 2.10 Median Income of Year-Round Full-Time Workers by Race and Gender, 1993

RACE/GENDER	EARNINGS	EARNINGS AS A PERCENTAGE OF WHITE MALE EARNINGS
White men	$31,832	100%
Black men	23,566	74%
Hispanic men	20,423	64%
White women	$22,979	72%
Black women	20,315	64%
Hispanic women	17,112	54%

Source: U.S. Bureau of the Census, *Statistical Abstract of the United States, 1995*, Table 739, p. 477. Author's calculation of percentages.

of this book were to win successive large lotteries, for example, winding up with millions of dollars, that in itself would not make them powerful. Access to powerful positions is based on being part of the social networks from which the elites are recruited.

There is an organizational aspect to power. Bureaucracies dominate life in the United States. Those who run the bureaucracies have great power by occupying what sociologist, C. Wright Mills called the "command posts." Although there are over 120 million jobs in the United States, only a tiny fraction of these are "command post" occupations: 5,416 positions or about .005 percent of the total occupations.[20] The most powerful positions are those at the top of the corporate pyramid. Much of the violence in the United States is linked to the decisions of those in the economic and political command posts with corporate bureaucracies being the most powerful in the United States.

CORPORATE DECISION MAKING

Are corporate executives and the politicians who enact policies leading to violence hard-hearted, evil people? The problem is not with the personalities of individuals but with a structure of inequality that creates conditions conducive to structural violence.

The goal of corporations is to maximize profit. It is in the self-interest of executives and managers to do this.[21] Summarizing the results of their study on why top corporate executives were dismissed, researchers David James and Michael Soref state, "Profit criteria appear to be the most important standard by which corporate chiefs are judged and dismissal is the ultimate sanction that conditions their behavior."[22]

Capitalist culture encourages materialism, such as looking out for oneself, and so on. Of course, people learn many other values as well. Those who are most accepting of material success as a life goal are likely, if they have the opportunity, to move into the business world. Those with alternative value systems are less likely to seek management positions.[23]

Corporations are increasingly administering various tests to applicants for executive positions to ascertain that they have the appropriate values and personality traits to meet the needs of the organization.[24] The CIA, discussed elsewhere in this book, also administers personality tests. They are looking for a person who, in the words of former agent Ralph McGehee, is a doer, not a thinker, who is "self centered and insensitive to others" and is "chameleon like . . . all things to all people [with] the ability to spot weaknesses in others and use these to his advantage."[25]

Once placed in a management role, whether at the middle or the top, executives face pressures to accept and to reach the goals of the company. By the time they reach the top of the hierarchy, most executives have many years of acting on behalf of an organization rather than on the basis of their own morality, should there be any conflict.[26]

Several psychological experiments indicate that the role into which one is placed will influence behavior, regardless of one's personality. In one such study, students played the roles of a drug company's board members. They were confronted with a problem such a company actually had: their organization had created a drug that was both profitable and dangerous. In this simulation, the students, like their real-life counterparts, tried to prevent the government from banning the product and would not withdraw it from the market.[27]

One of the most famous role-taking experiments is Stanley Milgram's studies of obedience. Disturbed by the Adolph Eichmann trial, and the typical Nazi justification of "I was only following orders," Milgram placed subjects in a situation where they were ordered to give shocks to a person, actually a confederate who was not really being shocked, supposedly to see the effect pain had on that person's capacity to memorize. Milgram wanted to know if subjects in a laboratory situation would obey a person whose only real authority came from being presented as a scientist. He was very disheartened to discover that a majority of the subjects, in spite of their own personal discomfort at their acts, did follow orders and gave what they thought were very painful shocks. Milgram discovered something else that is relevant to behavior in bureaucracies: the subject's action was influenced by the behavior of his or her peers. If the peer did not follow orders, the subject's obedience was much less likely; when peers did follow orders, the obedience rate rose. Milgram concluded:

> When an individual wishes to stand in opposition to authority, he [sic] does best to find support for his [sic] position for others in his group.

The mutual support provided by men [sic] for each other is the strongest bulwark we have against the excesses of authority.[28]

Turning from the laboratory to real-life, a survey of four hundred corporate managers in eighteen industries found a high proportion (from 50 to 84 percent) agreeing with the statement that "managers today feel under pressure to compromise personal standards to achieve company goals."[29]

In January 1986, excitement turned to horror as the space shuttle, *Challenger*, exploded seventy-three seconds after liftoff. Seven astronauts died, including Christa McAulliffe—a grade school teacher. Later an investigation revealed that Morton Thiokol, a major *Challenger* contractor, had allowed defective booster seals to be placed on the shuttle even though company engineers had warned that these might not hold at the low temperatures the craft would encounter.

> Under strong pressure from a team of senior-level executives and NASA officials to make the shuttle launch—and procure the renewal of the lucrative $400 million solid booster contract at stake—the vice-president for engineering at Thiokol testified that he changed his position regarding the safety of the flight after being told "to shed his role as an engineer and take the role of a management person."

Morton Thiokol was not the only culprit. Managers at Rockwell International, another shuttle contractor, had falsified reports on defective welding "to avoid the costs of rewelding" according to NASA's Inspector General's Office.[30]

BUREAUCRACY AND VIOLENCE

Corporations have powerful sanctions at their disposal. Keeping one's job, getting promoted, receiving material rewards or punishments, and peer approval or disapproval are all considerations for top and middle management. Self-interest for the decision makers, profit as a goal for the organization, and the structure of the organization come together to produce the conditions that are associated with violence.

We can identify five major features or processes in this regard: sanctions, the chain of command, social distance, a shared worldview, and neutralization techniques.

Sanctions: Positive and Negative Executives who help the organization to meet its goals can expect large material rewards that can compromise their personal values. An example comes from an interview conducted with Benton Harlow, an employee of a Midwest pharmaceutical company that distributed an unsafe anticholesterol drug, HE/14. Laboratory animals given the drug developed cataracts and lost their hair. But a lot of money had been invested, and there was a $2 million inventory of the drug, making withdrawal from the market unappealing. When the Justice Department investigated this case, Harlow accepted responsibility, was convicted, and given six months' probation. He was later interviewed and asked how the company reacted to his conviction. Harlow replied:

> They knew someone had to take responsibility. If I refused then my case as well as a score of others would have gone to trial, which would have been disastrous both for me personally and the company.... I was given a substantial raise.[31]

Life can be made very uncomfortable for those who follow their conscience. The term "whistle-blowers" describes employees who call attention to wrongdoing at their workplaces. They are motivated by a sense of social responsibility; by concern for their own friends, families, and communities; professional ethics; and/or a desire to see wrongdoing stopped. Their stories are sometimes very dramatic, and some have been made into movies, for example, Karen Silkwood who worked for Kerr-McGee, and Frank Serpico, a New York City cop. Other famous whistle-blowers include Daniel Ellsberg, who leaked what came to be called the *Pentagon Papers* during the Vietnam War.

It takes courage to blow the whistle. There are numerous cases of such people accused of incompetence and disloyalty, who were punished by their employer. Three engineers who had worked on the *Challenger* testified before a federal commission investigating the disaster and related their doubts about the spacecraft's safety. According to a *New York Times* story, they were "stripped of their authority, deprived of their staffs and prevented from seeing critical data about the investigation."[32] General Electric, whose motto is "we bring good things to light," fired health physicist Frank Bordell in 1988, after he took his worry about radiation exposure and lack of adequate reporting to the Department of Energy (DOE). When the company took no notice of his concerns, he went to the DOE directly, and he was subsequently fired. Three years earlier, GE punished Jack Shannon, manager of industrial safety and hygiene at another site. Shannon was troubled by problems with asbestos and fire. When he reported these problems, the company demoted him, harassed him, and placed him on "permanent disability."[33]

In Tempe, Arizona, a hazardous waste officer, Jay Golden, did his job by arresting a circuit board manufacturer who was dumping toxic wastes. Instead of rewarding him for his responsible actions, the Tempe Police Department sent him out to monitor traffic.[34]

There are also more serious repercussions. D. Varnadore worked at a Martin

Marietta operated facility at the federal nuclear facility in Oak Ridge, Tennessee. Varnadore, a victim of colon cancer, appeared on a March 1991 CBS news show where he described elevated cancer levels among people working at the facility. After this, he was isolated from other workers and given an office filled with radioactive wastes. A spokesperson for the Government Accountability Project, a nongovernmental organization that tries to protect whistle-blowers, said, "What they did borders on attempted murder, knowingly putting a cancer patient with a suppressed immune system in there."[35]

There may even be examples of direct murders of whistle-blowers. Karen Silkwood, fearful of Kerr McGee's mishandling of plutonium at their Oklahoma plutonium processing plant, tried to interest the Atomic Energy Commission in the situation but became impatient with their lack of adequate response. She collected documentation of safety problems but was killed in 1974 in a suspicious car accident on her way to meet with a reporter from the *New York Times* and an official from the Oil, Chemical and Atomic Workers' Union. Her collection of documents was never found. A week before she died, she, along with three hundred other workers, were contaminated by plutonium as a result of a plant accident.[36]

In 1985, a shotgun blast killed Judith Penley, a critic of safety at the Commanche Peak nuclear facility, part of the Tennessee Valley Authority energy complex. Her murder, never solved, came "shortly after she had met with interviewers from ... a private firm hired by the government to investigate complaints at the nuclear facility."[37]

Personal vindictiveness is not the main reason for these punishments. Rather those who order them are acting on behalf of their organization. Myron and Penina Glazer, who did an extensive study on whistle-blowing, summarize the reasons for the harsh treatment, list the punishments corporations can use, and give reasons for these retaliatory actions:

> Retaliation is, in fact, part of a rational and planned process initiated by an organization to destroy the resister's credibility as a witness. To achieve this aim, management often invokes such harsh measures as blacklisting, dismissal, transfer and personal harassment.... There are several reasons for these excessive punishments. First, management insists that employees do not have a right to ... challenge organizational policies publicly. Attempts to overturn decisions made by those at the top are defined as acts of insubordination and are considered a threat to the orderly procedures required to operate in a businesslike fashion.[38]

In addition, there are fears that the whistle-blowers may become role models, examples of moral courage, to their fellow employees.

There are also efforts to protect whistle-blowers and to find ways to ensure that the public will not be at the mercy of corporate practices. Public-interest groups, congressional hearings, sympathetic journalists, all play an important role in supporting the conscientious employee and making some efforts to rectify the problems.[39] Because of public pressure, federal laws have been passed to protect whistle-blowers in at least some areas, such as those working in nuclear facilities and those reporting environmental problems. In addition, "twenty-six states have granted . . . a policy that limits an employer's right to fire at will, further legitimizing the role of the employee who refuses to comply when management insists on engaging in lawless behavior."[40]

The Chain of Command The structure of bureaucracies, corporate or government, means that some people in the organization carry out decisions made by those above them, while delegating responsibilities to subordinates. It is easier to deny responsibility for the consequences of decisions one has not made or for actions that one has not personally carried out. Because of the chain of command, employees routinely concentrate on their own jobs and can avoid thinking about the implications of their activities.

James Carey, who provided us with the example of Benton Harlow above, points out that for the executives marketing the dangerous anticholesterol drug "there was no strong repugnance or even opposition. . . . Rather, they all seemed to drift into the activity without thinking a great deal about it."[41] When a lab technician at B. F. Goodrich confronted his supervisor over covering-up faulty airplane brakes, the supervisor responded "it's none of my business, and it's none of yours. I learned a long time ago not to worry about things over which I have no control. I have no control over this." When the technician pressed the point, the supervisor continued his justification of his own actions, saying, "I just told you I have no control over this thing. Why should my conscience bother me."[42]

Social Distance Bureaucratic decision makers do not usually see the consequences of their actions. They are isolated by their own social position from ever confronting the suffering their decisions have caused. Roger Smith, former General Motors chairman, presided over the devastating closing of a number of General Motors plants, including one in Flint, Michigan, and the leveling of a close-knit Polish neighborhood, Poletown, in Detroit to build a factory and a parking lot. Requested to visit these communities to see their pain and possibly reconsider his decisions, he refused, and there was no way to force him.[43]

The private lives of CEOs, as well as their corporate lives, encapsulate them in a sealed world of shared views. Executives themselves are aware of this. Sociologist Robert Jackall studied decision making by corporate executives, and he quotes one on the possibilities of a chemical subsidiary causing cancer:

Suppose ... you knew that fifty specific people were going to get skin cancer because you produced chlorofluorocarbons. You would just stop production. But suppose that you didn't know the fifty people and it wasn't at all clear that CFCs were ... entirely at fault? What do you do then?[44]

Workers also understand the consequences of social distance. For example, Donna Miller-Doyle, a New Jersey AT&T employee, feared being fired as the company laid off thousands of workers around the country. Workers at the giant communications corporation previously had taken job security for granted. Donna Miller-Doyle was laid off but rehired. Reflecting on her future, she said, "I am glad to be back, but I wonder if the ax swings again if I'll be so lucky. I don't think upper management realizes what's happening. They seem too far removed."[45]

Shared Worldview Managers in bureaucracies spend their workdays surrounded by people who see the world in similar ways; each person reinforces the views of everyone else. This mental conformity is sometimes referred to as "group-think," which has been described as referring to "the deterioration of mental efficiency, reality testing and moral judgment that results from in-group pressures."[46]

When they go home, the decision makers are still surrounded by likeminded people. The editor of *Car and Driver* magazine quotes a former General Motors executive's description of a life he shared with his peers in the posh Detroit suburb of Bloomfield Hills. "They live together, they play golf together, they *think* together."[47]

Neutralization Techniques There are a number of ways of talking and thinking about ethical problems that permit decision makers to feel blameless: appeal to a higher authority, condemn the condemner, and the use of "doublespeak." In the appeal to a higher authority, the decision maker claims to be acting in the interest of a widely accepted moral principle. For example, the tobacco company, R. J. Reynolds, had an advertising page in the *New York Times* with photos showing the Berlin Wall crumbling, the ending of apartheid in South Africa, and Russia's new constitution while in the United States, freedom is ominously threatened. A photo caption read, "Reins on Smokers' Freedom Tighten." The ad went on to say that the rights of all Americans "could be compromised" if the rights of smokers are violated.[48]

Progress is an oft-cited value. If there are costs to a corporate action, progress justifies it. In a lecture to the Arizona Business Forum, Paul Oreffice, then CEO of Dow Chemical Company claimed that environmentalists "have now made a profession of standing in the way of any progress." Regarding General Motor's leveling of Poletown, a community of over three thousand people, Roger Smith said, "I'm sorry that people had to get displaced....

We have to build freeways; we build power lines. People do get displaced in the name of progress."[49] Of course, people living in Bloomfield Hills are not likely to "get displaced."

Higher authority may be a value, but it can also mean scientists who question the findings of product danger by their colleagues. Because scientific findings are, by their nature, tentative, and scientists, like other people, can be influenced by material rewards, there is always a possibility of finding some alleged experts whose research is supposed to be more valid than those of the corporate critics. A survey compared the views of corporate-employed scientists with those of academic scientists on what constituted a safe level of exposure to carcinogens. Sixty percent of the academic scientists felt there is no safe level at all, while 80 percent of industry scientists felt there is no health risk at certain exposure levels.[50] In another tobacco industry example, Philip Morris placed a full-page ad in the *New York Times* claiming that "many authoritative sources" question the EPA's conclusions that secondhand smoke is a danger.[51]

The corporate critic may come under attack. Those who claim a company is behaving unethically are condemned for their alleged moral flaws and are labeled as persons not to be taken seriously. Paul Oreffice, former CEO of Dow Chemical, in addition to claiming environmentalists are against progress, condemned them for being a "well-organized, often unscrupulous professional force . . . fiendishly clever people."[52] He believed they were frightening the public with their dire tales of what the chemical industry's products could do to the human organism. Oreffice told consumer advocate Ralph Nader, "Frankly, I think you and I have exposed ourselves this morning to more carcinogens by drinking a cup of coffee and a cup of tea than we do from most things that come out of [chemical] plants."[53]

Critics of companies have been branded as criminals. When Debbie McQueen, a local environmental activist in Phoenix, Arizona, tried to raise public awareness of the dangers caused by Marsh Aviation's crop-dusting activities, the company falsely accused her of shooting at their aircraft and the state Department of Environmental Quality kept a file on her, which, among other things, labeled her as a sabotage suspect.[54]

In doublespeak, language is used that does not have the connotations of pain and suffering of usual vocabulary. (The military frequently uses doublespeak, as we will discuss in chapter 7, concentrating here on corporate language manipulation). Instead of speaking of mass firings, managers speak of "downsizing," "restructuring," "workforce adjustments," "headcount reductions," and "negative employee retention."[55] When General Motors shut down its assembly plant in Framingham, Massachusetts, in 1987, they called it "a volume-related production schedule adjustment." With equal creativity, Chrysler referred to its laying off of five thousand auto workers in

Kenosha, Wisconsin, as "a career alternative enhancement program."[56] Some other examples of euphemisms would be calling the near meltdown at Three Mile Island an "abnormal evolution" and a "plant transient," while the Department of Agriculture honored the food industry's request to call "powdered bone," "calcium" on food labels.[57]

How Capitalists Influence the Government

To achieve their economic goals, corporations and their owners (shareholders) need to have government as their ally. Our economic system may be undemocratic, but we have a democratic political system: we can exercise certain basic freedoms and we can vote. What if the vast majority of us use our right to vote, to criticize, to organize, and so forth to limit the wealth and income of those at the top, to create a more equitable distribution of economic resources, and to make those in the command posts more responsible and accountable for their actions?

There are four specific processes through which economic elites influence political decisions so that the general public's exercise of rights does not unduly hinder profit seeking. These processes are lobbying, financing of parties and candidates, staffing of political positions, and formulating policy.[58]

Lobbying is how organizations or groups try to pressure elected officials to take a particular stand. Of the four processes discussed here, lobbying is where ordinary citizens can have the greatest impact. Anyone can write a letter or visit a congressperson alone or with a group. After all, votes determine who gets into office, and congresspeople can be made to feel some responsibility to their constituents. Citizens also support organizations that lobby in their behalf, but these often do not have much money compared with business lobbying groups.

Corporate resources for lobbying are much greater than for the rest of the population. Corporations can hire people to do their lobbying, and they can offer financial rewards and other perquisites to those they are trying to influence. Furthermore, as investigative journalist William Greider notes, citizens are likely to be

> temporarily aroused by an issue, see reforms enacted and then move on to other concerns. But the corporations do not go away from the legislative debate, even in the off-seasons. By their nature, the people and institutions with large amounts of money at stake are always at the table. It is their business to be there. Their profits depend on the outcomes.[59]

He points out that a Senate study found that "on some important matters, industry would invest fifty to one hundred times more resources than the public-interest advocates could muster."[60]

Wall Street Journal reporter Jeffrey H. Birnbaum, who has studied lobbying, writes, "The fact that lobbyists are everywhere all the time, has led official Washington to become increasingly sympathetic to the corporate cause. This is true among Democrats as well as among Republicans."[61]

With their resources, corporate lobbyists are able to develop ties with political figures. Politicians do not usually socialize with, or routinely meet with, groups of working people. On the other hand, they go to parties, resorts, and business gatherings that are dominated by the corporate elite. In 1989, for example, business lobbyists paid for a $250,000 weekend trip for 142 representatives and their families to the Greenbrier resort in West Virginia. Real estate lobbyist Wayne Thevenot explained that vacations like these "put you into proximity with some members of Congress—the major players. They get to know who you are. [And you] get to know who they are, something about them personally. Their likes, their dislikes, their family. Getting [sic] to develop a personal relationship with them."[62]

Corporations also create lobbying organizations to represent their joint interests. One example of this is the Association of Private Pension and Welfare Plans, which lobbies for a number of Fortune 500 companies and which mobilized to keep down the size of the federal Medicare program.[63]

Lobbyists for insurance companies, the hospital industry, and some medical associations have spent millions of dollars lobbying on health care. According to Ellen Miller, director of the Center for Responsive Politics, "this is the biggest-scale lobbying effort that's ever been mounted on a single piece of legislation both in terms of dollars spent and people engaged." Citizen Action, a consumer-advocate organization, estimates that since 1980, the insurance and health industries have given over $150 million to Congressional candidates to "keep health reform off the national agenda."[64]

In March 1994, following President Clinton's criticism of the high prices of pharmaceuticals, the companies mounted an effort to prevent any government interference in their pricing policies. The *New York Times* reported "hefty campaign contributions to members of congress and intense lobbying of the lawmakers who receive those donations." Citizen Action claimed that in 1993 political donations from this industry were up by 20 percent from 1992. According to *New York Times* reporters, "this situation is a case study of how one industry has been working to thwart an important part of the Clinton health plan, the effort to hold down drug costs." Especially valuable as allies to the pharmaceutical industry are senators and representatives from New Jersey, home to several major pharmaceutical companies. Together the Democratic senators from New Jersey, Frank Lautenberg and Bill Bradley, received over $200,000 from industry Political Action Committees

(PACs) between 1983 and 1993. During his 1990 senatorial campaign, Bradley "received about $59,900 from the prescription drug industry." Although he denied that their contributions affected his political actions, he "led a successful fight against legislation that would have prevented companies from raising prescription drug prices more than the Consumer Price Index and he helped retain much of the valuable drug company tax breaks for manufacturing in Puerto Rico."[65]

There are periodic attempts to reform this process. In 1995, Congress passed a bill that would require lobbyists to disclose what issues they are working on, who is paying them, and how much they are receiving. However, a new kind of corporate lobbying effort, "grassroots" lobbying, sometimes called "astroturf" lobbying, is not affected by the legislation. This is where corporate lobbyists organize ordinary citizens to write letters and make calls to congresspeople. This makes it appear as though there is popular support for or against a particular measure.[66] In New Jersey in 1996, tobacco companies were calling smokers to suggest they in turn contact their state legislators to fight against a proposed hike in cigarette taxes.[67]

Running campaigns has become an increasingly expensive enterprise in this country. Public Citizen, an organization founded by Ralph Nader in 1971, estimated that over $2 billion was spent on the 1996 federal elections alone, not counting state or local races.[68]

Laws were passed in 1974 stipulating that individuals could give only $1,000 to presidential candidates, and PACs could give no more than $5,000. Donations, however, can be made to the parties and not directly to the candidates, allowing circumvention of these laws. These contributions are called "soft money." Charles Lewis, executive director of the Center for Public Integrity, explains that the reason for the word "soft" is because this money is "squishy"—it is difficult to follow its path. He points out that these funds "can grease the skids in Washington for some powerful companies while the average citizen doesn't have access." A Democratic fund raiser, Alfred C. DeCotis, who has himself raised millions for the party, admits, "If you write a large check, you get to be well known in the party and you get a certain amount of access."[69]

Running increasingly expensive media-based campaigns, parties and their candidates need financial backing that they will not get by attacking the interests of potential large contributors. Both the Democratic and Republican parties receive funds from the same large corporations, although the Democrats also get support from more diverse groups in the population, including labor organizations. Contributions are made to candidates at all levels, as well as to the two parties. It is obviously much more difficult for other parties to raise comparable funds.

Companies will give money to the party they think will do them the most good at a particular time, a process some political analysts call "switch-hitting." Tobacco companies are a case in point. As of September 1996, this industry had given $3.9 million to the Republicans, and $714,000 to the Democrats. The discrepancy is explained by Darienne Dennis, communications director at Philip Morris: "Philip Morris supports those who share our thoughts. We have a responsibility to our employees and shareholders to be in the political process and we are happy to do so." Gerald Lowrie, a senior vice president in AT&T's Federal Government Affairs Office also described why these contributions are so important, "Government can change the way you live and how you work. If you ignore who is in office it can be at your peril."[70] Some of the contributions corporations make are tax deductible.

For the past twenty years, PACs have been the main route by which campaign money is contributed.[71] The money links the candidates' or parties' interest with that of the contributor. As one executive put it:

> The PAC gives you access. It makes you a player. These congressmen, in particular are constantly fundraising.... It profits us ... to be able to provide some funds because in the provision of it you get to know people, you help them out.[72]

There are four kinds of PACS recognized by the Federal Election Commission that regulates them: labor, corporate, those termed trade-health-membership, and nonconnected. The last are formed to raise money for a specific issue. Some of these do have a tie to an existing organization that pays their expenses and has control over the money so they are not totally unconnected.[73]

However, in the world of political contributors, there is also inequality. Three sociologists who researched PACs summarize why the corporate PACs are the most important contributors.

> First, they are the largest concentrated source of campaign money and the fastest growing. In 1988 corporate PACs contributed more than $50 million, all trade-membership-health PACs combined less than $40 million, labor PACs less than $35 million, and nonconnected PACs less than $20 million. Moreover, these figures understate the importance of corporate decisions about money because industry trade associations are controlled by corporations and follow their lead. In addition, corporate executives have high incomes and make many individual contributions; a handful of labor leaders may attempt to do the same on a reduced scale, but rank-and-file workers are unlikely to do so. Second, corporations have disproportionate power in U.S. society, magnifying the importance of the money they contribute. Finally, corporate PACs have enormous untapped fundraising potential. They are in a position to coerce their donors in a way no other kind of PAC can.[74]

The last point refers to the corporation's ability to pressure employees to make contributions. No other organization has the same kinds of influence as does a large company vis-à-vis its employees. Unions, for example, can put social pressure on members and provide them with information about candidates, but they have no material sanctions at their disposal.[75]

Corporations have additional ways to assist favored political figures. They may host gala events for favored political figures. Prior to the Republican National Convention in 1988, General Motors gave a party for Senator Robert Dole and his wife, Elizabeth. Among the refreshments was a two-pound tub of caviar worth about $1,000. The automobile company did not slight the Democrats, however, also hosting a reception for Representative John Dingell of Michigan, who was described by the *New York Times* as "one of the auto industry's strongest allies in Congress."[76]

Speaking engagements with large honoraria, an all expense-paid trip, or simply personal gifts are additional carrots that can be dangled in front of lawmakers. Companies can also make facilities available. At the 1996 Republican convention, there were photocopiers provided by Xerox and office space courtesy of AT&T. At their Chicago convention, Democrats had access to vehicles provided by General Motors.[77]

Capitalists do not personally hold most of the elected offices in this country, but they do hold a significant number, and members of this class are appointed to positions of great influence. In 1981, at least twenty-nine senators were worth over a million dollars each, as were several members of the House of Representatives.[78]

Reagan and Bush were both millionaires who became presidents, and they were not the first very rich individuals to hold that position. The Supreme Court is a highly unrepresentative body, not only in terms of race and gender but also in class. Justices Sandra Day O'Connor, John Paul Stevens, and Ruth Bader Ginsberg are all worth over a million dollars; the other justices have assets valued in the hundreds of thousands.[79]

Members of the capitalist class are often the ones who hold cabinet posts.[80] There is a revolving door between government and business. Corporate directors or those with close ties to them often run government agencies that are supposed to regulate industries, or they serve as advisors to such agencies. Government officials move to top corporate positions when they leave their political jobs. For example, in 1990, an Environmental Protection Agency panel was set up supposedly to investigate the effects of secondhand smoke. The chairman and five of the panel's sixteen other members came from the Center for Indoor Air Research whose funds are provided by Lorillard Inc., R. J. Reynolds, and Philip Morris. Philip Morris also used its influence to appoint a seventh member. A doctor from an antismoking organization, Doctors

Ought to Care, remarked, "They've stacked the deck with people who have close ties to the tobacco industry. It's pathetic." Dr. David Burns, an expert on secondhand smoke, was removed from the panel at the urging of the tobacco companies.[81]

The same advisors are often used regardless of which party is in office. A recent example was President Clinton's appointment of David Gergen as national security advisor following Gergen's similar role to three Republican presidents.[82]

A prime example of class and political power is John J. McCloy, who died in 1989. McCloy was chairman of Chase Manhattan Bank and on the board of a number of other corporations, including E. R. Squibb and Sons. A Harvard Law School graduate, he represented numerous companies, including those in the oil industry. He served as an advisor to seven presidents: four Democrats—Roosevelt, Truman, Kennedy, and Johnson—and three Republicans—Eisenhower, Nixon, and Reagan. One of his acts in the Roosevelt administration was to oversee the internment of Japanese Americans in 1942, an act he vigorously defended, although he unsuccessfully opposed compensation of the internees. In the late 1940s, as high commissioner for Germany, he was instrumental in the pardoning of high-ranking Nazis. Richard Rovere, the political analyst, aptly described McCloy as the "chairman of the Establishment" that "fixes major goals and constitutes itself a ready pool of manpower for the ... labors of leadership."[83]

Another example of an individual who has worked with both parties is the now Democratic senator from New York, Daniel Patrick Moynihan. He was the urban advisor for Republican president Richard Nixon and later Nixon appointed him ambassador to India. He was also the chief delegate to the United Nations during Republican President Ford's term.[84]

The aspect of decision making called policy formation is probably the least well known to the public, and it has received relatively little analysis from social scientists. The policy formation establishment consists of foundations, councils, commissions, and so on, which discuss issues and develop strategies for dealing with these. They are sometimes called "think tanks," a term coined during World War II to describe a place where discussions of the war effort could be secretly conducted. Funding for projects frequently comes from government grants but also from corporations that have been increasing their contributions in recent years.[85]

In these associations, academics, corporate leaders, and government officials meet to develop policies that protect the interests of the capitalist class. John J. McCloy was a president of the Ford Foundation and a one-time head of the Council on Foreign Relations.

G. William Domhoff, who has written extensively on power in the United States, described the policy formation process as beginning in corporate board rooms and executive suites. It ends in the innermost private offices of the government in Washington, where reporters and sociologists never tread. In between the beginning and the end there are a handful of foundations that provide the experts with money for research ... and influential newspapers and magazines are important in bringing the views of the policy groups to the attention of government personnel.[86]

Some of the most important of the policy-making organizations are the Council on Economic Development, the Business Council, the Council on Foreign Relations, the Ford and Rockefeller Foundations, the Brookings Institution, the Hoover Institute, and the Heritage Foundation. During the Reagan years, the Heritage Foundation established in 1973 by the brewer Joseph Coors played an especially prominent role.[87] In 1980, the Foundation prepared a 1,093-page volume of recommendations for the new president, and over twenty of the writers became part of the Reagan administration. They have worked closely with the Republicans in Congress, seeking cuts in social programs, deregulation of business, and increases in the military budget, all relevant for issues discussed throughout this book.[88]

Temporary groups are also formed to arrive at policies which are then presented to the general public. An example of this was the Jackson Hole Group, originally formed in 1990 and named after the Wyoming resort where its members first met. This group rejected the idea of a comprehensive national health care plan. Instead they promoted "managed competition," whereby doctors and hospitals and insurance companies form organizations that will compete for patients on the basis of price and quality. Unfortunately for those with health problems, this can mean not being given more expensive treatments and less choice of physicians as well. Dr. Steffie Woolhandler, a founder of Physicians for a National Health Program, describes this system as an "effort to preserve a role for the insurance industry in health care."[89] The lack of affordable, accessible health care is very related to structural violence, as will be shown in chapter 6.

The Jackson Hole Group has included Hillary Clinton; representatives from life insurance companies (Prudential, Aetna, Metropolitan, Cigna, and Blue Cross & Blue Shield); pharmaceutical companies and their trade organization, the Pharmaceutical Manufacturers Association; some medical organizations; and Pepsico and General Electric.

THE CULTURAL APPARATUS AND VIOLENCE

In addition to having a disproportionate influence on the political process, corporations have the power to shape public opinion. Corporate executives are at the top of what C. Wright Mills termed the "cultural apparatus," where information, interpretations of reality, and entertainment are produced and distributed.[90]

The cultural apparatus influences our thinking about violence. Interpersonal violence is described as much more of a problem than what we are calling structural violence, and crime and street violence, for example, are usually equated, even though most crime is nonviolent. Much more attention is given to street crime than to corporate wrongdoing.

For example, in January 1994, *U.S. News and World Report* had a cover story on crime that claimed crime has been increasing since 1960, a distortion of the data. *Time* magazine's 23 August 1994 cover story was "America the Violent," with a subheading that noted "crime is spreading and patience is running out." The bright red cover was a lurid illustration of a sinister looking young man, with a frightening, inhuman face, not a well-dressed executive with a briefcase. Inside the reader was told that people are in danger while doing the ordinary things of life: going to the hospital, a fast-food restaurant, or the shopping mall. As its front page headline, *New York Newsday* had "Murder Victim Number 1,429"—the headline for a story about the shooting of thirteen-year-old Geovanny Santiago, who was shot while shopping for his mother.

Television news is increasingly dominated by crime stories in the belief that this will increase ratings. The motto of television news producers seems to be "if it bleeds it leads," that is, "a lurid crime report with a high body count will ... become the lead story, no matter how insignificant its actual news value."[91] Media commentators sometimes use the phrase "body-bag journalism" to convey how news programming aims toward the sensationalistic.

Although crime rates do not change much, television crime coverage has. According to the media-watch group Fairness and Accuracy in Reporting (FAIR), from January 1989 to January 1992, the three major networks spent an average of "67 minutes a month on crime stories." In the period from October 1993 to January 1994, they were spending over 157 minutes a month on this topic. Between 1993 and 1994, the Center for Media and Public Affairs estimated there was a doubling of the time news shows allotted to violent crime compared with the previous year. An increasing number of news magazine shows have appeared, which are also full of tales of lurid and violent crimes.[92]

In Los Angeles, researchers sampled thirty-five hours of news coverage on local TV, finding that crime stories made up "23 percent to 54 percent of all news coverage." It was news presented as entertainment with little analysis. Much less attention was given to upcoming elections in California. "Of 2,059 minutes of news, just over eight minutes concerned the gubernatorial primary."

A report issued by Arizona State University's School of Justice, "Confronting

Violent Crime in Arizona," claims that "corporate crimes, which are not only prevalent but physically dangerous, even deadly, receive little attention and may not be covered as crime at all, but rather as a business matter."[93]

Earlier we presented data showing the extent to which people feel threatened by crime, feelings that are encouraged by the media. A *Los Angeles Times* survey, for example, reported that 65 percent of respondents got their information about crime from the media. Between June 1993 and February 1994, the percentage of those telling *Washington Post* pollsters that crime was the most important issue facing the country rose from 5 percent to 31 percent.[94] National survey data also show a steep rise in the general feeling that crime is the most important problem in the nation. Thus, between January 1993 and January 1994, the percentage of respondents identifying crime as the most important problem in the country rose from 9 to 37 percent, a 400 percent increase, clearly not a reflection of any drastic increase in crime rates.[95]

The mainstream media's slant on crime may actually contribute to the incidence of interpersonal violence. Fearful of being attacked, even in their own homes, and with easy access to firearms, people in the United States are buying weapons. Sixteen million handguns were owned in 1960, and by 1995, this number had risen to 79 million. According to the Bureau of Justice, counting handguns, rifles, shotguns, and so on, there are at least "223 million guns available to the general public." A 1980 study in Washington state found that in homes with guns, owners, residents, and friends were forty-three times more likely to be killed than any intruder.[96]

Some examples will illustrate how fear plus gun ownership can lead to death. In 1995, Sam Walker's wife called him, saying their security company had notified her that their burglar alarm had gone off. He went to their Texas home, found the door unlocked, and got his recently purchased .38 caliber revolver. Checking the house, he went into his daughter's room, saw someone that he didn't instantly recognize and fired, killing sixteen-year-old Sheree who had skipped school. A similar incident occurred in 1994 in Louisiana when a fourteen year old decided to play a prank on her father. She made some noises in her closet, and when he entered the room to see what was happening, she jumped out of her hiding place. Her startled parent, thinking she was an intruder, shot and killed her. In Mississippi in December of 1995, a three year old got up to look at the family's Christmas tree lights while his parents were sleeping. He accidentally tripped a motion detector, setting off an alarm. His frightened stepmother went downstairs with a gun, fired at the movement she saw, and killed the little boy. Each year approximately five hundred young people die as the result of accidental shootings.[97]

Sixteen-year-old Japanese exchange student Yoshihiro Hattori and a friend were on their way to a Halloween party in Baton Rouge, Louisiana, in 1992. Yoshihiro wore a costume based on the movie *Saturday Night Fever*, his friend was uncostumed. Looking for the party, they rang the doorbell at the Peairs's family home. Bonnie Peairs answered the door and called to her husband Rodney to come with his gun, a .44 caliber magnum. It seems the student did not understand Rodney Peairs's shout of "freeze" and so did not stand still. The homeowner killed him. In 1993, Peairs was acquitted of manslaughter; the jury apparently found his actions were based on justifiable fears. In 1994, a judge awarded Yoshihiro's parents $650,000 in damages and for funeral costs. The case became a cause célèbre in Japan, where there were seventy-four shooting deaths in 1991; sixty-seven of this number were members of organized crime groups. The United States, with twice Japan's population, had about thirty-eight thousand firearm deaths.[98]

Although a careful reading of the media can provide useful information, there is much that is missing or distorted in the analysis we get from the newspapers, magazines, radio, and television. For instance, the relationships between corporate goals and resources, political decisions, and the conditions that give rise to interpersonal violence are rarely discussed. These connections will be the subject of the next two chapters.

Notes

1. Jason DeParle, "Sharp Increase Along the Borders of Poverty," *New York Times*, 31 March 1994, p. A18.
2. Discussions of this term can be found in James Jennings, *Understanding the Nature of Poverty in America* (Westport, Conn.: Praeger, 1994), pp. 123–32; Michael B. Katz, ed., *The "Underclass" Debate: Views from History* (Princeton, NJ: Princeton University Press, 1993); Bill E. Lawson, ed., *The Underclass Question* (Philadelphia: Temple University Press, 1992); William J. Wilson, *The Truly Disadvantaged: The Inner City, the Underclass and Public Policy* (Chicago: University of Chicago Press, 1987); William J. Wilson, ed., *The Ghetto Underclass: Social Science Perspectives*, in January issue of the *Annals of the American Academy of Political and Social Science* 501, 1989.
3. Jacqueline Jones, *The Dispossessed: America's Underclasses from the Civil War to the Present* (New York: Basic Books, 1992), p. 2; Herbert Gans, "Deconstructing the Underclass," in *Race, Class and Gender in the United States*, ed. Paula Rothenberg, 3d ed. (New York: St. Martin's Press), pp. 51–57.
4. Gary Burtless, "Introduction and Summary," in *A Future of Lousy Jobs: The Changing Structure of U.S. Wages*, ed. Gary Burtless (Washington, D.C.: The Brookings Institution, 1990), pp. 2, 18; Edward N. Wolf, *Top Heavy: A Study of the Increasing Inequality of Wealth in America* (New York: The Twentieth Century Fund, 1995), pp. v–vi.
5. Global Exchanges 27 (Summer 1996) "Globalization and the Downsizing of the American Dream," special insert, p. 2.
6. Wolf, p. 7.

7. Derek Bok, *The Cost of Talent: How Executives and Professionals Are Paid and How It Affects America* (New York: Free Press, 1993), p. 95; Editorial, *The Nation*, 8 April 1996, p. 3; Keith Bradsher, "A Surge in Hiring Cheers President but Roils Markets," *New York Times*, 6 August 1994, p. 1.
8. Bok, pp. 65, 95. Author's calculation of executive hourly wage.
9. Author's calculations on data from, "The Corporate Elite," *Business Week*, 11 October 1993.
10. McKinley L. Blackburn, David E. Bloom, and Richard B. Freeman, "The Declining Economic Position of Less Skilled Men," in Burtless, pp. 60–62.
11. Lawrence Mishel, and Jared Bernstein, *The State of Working America, 1992–1993* (Armonk, N.Y.: M. E. Sharpe, Inc., 1993), p. 187. See also Richard B. Freeman, "How Much Has De-Unionization Contributed to the Rise in Male Earnings Inequality," in *Uneven Tides: Rising Inequality in America*, eds. Sheldon Danziger and Peter Gottschalk (New York: Russell Sage Foundation, 1993), pp. 133–63.
12. Edna Bonaich, and David W. Waller, "Mapping a Global Industry: Apparel Production in the Pacific Rim Triangle," in *Global Production: The Apparel Industry in the Pacific Rim*, eds. Edna Bonaich, Lucie Cheng, Norma Chinchilla, Nora Hamilton, and Paul Ong (Philadelphia: Temple University Press, 1994), p. 23.
13. Figures for 1972, U.S. Bureau of the Census, *Statistical Abstract of the United States, 1980*, Table 713, p. 428; figures for 1993, *Statistical Abstract of the United States, 1994*, Table 682, p. 438. These two unions have merged into the American Clothing and Textile Workers Union.
14. Dan Clawson, Alan Neustadtl, and Denise Scott, *Money Talks: Corporate PACS and Political Influence* (New York: Basic Books, 1992), pp. 91–96.
15. Mischel and Bernstein, p. 117.
16. Michael Parenti, *Democracy for the Few*, 6th ed. (New York: St. Martin's Press), p. 81; Kevin Phillips, *The Politics of Rich and Poor: Wealth and the American Electorate in the Reagan Aftermath* (New York: HarperPerennial, 1990), p. 78.
17. Jonathan Kozol, *Savage Inequalities: Children in America's Schools* (New York: HarperCollins, 1991).
18. A 1996 Supreme Court decision that disallows creating voting districts to ensure minority representation is likely to reduce the number of people of color in Congress in the future. Linda Greenhouse, "High Court Voids Race-Based Plans for Redistricting," *New York Times*, 14 June 1996, pp. A1, A25. For more detail on this issue, see Bernard Grofman and Chandler Davidson, eds. *Controversies in Minority Voting: The Voting Rights Act in Perspective* (Washington, D.C.: The Brookings Institution, 1992).
19. Government statistics use the term "Hispanic" for people of Spanish-speaking ancestry. Some object to this term, believing it denigrates their Indian and/or African heritage and preferring the term "Latino," which we will use as well.
20. David R. Simon, and D. Stanley Eitzen, *Elite Deviance*, 4th ed. (Boston: Allyn and Bacon, 1993), p. 15. Percentage calculated from total number of occupations in the United States, U.S. Bureau of the Census, *Statistical Abstract of the United States*, 1995, Table 649, p. 411.
21. Paul Blumberg, *The Predatory Society: Deception in the American Marketplace* (New York: Oxford University Press, 1989), p. 4.
22. "Managerial Theory: Unmaking of the Corporation President," *American Sociological Review* 46 (1981): 16.

23. Bok, pp. 79, 90.
24. Judith H. Dobrzynski, "Executive Tests Now Plumb New Depths of the Job Seeker," *New York Times*, 2 September 1996, pp. 1, 38.
25. Ralph McGehee, *Deadly Deceits: My 25 Years in the CIA* (New York: Sheridan Square Press, 1983), p. 6.
26. James W. Coleman, *The Criminal Elite: The Sociology of White-Collar Crime*, 3d ed. (New York: St. Martin's Press, 1994), p. 190; M. David Ermann, and Richard J. Lundmann, "Overview," in *Corporate and Governmental Deviance*, eds. Ermann and Lundman, 4th ed. (New York: Oxford University Press, 1987), p. 7.
27. Coleman, p. 194.
28. Stanley Milgram, *Obedience to Authority* (New York: Harper and Row, 1969), p. 21.
29. Stuart L. Hills, "Epilogue," in *Corporate Violence: Injury and Death for Profit*, ed. Stuart L. Hills (Totowa, N.J.: Rowman & Littlefield, 1987), p. 192.
30. Ibid., pp. 192–93; see also Russell Boisjoly, Ellen Foster Curtis, and Eugene Mellican, "Ethical Dimensions of the Challenger Disaster," in Ermann and Lundman, pp. 111–36.
31. James T. Carey, "Benton Harlow: Distributor of Unsafe Drugs," in Hills, pp. 164–65.
32. Quoted in Myron Peretz Glazer and Penina Migdal Glazer, *The Whistleblowers: Exposing Corruption in Government & Industry* (New York: Basic Books, 1989), p. 10.
33. Russell Mokhiber, Julie Gozan, and Holly Knaus, "The Corporate Rap Sheet: The 10 Worst Corporations of 1992," *Multinational Monitor* (December 1992), pp. 12–13.
34. Ronald A. Hardert, "Environmental Whistle-blowers, Anger and the Power Elite," working paper presented to the Pacific Sociological Association, San Diego, Calif., April 1994, p. 11.
35. Quoted in Matthew L. Wald, "Nuclear Laboratory Whistle-Blower Is Disciplined for Questioning a Test," *New York Times*, 5 February 1992, p. A16; Mokhiber, Gozan, and Knaus, p. 14.
36. Deena Weinstein, *Bureaucratic Opposition: Challenging Abuses of the Workplace* (New York: Pergamon Press, 1979), p. 82.
37. Glazer & Glazer, p. 146.
38. Ibid., pp. 134–35.
39. Ibid., pp. 59–63.
40. Ibid., p. 66.
41. Quoted in Carey, p. 191.
42. Quoted in Hills, p. 194.
43. Shown in Michael Moore's film, *Roger and Me*; Ralph Nader, and William Taylor, *The Big Boys: Power and Position in American Business* (New York: Pantheon, 1986), pp. 120–28.
44. Quoted in Robert Jackall, *Moral Mazes: The World of Corporate Managers* (New York: Oxford University Press, 1989), p. 127.
45. Quoted in Amalia Duarte, "Workers and AT&T Both Grapple with the Reality of Layoffs," *New York Times*, 28 August 1994, Section 13, p. 1.
46. Quote from Irving L. Janis, *Victims of GroupThink: A Psychological Study of Foreign Policy Decisions and Fiascoes* (Boston: Houghton Mifflin Company, 1972), p. 9.
47. Quoted in Nader and Taylor, p. 77, emphasis in original.
48. 25 October 1994, p. A17.

49. Oreffice quoted in Nader and Taylor, p. 169; Smith quoted p. 127.
50. William Greider, *Who Will Tell the People: The Betrayal of American Democracy* (New York: Simon and Schuster, 1992), p. 56.
51. 27 October 1991, p. A25.
52. Nader and Taylor, p. 169.
53. Ibid., p. 163.
54. Hardert, p. 10.
55. William Lutz, *Doublespeak: From "Revenue Enhancement to Terminal Living": How Government, Business Advertisers and Others Use Language to Deceive You* (New York: HarperPerennial, 1989), p. 128.
56. Lutz, p. 129.
57. Robert Jackall, *Moral Mazes: The World of Corporate Managers* (New York: Oxford University Press, 1988), p. 136.
58. These are somewhat modified from G. William Domhoff, *The Powers That Be: Processes of Ruling Class Domination in America* (New York: Vintage, 1979).
59. Greider, p. 43.
60. Ibid., p. 58.
61. Jeffrey H. Birnbaum, *The Lobbyists: How Influence Peddlers Work Their Way in Washington* (New York: Times Books, 1993), p. 4.
62. Quoted in Birnbaum, p. 25.
63. Robert Pear, "Many Health Groups Fight House Democratic Leaders Plan," *New York Times*, 31 July 1994, p. 14.
64. Katharine Q. Seelye, "Lobbyists Are the Loudest in the Health Care Debate," *New York Times*, 16 August 1994, pp. A1, A12. Quotes from Miller and Citizen Action, p. A12.
65. Neil A. Lewis, and Robert Pear, "Drug Companies Are Fighting Image as Price Gougers," *New York Times*, 7 March 1994, pp. A1, B6.
66. Adam Clymer, "Congress Passes Bill to Disclose Lobbyists' Roles," *New York Times*, 30 December 1995, pp. A1, B12. For an example of astroturf lobbying, see Laura Flanders, "Is It Real . . . Or Is It Astroturf: PR Firm Finds 'Grassroots' Support for Breast Implants," *EXTRA!* (July/August 1996), p. 6.
67. This example comes from my own experience. I am not a smoker, but I am on the mailing lists of several tobacco companies, and I am sure that is why I was contacted.
68. *Public Citizen*, November/December 1996, p. 13.
69. Quotes from Leslie Wayne, "Loopholes Allow Presidential Race to Set a Record," *New York Times*, 8 September 1996, p. 26.
70. Quotes from Wayne, p. 26.
71. On the history of PACs, including the thwarting of reform efforts, see Clawson, Neustadtl, and Scott, pp. 28–33.
72. Ibid., p. 1.
73. Ibid., p. 11.
74. Quoted in ibid., p. 12.
75. Ibid., pp. 36–44.
76. Richard L. Berke, "Companies Supply Parties Lifeblood," *New York Times*, 16 August 1988.
77. Wayne, p. 26.
78. "New Data Show Richest Senator Is Either Heinz, Danforth or Pell," *New York Times*, 21 May 1981; "Several House Members Disclose Assets Valued at Over $1 Million," *New York Times*, 19 May 1981.
79. "Now 2 Millionaires on High Court," *New York Times*, 18 May 1990, p. A32;

Neil A. Lewis, "High Court Nominee Defends Judge's Use of Broad Powers," *New York Times*, 7 July 1993, p. A12.
80. For many examples, see Thomas R. Dye, *Who's Running America: The Conservative Years* (Englewood Cliffs, N.J.: Prentice-Hall, 1986), pp. 59–112.
81. "6 Members of Panel on Smoking Have Ties to Tobacco Group," *New York Times*, 10 November 1990, p. 9.
82. Elaine Sciolino, "State Department Awaits Gergen with Trepidation," *New York Times*, 9 June 1994, p. A18.
83. John J. McCloy, "Repay U.S. Japanese?" *New York Times*, 10 April 1983; "John J. McCloy, Lawyer and Diplomat, Is Dead at 93," *New York Times*, 12 March 1989, p. 44; Kai Bird, *The Chairman: John J. McCloy and the Making of the American Establishment* (New York: Simon and Schuster, 1992).
84. Todd S. Purdham, "The Newest Moynihan," *The New York Times Magazine*, 7 August 1994, p. 26.
85. Greider, p. 48.
86. Domhoff, p. 62.
87. Russ Bellant, *The Coors Connection: How Coors Family Philanthropy Undermines Democratic Pluralism* (Boston: South End Press, 1991).
88. "What Heritage Foundation Does," *New York Times*, 18 November 1994; Norman Solomon, "The Media's Favorite Think Tank: How the Heritage Foundation Turns Money into Media," *EXTRA!* (July/August 1996), pp. 9–12.
89. Robin Toner, "Hillary Clinton's Potent Brain Trust on Health Reform," *New York Times*, 28 February 1993, Section 3, pp. 1, 8.
90. C. Wright Mills, "The Cultural Apparatus" in *Power, Politics and People: The Collected Essays of C. Wright Mills*, ed. Irving L. Horowitz (New York: Ballantine Books, 1963), pp. 405–22. Useful discussions of corporate control of the media can be found in Michael Parenti, *Inventing Reality: The Politics of News Media*, 2d ed. (New York: St. Martin's Press, 1993); Edward S. Herman, and Noam Chomsky, *Manufacturing Consent: The Political Economy of the Mass Media* (New York: Pantheon, 1988). *The Nation* magazine for 3 June 1996 devotes most of its pages to this topic.
91. Susan Ruel, "Body Bag Journalism: Crime Coverage by the U.S. Media," paper presented at International Conference on Violence in the Media, St. John's University, New York, 3–4 October 1994, p. 6; Walter Goodman, "Crime and Black Images in TV News," *New York Times*, 23 December 1993, p. C14.
92. Janine Jackson, and Jim Naureckas, "U.S. News Illustrates Flaws in Crime Coverage," *EXTRA!* (May/June 1994), p. 10; Ruel, pp. 13, 7–10.
93. Barbara Bliss Osborn, "If It Bleeds It Leads—If It Votes It Don't: A Survey of L.A.'s Local News Shows," *EXTRA!* (September/October 1994), p. 15; *Extra* (May/June 1994), p. 27.
94. Jackson and Naurekas, p. 10.
95. U.S. Department of Justice, *SourceBook of Criminal Justice Statistics—1994*, Table 2–1, p. 140.
96. Erik Larson, *Lethal Passage: How the Travels of a Single Handgun Expose the Roots of America's Gun Crisis* (New York: Crown Publishers, 1994), pp. 19, 21; Marianne W. Zawitz, U.S. Department of Justice, Bureau of Justice Statistics, *Guns Used in Crime*, 1995, pp. 1–2.
97. Sam Howe Verhovek, "Unwanted Gun Unimagined Result," *New York Times*, 13 December 1995, p. A18; "A Parent Kills Child Mistaken for a Burglar," *New York Times*, 12 December 1994, p. 18.

98. Adam Nossiter, "Judge Awards Damages in Japanese Youth's Death," *New York Times*, 16 September 1994, p. A12; David E. Sanger, "After Gunman's Acquittal, Japan Struggles to Understand America," *New York Times*, 25 May 1993, pp. A1, A17. Gun ownership does not necessarily produce a high death rate. On this, see Nicholas D. Kristof, "Guns: One Nation Bars, the Other Requires," *New York Times*, 10 March 1996, Section 4, p. 3.

3 / Interpersonal Violence: Street Crime

Many owners of grocery stores in poor, inner-city neighborhoods put on a bulletproof vest and make sure there's a gun at hand before going to work. Unlike supermarkets, there are few customers or workers around at any given time. The stores, open late and one of the few local money-making enterprises, are tempting to thieves looking for some quick cash, even though the net proceeds are sometimes as little as $20.00. In 1993, in New York alone, fifty grocers or their employees were killed during hold-ups at these stores, the highest number of murders for any occupation in that city.[1]

In more affluent, largely white suburbs, teenagers worry about getting into a good college. But in Camden, New Jersey, one of the poorest cities in the United States, the preoccupations are different. At a youth center, a seventeen year old writes a poem about being an astronaut. He is not contemplating a future career so much as imagining a place away from the routine violence in his neighborhood:

> Away from guns and ride-by's and
> everyday fights.
> Away from gangs and drugs and
> burned out houses and speeding
> cars that run down little kids.

Other Camden youngsters draw pictures of children hiding under their beds, and pictures of friends who have been shot. Many can even recount the details of their friends' funerals.[2]

Crime rates and fear of crime are greatest in neighborhoods of color. In 1991, the American Housing Survey asked a sample of respondents to identify what bothered them about their neighborhood. Seventeen percent of African-American households, 12 percent of Latino households, and 6 percent of white households answered crime. In 1992, 50 African-American households per 1,000 experienced violent crimes. The figure for whites was 30.[3]

Why do African-American communities experience higher rates of criminal violence? Answering this question involves looking at how racial inequality interacts with economic and political inequality.

Unsafe Streets: Nothing New

Ethnic stereotyping has been used to explain urban crime in the United States for well over a century. David Dinkins, the former mayor of New York, in his new position teaching political science at Columbia University, read a description of New York to his students:

> Two or three murders take place every day, before breakfast. You risk your life by walking the streets late at night. Homeless people lie in the gutters. Prostitution runs rampant. There are useless expenditures of public money, overtaxation, and improper contracting. The streets are filthy and in disrepair and filled with drivers reckless of human life. There is inadequate health care and TB has reached epidemic proportions and illegal immigrants are entering from ships onto our shores.

This description, which might sound like it came from this morning's newspaper, was in fact from 1856.[4] As European immigrants came to the United States from the 1840s to about 1915, they discovered that jobs were sometimes hard to find and discrimination rampant. Some of those who were locked out of mainstream opportunities found alternative openings in entertainment, sports, and crime, each offering potentially big payoffs. All, however, have serious drawbacks; success is rare and often short-lived, while crime and many sports are physically dangerous.

The Irish, the first large immigrant group in the early nineteenth century, were also the first ethnic group associated with these problems. *Harper's Magazine*, at the time of the Civil War, claimed, "Fully 75 percent of the crimes of violence ... are the work of Irishmen."[5] Later, as Italians and Eastern European Jews came in large numbers to American cities, they were similarly portrayed. For example, in 1890, a prison expert said of the Italian: "The knife with which he cuts his bread he also uses to lop off another 'dago's' finger or ear. . . . He is quite as familiar with the sight of human blood as with the sight of the food he eats."[6]

A 1906 description of Chicago's "Jewtown" claimed that more "murderers, robbers and thieves of the worst kind" came from this area than any other neighborhood. During Prohibition (1919–33), when the opportunity to make big money by illegally supplying liquor arose, one judge went so far as to describe bootlegging as a "Jewish crime wave."[7] Although most Jews were not criminals, there were Jewish-run, organized-crime groups at a time when anti-Semitism limited opportunities for Jewish social mobility.

Then, as now, crime was a result of economic conditions. Criminologist Jeffrey Fagan describes those recruited into the bootlegging business as "young males, in their late teens or early twenties, often children of immigrants raised in slums." They were part of a "surplus labor force," and crime "promised incomes far beyond what they might expect in a declining industrial economy."[8] Like today, a large proportion of those arrested were young, between fifteen and thirty. In another modern parallel, commentators at the time, instead of criticizing the distribution of wealth and power, lamented alleged family disorganization, which they held responsible for delinquency.[9]

THE AFRICAN-AMERICAN CRIMINAL STEREOTYPE

African-Americans are the feared ethnic group of today. Black men get stopped in the streets for being in the "wrong" (i.e., white) neighborhoods, taxis pass them by, and they are followed around stores by salespeople. In 1994, for example, in my class on the sociology of violence, one of my white students, then employed in a New Jersey men's clothing store, recounted how his manager ordered the sales staff to announce a black man's entrance. The first one to spot the unwelcome customer was to tell the others, "Mr. Johnson's here." "Mr. Johnson" was then to be watched. Similar incidents have been described by other students working in retailing, and minority students have described being the victims of unwarranted scrutiny.

Surveys show that whites see blacks as more prone to committing acts of crime and violence. Many might agree with Boston City Councilman James Kelly's statement: "People feel very intimidated by these black males in hooded sweatshirts."[10] Some whites have even used this stereotype to their own advantage. For example, the 1988 George Bush presidential campaign exploited fears of violent blacks in the Willie Horton ads. In the ads, Democratic candidate Michael Dukakis, then governor of Massachusetts, was accused of allowing an African-American inmate a prison furlough during which he murdered a white woman. The Bush ads implicitly promised protection from violent black criminals.

In several incidents, whites have used the violent stereotype of African-American men to cover their own crimes. In 1989, a Boston man, Charles Stuart, shot his pregnant wife, saying it had been done by an African-American man. This touched off a massive manhunt in which many young black men were stopped and questioned by the police. One was actually charged with the killing and arrested. He was released when Stuart's brother revealed who had done the shooting. Stuart subsequently committed suicide. In Milwaukee, in 1992, Jesse Anderson falsely claimed two black men had stabbed his wife to death. The evidence indicated he was the killer.

Table 3.1 Arrest Rates for Violent Crimes per 100,000 Persons

YEAR	UNDER 18		18 AND OLDER	
	WHITE	BLACK	WHITE	BLACK
1970	42	465	104	988
1992	126	678	216	1,361

Source: U.S. Department of Justice, *SourceBook of Criminal Justice Statistics—1994*, Table 4.18, p. 403.

In Yonkers, New York, in 1993, six officers were involved in covering up a fight between two of them. They accused a young black man of the assault to explain one cop's injuries. In 1994, Susan Smith, a South Carolina mother, drowned her two sons; at first, she claimed a black man had stolen her car and children. Dr. Alvin Poussaint, a psychiatrist who has written on racism in the United States, described Susan Smith as knowing "what would work best to direct attention away from her: point the finger at a black man."[11]

Responding to the South Carolina case, African-Americans expressed their feelings about the false accusations. Inez Chappel, a sixty-seven-year-old Baltimore woman, felt the story "just goes to show that racism is alive and well and free in America." In Boston, a young hospital orderly, Kevin Pippins, reminded of the Stuart killing, said, "It was the exact same thing.... Why'd she try to blame it on a black man ... to cover up their hoax they use a black man. That's not good at all." At Northwestern University, an African-American professor commented on how the Smith case revealed

> once again the stereotypical view of black men in America, ... they are the other, ... they are dangerous ... and they should be imprisoned. It is the same view that causes black men to be stopped, searched and harassed on a routine basis by the police.[12]

It is true that African-Americans account for a disproportionate number of those arrested for violent crimes. Table 3.1 compares violent crime arrest rates for blacks and whites in 1970 and 1992. Table 3.1 shows that for both time periods and both age groups, African-Americans have higher arrest rates than whites, although arrest rates for whites are increasing. The arrest rates, however, reflect not only greater violence by blacks but a greater probability they will be arrested.

The greater likelihood of arrest is partly due to what criminologists call the social ecology of crime. Poorer African-Americans generally commit crimes in more public places than other groups, making their acts more visible and them more subject to apprehension. This will be discussed further below. They are more likely to live in neighborhoods with more geographic mobility. In such areas, with lots of people moving in and out, it is easier for undercover agents to operate than in more stable communities where people have known one another for a period of time.[13]

There is also racial bias in the criminal justice system at every level. Nonetheless, blacks, who are about 12 percent of the population, do seem to account for more violent crime. In 1993, blacks were 58 percent of those arrested for murder. This last statistic is probably the most reliable, because a large proportion of all murderers are arrested.[14]

Despite the appearances, it is not race but class that accounts for the overrepresentation of African-Americans in violent crime arrests. When social class is controlled, there is little difference between whites and blacks in the commission of violent crimes. The dean of Boston's Northeastern University College of Criminal Justice found that when you take income into account, "the discrepancy at which whites and blacks commit crime disappears." Lower-income groups, regardless of ethnicity, commit more street crimes, but as young lower-income white males get older, they are more likely to find legitimate work.[15] Latinos also have lower-average incomes and higher-unemployment rates than whites, and the discussion below on unemployment and crime is relevant to them.

Some historical background is needed to explain how past economic and political policies have created an underclass that is kept off the opportunity ladder, increasingly put into prisons, and disproportionately comprised of people of color.

SEPARATE AND UNEQUAL: APARTHEID, U.S. STYLE

Many descendants of European immigrants achieved middle-class lifestyles despite the initial hardships of their ancestors. We are taught that such success is a result of hard work, a two-parent family structure, or some other characteristic supposedly lacking among blacks. These explanations, however, overlook the depths and impact of American racism.

The offspring of white immigrants are correct in their belief that their relatives often faced great difficulties in their new country. Many also share the sentiments of Catherine Nielsen, who lives in the all-white Chicago neighborhood of Mount Greenwood and thinks discrimination is past history: "It's up to them to paddle their own canoe. They shouldn't always think about the fact that they were slaves."[16]

The racism faced by African-Americans, however, extends beyond anything experienced by other ethnic groups and results in the inequalities discussed in chapter 2. Political and economic decisions have created a highly racially segregated society. This segregation is crucial to our understanding of certain aspects of both interpersonal violence and structural violence.

As industrialization increased following the Civil War, European immigrants provided cheap labor for an expanding economy. For many of them, this economic growth eventually provided opportunities that are far less available to African-American and Latino urban populations. As immigrants poured into cities, they took jobs in factories and participated in the construction of the urban centers in which they were settling.

Italians, for example, were the major ethnic group that built the New York subways. They composed three-quarters of the building laborers in New York.[17] Sociologist Stephen Steinberg describes the advantages of Jewish immigrants who already had "industrial experience and concrete occupational skills that would serve them well in America's expanding industrial economy." They were especially concentrated in the garment trade, which was the most rapidly growing of U.S. industries just before the First World War.[18] Earlier Irish immigrants had found jobs in municipal government, and in police and fire departments, which is why so many police and fire persons march in St. Patrick's Day parades. In New York City, a tuition-free city college system between 1847 and 1976 facilitated immigrant children's social mobility. Farther west, German and Scandinavian immigrants benefited from the lands taken from the native population.

While Europeans were finding economic niches, the descendants of African slaves were working as agricultural laborers in the South. As long as their labor was needed, the Southern elite made it difficult for them to leave. African-Americans had less freedom of movement than did immigrants. They were kept tied to the land by the system of sharecropping, denied education, and the vote that had been promised by the Fifteenth Amendment. Brutality and lynching were used as means of intimidating those who might attempt to challenge the racial hierarchy.

Around the time of the First World War, an infestation of boll weevils lessened the need for black labor in the cotton fields. At the same time, the war curtailed the supply of immigrant labor, and blacks could hope to find jobs in manufacturing. The Second World War similarly promised opportunities. Following the war, mechanization in Southern agriculture meant Southern employers again had less need for field workers. These push-pull forces led to waves of migration out of the South. Like the Europeans who left their homes to find a better life, millions of African-Americans moved North, to a region they called "the promised land."[19]

Over time, the immigrants and their descendants were able to achieve a certain level of comfort. The creation of unions that improved their wages and working conditions was instrumental in this. African-Americans, however, were excluded from many of the craft unions established by the immigrants. This exclusion was accompanied by residential segregation.

"CHOCOLATE CITIES, VANILLA SUBURBS"[20]

Immigrants from one European country lived in communities with immigrants from other countries. Their white children moved into even more ethnically integrated, although still white, neighborhoods. But when African-Americans moved in, whites moved out of the neighborhood, and increasingly out of the cities.

Political and economic decisions have produced a highly segregated society. This segregation is crucial to understanding certain aspects of both interpersonal violence and structural violence, which will be discussed further in subsequent chapters. Douglas S. Massey, director of the University of Chicago's Population Research Center and coauthor, with Nancy Denton, of a major study on contemporary urban segregation, describes how important residential separation is:

> Where you live determines the chances you get in this world. It determines the school your children go to, the crime you're exposed to, the peer influences on your children. If you're isolated from the mainstream, it's not a fair world, it's not a fair contest. Segregation is structural underpinning of the underclass.[21]

Both the government and private business played active roles in promoting the flight of whites to the suburbs as African-Americans were concentrated in the inner cities. The Federal Housing Administration (FHA) and the Veterans' Administration (VA) were especially prominent. From its inception, for example, the FHA accepted segregation, even stating in its 1939 *Underwriting Manual*, "if a neighborhood is to retain stability, it is necessary that properties shall continue to be occupied by the same social and racial classes."[22]

The FHA and the VA made millions of dollars available for housing loans. The FHA lowered risks to banks by providing loan guarantees and extended loan repayment periods so that a home buyer could have lower, more affordable monthly payments. FHA loans were more available for buying a new home than for remodeling an existing city dwelling. Government policy, in other words, allowed urban housing conditions to deteriorate.

When soldiers returned from World War II, the Serviceman's Adjustment Act (the G.I. Bill) administered by the VA made it financially possible for many veterans to buy their own homes. White veterans, however, could more easily obtain VA mortgages, and many moved from the cities. By 1960, the suburbs were about 90 percent white, and that figure has not appreciably changed.[23]

The federal government also subsidized highway systems, which had the effect of encouraging the development of suburbs. From 1956 to 1972, the government spent over $55 billion on the interstate highway system alone.

In contrast, only $3.1 billion was allocated from 1970 to 1975 for urban mass transit. This pattern has continued with help (and pressure) from the auto industry. Between 1990 and 1995, for example, the federal treasury provided nearly five times as much to highways as it did to urban mass transit, about $98 billion to $22 billion.[24]

Private lending agencies also helped establish and perpetuate residential segregation. Restrictive covenants were a device used for years to maintain a color barrier; deeds to property had a clause that the owners would not sell to a group considered "undesirable." The Supreme Court declared these agreements unconstitutional in 1948, but numerous discriminatory practices have continued, for example, the practice of not showing African-Americans homes or apartments in certain areas, or lying about the availability of a dwelling. Larger security deposits or down payments have also sometimes been required from African-Americans than from whites.

Banks are involved as well, engaging in a practice called "redlining": denying loans to certain areas of the city. This practice was initiated in the 1930s by the federal Home Owners Loan Corporation (HOLC), which had an *explicit* policy of keeping funds away from black neighborhoods. In fact, lower-income whites, in some localities, have found it easier to get bank loans than more affluent African-Americans. Recent studies have found that although about a third of African-American mortgage applicants are rejected, for whites the figure is 14 percent.[25]

Over the years, African-Americans have been discouraged from moving out of their neighborhoods by white homeowners themselves. African-American families moving into white neighborhoods are still sometimes greeted by bricks through their windows, crosses burnt on their lawns, or racist graffiti painted on the exteriors of their homes.

In 1968, following the urban disorders of the 1960s, Congress passed the Fair Housing Act banning discrimination. Although it is an important statement of values, the act has not been enforced with any regularity.

SEGREGATED CITIES, SEGREGATED JOB MARKETS

Federally subsidized highways, discussed earlier, made it possible for suburbanites to commute to their city jobs. The suburbs themselves eventually became attractive to companies; taxes were lower, property cheaper, and suburban housewives constituted a pool of educated women available for employment in the expanding service sector. For example, during the 1970s, New York City's suburbs gained half a million jobs while the city itself lost 95,000. In Chicago's suburbs, 630,000 jobs were created during a period when that city lost 88,000.[26]

The movement of jobs into the suburbs put African-Americans at a further disadvantage. Housing discrimination makes it difficult, for even those African-Americans who could afford it, to follow their employer. If the jobs move and transportation is a problem, then for all practical purposes, the jobs are not available.

The effects of suburbanization have been compounded since the 1970s by a decrease in manufacturing, called *deindustrialization*, which has meant the loss of many good paying blue collar jobs. A study of manufacturing plants with one hundred or more employees for the years 1978–82 found that in each of those years an average of nine hundred thousand jobs were lost to plant closings, translating into more than 3 million jobs in four years. African-American men have been especially hard hit by economic change, as they were usually the last hired and the first fired when cutbacks occurred. Throughout the United States between 1979 and 1984, for example, "nearly a third of all black men working in durable goods manufacturing in the United States lost their jobs."[27]

New Jersey, my home state, has some of the poorest cities in the United States due to the economic changes. The New Jersey Council of Churches reported that "between 1970 and 1985 total employment in the six major cities decreased by almost 28 percent." In this same period, there was job growth in suburban areas.[28] In the decade 1970–80, close-by Philadelphia lost 35 percent of its manufacturing jobs. At the end of that period, African-Americans had become 40 percent of the city's population, as whites continued to move beyond the city limits.[29] A specialist on urban development, John J. Kasarda, summarized the situation for four cities:

> Between 1967 and 1987, Chicago lost 60 percent of its manufacturing jobs, Detroit 51 percent, New York City 58 percent and Philadelphia 64 percent. During this same period, New York City added over 110,000 manufacturing jobs in suburban rings and Chicago 34,000.[30]

Lawrence Hunter, a forty-eight-year-old Milwaukee, Wisconsin, resident, looks back to the days when "you could go a foundry and get a job any day." Those days are gone. In Milwaukee, a highly segregated city, between 1979 and 1990 there was a loss of 46,800 manufacturing jobs in the old smoke-stack industries with more devastating effects on African-Americans than whites. Isabel Wilkerson described why this was so in the *New York Times*.

> At factories that laid off only some workers, whites often had seniority and were retained. And even for whites who were laid off, the prosperity of the white parts of the city insured that new businesses would spring up there, offering jobs suitable for former assembly line workers. Such jobs have generally not appeared in black sections. The result is a city of 628,000 people where black men stand idle on street corners just blocks from the breweries and factories that used to employ them,

while well-dressed white collar workers sell insurance or computers out of some of those same factories now converted into office parks.[31]

The *spatial mismatch hypothesis* is used by some social scientists to explain how the movement of jobs away from industrial cities has led to high levels of unemployment among African-American males.

A study in Chicago, where this hypothesis has often been used to explain urban problems, showed that there are other variables besides job movement that help account for black male unemployment. The 1986–87 study compared a sample of black, white, Mexican, and Puerto Rican males, finding that especially for blacks, the problem of job movement is compounded by a lack of transportation alternatives to seek the now more distant jobs and a lack of relevant skills as a result of lower-quality education.[32] The researchers also found that employers prefer Mexican immigrants to African-Americans, even with low levels of education for lower-paying jobs where language skills are not too important. In addition, these jobs are filled through informal networks; those already holding them, unlikely to be African-Americans, bring in friends or relatives as new openings occur. This is done with the encouragement of the employer.[33]

Racist stereotyping still often affects job opportunities. An Urban Institute study of Chicago factory employers found that African-American men were considered "unstable, uncooperative, dishonest, and uneducated."[34] A white businessman in that city claimed, "Basically, the Oriental is much more aggressive and intelligent and studious than the Hispanic. The Hispanics, except Cubans of course . . . are mañana, mañana, mañana—tomorrow, tomorrow, tomorrow." But, for him, the least desirable non-whites were African-Americans, whom he described as "the laziest of the bunch."[35]

In a Chicago suburb, the manager of a drugstore was not likely to hire an inner-city job applicant, claiming, "You'd be afraid they're going to steal from you. They grow up that way. They grow up dishonest and I guess you'd feel like, geez, how are they going to be honest here?"[36]

Chicago is not unique. Job audits in other cities, where matched whites and African-Americans applied for the same job, have also found stereotyping and discrimination lessen black employment prospects.

Decrease Jobs: Increase Crime

Prisoners in the United States are disproportionately drawn from the ranks of the disadvantaged: minorities, the less educated, those without full-time employment, and the poor. Table 3.2 illustrates some of the relevant characteristics of state and federal prison populations for 1991. Most prisoners are in the state system: 704,000 compared with 54,000 federal prisoners.

Table 3.2 Selected Characteristics of Federal and State Prison Inmates, 1991, Compared to U.S. Population

	STATE PRISONS	FEDERAL PRISONS	U.S. POPULATION
African-American	46%	30%	12%
Hispanic	17%	28%	9%
White	38%	35%	84%
Less than high school	41%	33%	25% (1990)
Not employed	33%	26%	6% (white)
Employed full time	67%	74%	81%
Less than $15,000 annual income	69%	54%	37% (males)

Notes: Over 90 percent of prisoners in both systems are male—the group described by these statistics. The U.S. population figures are for both genders. Employment and income status are at time of arrest.

Sources: Ethnicity, work status, income, U.S. Department of Justice, Bureau of Justice Statistics, *Comparing Federal and State Prison Inmates, 1991*, Tables 1, 2, p. 2; U.S. ethnicity, education, unemployment, income, *Statistical Abstract of the United States, 1994*, Table 12, p. 13; Table 236, p. 159; Table 723, p. 473; Table 616, p. 396. U.S. population full-time employment, Lawrence Mishel and Jared Bernstein, *The State of Working America: 1992–93* (Armonk, N.Y.: M. E. Sharpe, 1993), pp. 228–29.

Numerous studies show a causal relation between joblessness and crime: first unemployment rises, then the crime rate. Researchers Mary Merva and Richard Fowles found that from 1976 to 1990, in 30 metropolitan areas, each 1 percent rise in unemployment was matched by a 7 percent increase in homicides and a 3 percent rise in other violent crimes. Putting this into absolute numbers for 1990–92, they estimate that "increases in the unemployment rate may have been responsible... for 1,459 additional homicides [and] 62,607 additional violent crimes."[37]

The relationship between unemployment and homicide has also been found in a number of international studies. For example, in 1991 about half of English and Welsh prisoners were unemployed at the time of their arrest and were less educated than the general population.[38] Criminologist Elliot Currie summarizes the data on this point:

> The countries that developed humane and effective employment policies had both much lower unemployment and much less crime throughout the postwar period. Between 1959 and 1976 the average unemployment rate in the United States was nearly double that of... Italy and the United Kingdom, and between three and four times the average rate in countries like West Germany, Sweden, Norway, Austria and Japan; while its homicide rate ranged up to more than ten times that of these countries.... In a 1976 comparison of twenty-four countries... Marvin Krohn of the University of Iowa found that high rates of unemployment were predictably associated with high rates of homicide.[39]

THE ROLE OF INEQUALITY

Poverty in the United States is largely a consequence of decisions made by the more powerful organizations and individuals; their decisions ripple down into the lives of individuals. As discussed above, some of these decisions have also resulted in racial inequality and de facto segregation. This latter fact means not only that African-Americans are more likely to be without jobs but also that living in different communities makes it less likely that whites and blacks will join together to deal with common problems, which makes both groups weaker and allows the conditions that lead to violence, including the criminal violence described below, to persist.

Those most hurt by changes in the economy can realize there are alternatives to crime. For example, in April 1996, a group of predominately Latino teenagers, some of them gang members, met in Washington to discuss a plan for the government to create alternatives to crime, violence, and incarceration in their communities. Over two decades earlier, in 1972, sixty black gang leaders presented a similar set of proposals to the Los Angeles City Human Relations Conference, which included creating jobs and improving recreation, housing, and schools. In the words of journalist Mike Davis, the young people

> clearly understood that they were the children of deferred dreams and defeated equality. . . . Black and Chicano gang leaders have always affirmed, in the handful of other instances over the last eighteen years when they have been allowed to speak, decent jobs are the price for negotiating a humane end to drug dealing and gang violence.[40]

However perceptive their insight, these spokesmen lacked the political clout that could have produced social change. Their ideas were not implemented, and conditions in their communities deteriorated further.

Social programs and decent unemployment benefits can help decrease desperation, anger, and violent crime, but these programs are consistently opposed by business interests. At higher levels of unemployment, and with little public support, workers tend to be more competitive with one another and demand less of employers, factors discussed more fully in chapter 5. Between 1980 and 1990, even as crime was supposed to be our biggest problem, government spending on all employment programs decreased from $10.3 billion to $5.4 billion.

THEY WANT TO WORK

If people really want to work, surely they can find jobs, can't they? In 1982, with the official rate of African-American unemployment rising, then president Reagan was asked what advice he would give the unemployed. He replied that he had seen twenty-four pages of help wanted ads in the Sunday *Washington Post*. One reporter decided to check out ads in that paper and found that there were 1,059 listed at a time when there were officially 77,600 people unemployed in Washington, D.C. Looking closely, the reporter also found that some jobs were come-ons for courses, some were far out of town or overseas, and a number paid by commissions only. Others required craft skills, a license, or managerial or professional experience. A similar study had been conducted earlier, in 1978, by a *Fortune* reporter in Middletown, New York. Of the 228 jobs advertised, only 142 were full-time positions in the area, covering less than 2 percent of the 7,800 unemployed people in this community at the time. Again, many of the jobs were for highly skilled persons, such as for auto mechanics and nurses.[41]

Journalistic accounts of employment opportunities for disadvantaged youth in particular illustrate just how elusive a job can be. Salvatore Martinez lives in the poorest area of Los Angeles and has been looking for work as a laborer. As a high school dropout, ex-gang member, and former jail inmate, he is not likely to be attractive to employers. His quest took him to the Vargas Furniture Manufacturing Company where his father once worked, and they weren't hiring. The receptionist's comments on Salvatore contradict the myths about the unemployed as people who just don't want to work:

> If I gave this boy an application, the whole area around would hear about it and people would appear out of nowhere. When we do have jobs, we post them, and we get scores of people, lines and lines of people around the block.

Mike Davis and other journalists corroborate her observation.

> The scale of pent-up demand for decent manual employment was... vividly demonstrated a few years ago when *fifty thousand* predominately Black and Chicano youth lined up for miles to apply for a few openings on the unionized longshore in San Pedro [an area of Los Angeles].[42]

In lower-income white neighborhoods, there is still more work available than in minority communities. There are more economic enterprises, small businesses, some factories, and so forth. Neighborhoods populated by people of color are more likely to have small groceries (the bodegas mentioned earlier) than supermarkets, where local teenagers could find part-time jobs. A study in New York City found that in poor neighborhoods, there are 17,232 people per supermarket; in more affluent ones, the ratio is 6,580 for each chain market. Movie houses can be rare. In Newark, New Jersey, the central city celebrated in 1993, after twenty-five years, when a multiplex opened. Three years later, there was another celebration—this time because a Rite-Aid drugstore had been built. Public housing, a feature of many urban areas, offers less job opportunities to local residents than private housing, because hiring is done by civil service.[43]

People do want to work, but there are many more applicants than there are jobs. The unskilled and less educated stand in line, along with unemployed college graduates or experienced blue collar workers. They are victims of decisions they had no role in making.

When Marriot Hotels announced 296 openings for a new hotel being built on Long Island, New York, 4,508 people showed up. Some stood in line for seven and a half hours waiting for applications. In Cleveland, a press account told of 15,000 "unemployed workers, welfare mothers and teenagers, some standing in the freezing rain for four hours" hoping to be lucky enough to be hired for $4.50 an hour temporary jobs cleaning up city parks and vacant lots. In Chicago, 15,000 competed for 3,800 temporary jobs. In Baltimore, an announcement of 75 openings at the Social Security Administration drew at least 26,200 applicants, mostly African-American. With only 3 interviews per position, the agency was going to use a lottery system to choose applicants. A Social Security Administration spokesman remarked, "This proves what black leaders have been saying for years—people would rather have jobs than be on welfare."[44]

At 7:00 A.M. on 16 March 1995, Jeanne Wright stood in a line already two blocks long. Nine hundred people, mostly African-American and Latino, had come to a Labor Department office to apply for arduous temporary jobs, with no benefits, at a New York state General Motors plant. Some even arrived at four o'clock in the morning. But, as Ms. Wright explained to a reporter, waiting hours for an application was "still better than standing on the welfare line."[45]

Detroit Representative John Conyers, a member of the black congressional caucus, explained what should be obvious to all politicians:

> When survival is at stake, it should not be surprising that criminal activity begins to resemble an opportunity rather than a cost, work rather than deviance, and a possibly profitable undertaking that is superior to a coerced existence directed by welfare bureaucrats.[46]

On a bitter cold November day in 1993 in Detroit, job seekers, mostly African-American, lined up, hoping for work at a gambling casino that was not even approved yet. The 4,000 jobs, which will probably never materialize, would pay less than $20,000 a year. By day's end, over 10,000 had received their applications. Bessie Sibbaluca, on welfare and supporting two children, explained her presence on the line: "There's nothing else happening but crime."[47]

"GETTING PAID": CRIME AS AN ALTERNATIVE TO WORK

Anthropologist Mercer Sullivan studied employment opportunities and youth crime in three ethnically distinct New York City neighborhoods: white, Latino, and African-American. Employment was a problem in all three but mostly so in the African-American neighborhood. Youths in each neighborhood engaged in crime, referring to this as "getting paid," but there were differences. The employed white youths committed some of their crimes at their workplaces and were thus less observable. Although some of these young criminals were caught by their employers, none were ever turned in to the police. Therefore, they avoided having criminal records, which would later decrease their chances for employment.

In the white and Latino neighborhoods, young men found it easy to break into factories and apartments; but in the African-American community, there were no factories, and the newer project apartments were more secure. Young criminals in black neighborhoods more often accosted their victims in undefended public spaces such as elevators, stairwells, spaces between buildings, and the street. After honing their criminal skills in these places close to home, they applied their abilities further afield, in the subways and downtown area.[48]

Engaging in street crime is a way to make money if there are few other options. Economist Richard B. Freeman calculated average earnings from street crime at about $19 an hour. Others have estimated up to $30 an hour with a monthly income of about $2,000.[49] Crime has other attractions: You get to set your own hours, and you aren't constantly supervised. There is also a certain excitement to engaging in illegal behavior. Youth crime, in addition, provides a form of social identification as much of it is done in groups. This helps explain the appeal of gangs.

THE AFRICAN-AMERICAN FAMILY AND CRIME: FALSE CONNECTIONS

It has become fashionable to blame female–head-of-households for African-American crime. Single-parent families and high crime rates, however, often occur under the same condition: lack of decent jobs. As the unemployment rate for black males has risen so has the percentage of female–head-of-households in the African-American community. Poor employment opportunities, combined with high mortality rates and rates of imprisonment, means a sizable proportion of African-American males have low potential as good spouses.

One consequence of female–head-of-households is that there is one less adult in the household to supervise and control younger people. Adults in stable two-parent families can watch not only their own children but others as well. In Los Angeles, it is estimated that there are over a quarter of a million children between ages five and fourteen who have to take care of themselves from the time school ends until a parent returns from work. The city allots few resources for these children, leaving some to find entertainment as well as a substitute family in a gang.[50]

COMMUNITY STRUCTURE AND CRIME

Areas of prolonged unemployment are likely to be poor areas. Not all impoverished communities, however, have high crime rates. Poor rural communities, for example, usually have less crime than urban communities. This is probably because there is less opportunity and less anonymity. In contrast, there is more moving in and out of urban communities as people go where the work is. There are more strangers and less concern with what others are doing in the city.

As crime increases in a neighborhood, people become more fearful and retreat, as much as they can, from the streets. In one study comparing more stable communities in San Francisco with those that were disintegrating due to job loss, researchers concluded,

> Without substantive jobs it is only a matter of time before a community begins to disintegrate as a social unit. . . . On blocks where residents had control and a sense of ownership over public space, there is no crack trafficking or "hanging out." Children were able to play outside their homes; older residents kept a watchful eye during the day; and blinds and curtains were open to let sunlight in. In the declining and most depressed areas, children were kept inside their apartments. Despite relatively dense block populations, there were few people on the streets during the day or night. Curtains and blinds were closed 24 hours per day.[51]

Fear of crime may even keep people from looking more actively for work. This was the case with 230 welfare mothers living in Chicago housing projects. The women moved to the suburbs as part of the settlement of a federal housing segregation lawsuit. Researchers who were studying these women found that

> the women talked about how liberating it was to be able to go out at night and not feel danger. People remarked repeatedly how oppressive it was to live in the projects. They felt they couldn't get a job, because it wasn't safe to be out after dark. And they didn't want to leave their kids alone after school, because they were frightened they would be lured into the gangs.[52]

The women also noticed how many more jobs were available in the suburbs compared with the city.

WORK-FREE DRUG ZONES

Unemployment is damaging on an individual level, especially for men, and this will be discussed more in the next two chapters. Social movements can combat feelings of failure by offering larger explanations for joblessness. In the absence of such movements, however, drinking and/or drug use can be a way of alleviating demoralization. Drugs in particular are associated with crime and violence.

Unemployment and poverty help widen the market for drug users, and dealing drugs offers alternative economic opportunities just as illegal alcohol trafficking did during Prohibition (1919–33). Studies in Holland and England also show that as unemployment increases so does drug use. In the United States, drug use is higher in lower-income white areas than in more affluent minority areas. In some communities, drug trafficking is a major source of money for young people.[53]

Marietta Powell, a Gary, Indiana, mother of five, is aware of the relation between jobs, drugs, and violence. She told a reporter there are "no jobs in this city for young people, so they're killing each other up over drugs." Gary, Indiana, was once a center of the U.S. steel industry, the flames from the mills visible twenty-four hours a day from the highways skirting the city. In 1996, there were 5,000 working at mills that had 30,000 workers in the 1960s.[54]

Anthropologist Philippe Bourgois spent five years in Harlem doing research on "the underground economy," which includes drug dealing. He found that youths involved in crime have essentially the same values as the larger population but lack the opportunities to reach socially approved goals of a good material life and respect from others. He describes the dealers he met as "ambitious, energetic" and "attracted to the underground economy precisely because they believe in the rags-to-riches American dreams." Some see themselves as entrepreneurs setting up a small business that they hope will grow. With unemployment twice as high in Harlem, Bourgois concluded, the "economic incentive to participate in the burgeoning crack economy" was "overwhelming."[55]

Mel, a Harlem drug dealer until he was shot seven times when he was eighteen, could be one of the people described by Bourgois. At age twelve, Mel was supporting himself and a younger sister, making $400 a week selling drugs, often to "people from outside the block, outside the city. It was more white people than black people.... I figured there was only one way to take care of me and my little sister." As he moved up in the business, he earned $5,000 a week, after expenses, and employed ten others.

Those who control the drug trafficking make the most money and face fewer daily dangers than do the inner-city dealers. Even at the local level, there is a wide range of earnings. Dealers like Mel are making thousands a week. Others are paid less for renting out storage space in their apartments, being lookouts for the police, buying guns, transporting drugs, and so forth. Some work eight hour days and are paid weekly. For a brief while, Mel was making hundreds of thousands of dollars a year, but he's out of business now, spending his days in a wheelchair, paralyzed by a bullet in his spine.[56] There are no statistics on the occupational hazards of drug dealing, but dealers face much greater physical risks than legitimate business people, professionals, or politicians.

THE VIOLENT NARCOTICS BUSINESS

In a New York City courtroom, Nelson Sepulveda testified how his gang killed at least ten people, including a "regular customer" who tried to cheat him with counterfeit money. They also shot members of rival drug-selling gangs, killing several bystanders in the process. During his trial, he referred to drugs as "the work" and described the different tasks various "workers" in his gang did, from cutting and weighing to handling payments.[57]

Homicide rates in U.S. cities have increased dramatically as drug use and trafficking have increased, just as they increased during Prohibition. The FBI estimates that in 1993 a minimum of 1,280 murders were committed during the manufacturing or selling of narcotics. That's about 6 percent of the homicides for that year—a figure that does not include murders associated with robbery or intimidation that might be connected with drug dealing. A study of murders in the seventy-five most heavily populated U.S. counties found that in 1988 nearly 20 percent of the arrests involved some aspect of narcotics trafficking.[58]

Criminologist Scott Decker studied gun violence in eleven cities, five of which had the highest violent crime rates in the United States. Decker concluded that it is drug dealers and their associates who are most likely to be using guns, many of them acquired illegally, some traded for narcotics by addicts. Dealers need guns to protect themselves from theft, in Decker's view. New York City's chief narcotics prosecutor concurred with his basic findings, saying, "People have a common misperception, that drug users use guns to support their habits. That is true in some cases. But law enforcement has found it is usually the dealers who have the guns."[59]

In an article published by the National Institute of Justice, the U.S. Department of Justice's research wing, Alfred Blumstein notes that increased youth violence, especially since 1985, can be best explained by

> the rapid growth of the crack markets in the mid-1980's. To service that growth, juveniles were recruited, they were armed with the guns that are standard tools of the drug trade and these guns then were diffused into the larger community of juveniles.[60]

Illegal trades are likely to be violent. People who cheat you can't be taken to court for violating contracts. Physical violence, therefore, is sometimes the only effective way of assuring debts are paid; it helps maintain hierarchy within criminal organizations and is a common means of fending off competing gangs in the battle for markets. Markets can't be sustained or broadened by ads in magazines, billboards, or by paying to have your product shown in a movie or a television show, the techniques available to tobacco companies. Philippe Bourgois found that in East Harlem

> Regular displays of violence are necessary for success in the underground economy—especially the street-level drug-dealing world. Violence is essential for maintaining credibility and preventing rip-offs by colleagues, customers, and intruders. Thus behavior that appears irrationally violent and self-destructive to the middle- or working-class outsider can be interpreted, according to the logic of the underground economy, as judicious public relations.[61]

Crack-cocaine seems to be especially associated with violence. Several factors converge to cause this. Crack is relatively cheap and offers possibilities of new markets among those with the lowest incomes. As more dealers try to capitalize on these markets, they use violence to discourage the competition. Some crack dealers were already adept at using violence and transferred these skills to their new trade.[62]

Joan Moore, a sociologist who has studied gangs in East Los Angeles, notes

> the crack economy has vastly increased the number of drug dealers in several inner-city communities; the technology and availability of cocaine have coincided with a shriveling of decent job opportunities in many of these communities. And, according to recent evidence, crack dealing almost invariably involves violence; dealers threaten both each other and the community.[63]

JUST SAY YES TO DRUGS: GOVERNMENT AND BUSINESS COMPLICITY

In 1989, Senator John Kerry of Nebraska chaired hearings of the Foreign Relations Subcommittee on Terrorism, Narcotics, and International Operations. A summary of the committee's findings is an astounding indictment of the U.S. government's involvement in the illegal narcotics business:

> The subcommittee found that the secret Contra war provided numerous opportunities for drug traffickers to link up with the Contras, and they did.... The subcommittee found cases in which high U.S. officials intervened to stop law enforcement operations aimed at nailing drug kingpins. We found that a United States Ambassador to the Bahamas had shut down a Justice Department drug sting aimed at bringing down

corrupt Bahamian Government officials. We learned how high United States officials, including Lt. Col. Oliver North, went to the Justice Department to intercede on behalf of a man convicted of a narco-terrorist assassination plot against a Honduran President.... We were told by a former United States Ambassador to Costa Rica that a decision was made by the United States to "put Noriega on the shelf" and take no action against his drug trafficking until the Sandinista government had been overthrown. We also found out that the State Department chose four companies controlled by drug traffickers to provide assistance to the Contras. As a result, drug traffickers got funds out of the United States public treasury as part of our Contra humanitarian assistance program.[64]

Kerry's list makes it clear that U.S. foreign policy is implicated in narcotics trafficking, and his list can be extended. A CIA-created Haitian intelligence unit was engaged in drug dealing while receiving millions of dollars from our taxes. The United States funded and supplied the rebels against the Soviet backed government of Afghanistan, even though it was well known they were growing opium for heroin in areas they controlled. During the Vietnam War, the government, especially through the CIA, was involved with all phases of the narcotics business, even though one of the by-products of this business was the addiction of thousands of U.S. soldiers.[65]

Recently, investigative journalist Gary Webb, in a series for the *San Jose Mercury News*, compiled evidence that the CIA was instrumental in opening

the first pipeline between Colombia's cocaine cartels and the black neighborhoods of Los Angeles, a city now known as the "crack" capital of the world. The cocaine that flooded in helped spark a crack explosion in urban America... and provided the cash and connections needed for L.A.'s gangs to buy automatic weapons.[66]

Contra rebels, supported by the CIA, were selling cocaine in the 1980s and were supposed to be using the profits to buy weapons for overthrowing the Sandinista government in Nicaragua. The CIA provided support and protection for the operation.

A key figure in this endeavor was Oscar Blandon, a Contra leader. In 1986, Congress appropriated about $100 million for the Contra subversion efforts, and the drug money became less important. Blandon was then arrested but served only two and one-half years in prison. After his release, he became an informant with the Drug Enforcement Agency, which, at the time of Webb's stories, had paid him over $166,000.

Cocaine had been used mostly by the affluent, but if the market could be expanded, there was a potential for greatly increasing profits from the drug. Rick Ross, an entrepreneurial drug dealer, became the major disseminator of crack. Webb describes what happened.

[Blandon] and his compatriots arrived in South-Central L.A. right when street-level drug users [sic] were figuring out how to make the cocaine affordable: by changing the pricey white powder into powerful little nuggets that could be smoked—crack. Cocaine smokers got an explosive high unmatched by 10 times as much snorted powder. . . . Anyone with $20 could get wasted.[67]

Blandon sold the cocaine, on consignment, to Ross, whose sophisticated operation turned it into crack, which was then sold all over the country.

Ross was unaware of the source of the drug, and it might have made no difference to him had he known. His role, however, does not diminish that of the government whose responsibility it is to prevent drug trafficking—not abet it.

California Congresswoman Maxine Waters, representing South-Central Los Angeles, described her feelings regarding Webb's allegations.

As someone who has seen how the crack cocaine trade has devastated the South-Central Los Angeles community, I cannot exaggerate my feelings of dismay that my own government may have played a part in the origins and history of this problem. Portions of this country may have been exposed, indeed introduced, to the horror of crack cocaine because certain U.S. government or organized operatives smuggled, transported and sold it to American citizens.[68]

California Senator Barbara Boxer wrote in an August letter to CIA director John Deutch that "even the notion that the U.S. government was involved in trafficking is sickening."[69]

The narcotics business is a complex web of relationships in which drug use and dealing are only a couple of strands. Social conditions and psychological dispositions may lead some to a desire for narcotics. Other forces are involved in making narcotics *available* for illegal marketing. The notion of "criminal" then must be broadened beyond street criminals and organized crime if we are ever to understand the real roots of narcotics violence. Over thirty years ago, Malcolm X understood this clearly:

When a person is a drug addict, he's not the criminal; he's a victim of the criminal. The criminal is the man downtown who brings this drug into the country. Negroes can't bring drugs into this country. You don't have any boats. You don't have any airplanes. You don't have any diplomatic immunity. It is not you who is responsible for bringing in drugs. You're just a little tool that is used by the man downtown. . . . Big shots who are respected, who function in high circles—those are the ones who control these things. And you and I will never strike at the root of it until we strike at the man downtown.[70]

The "man downtown" includes elements in the CIA, the military, local police forces, banks, multinational corporations, and organized crime, collaborating and benefiting in various ways from narcotics trafficking. For the military and the armaments industry, "narco-terrorism" has become a convenient post–cold war rationale for continuing the arms buildup and padding the defense budget. A congressional staff person told a *Newsweek* journalist, "It's their new meal ticket now that the commies are not their big threat." General Maxwell Thurman confirmed this view, describing the war on drugs as "the only war we've got."[71]

Government officials at all levels are seriously concerned about narcotics. But too many powerful interests benefit from the continuation of this traffic. As will be discussed in chapter 6, U.S. foreign policy is designed to promote the interests of powerful multinational corporations. This sometimes leads to alliances with and the protection of high-level drug traffickers.

Banks receive billions of dollars from drug sales by organized crime; this is money they can then lend or invest. The banks are supposed to report transactions over $10,000 to the Treasury Department and to notify authorities when more than $5,000 is taken out of the United States, but they are lax in doing any of this and the penalties for noncompliance are very weak.

In 1984, the director of the federal Commission on Organized Crime commented, "Banks are part of the problem and . . . I mean brokerage houses, exchange firms and casinos, too." Financial organizations do not cooperate with law enforcement agencies, making them, in effect, partners in the drug trade in a de facto alliance with organized crime. A spokesperson for the banking industry was indignant about the Commission's recommendation that banks be more responsible about reporting questionable transactions, saying, "that leaves this country open to a witch hunt. . . . Where does it stop?" A lawyer for a prominent brokerage company, was worried that customers might be scared off by stricter regulation, because there would be "an element of Big Brother is watching you."[72]

Three Strikes and You Still Have Violent Crime

Between 1984 and 1994, there was a 129 percent increase in this country's prison population. Much of that increase was due to drug-related arrests.[73] As of November 1994, the U.S. prison population was over one million, with 180 people going to prison every day. Even though more prisons are being built, there is overcrowding. With overcrowding, prison violence increases. A "get tougher" with prisoners policy that doesn't reward prisoners for good behavior has a similar affect. Between 1993 and 1994, there was a 27 percent increase in attacks on guards in federal prisons alone.[74] Harry Butler, president of the American Federation of Government Employees local, which represents about half of prison personnel, noted the contradiction:

"Everybody wants to get tough on crime. I'm for getting tough too. But we can't just keep throwing people in prison and using 1920 tactics to try and control them."[75] To make room for new prisoners, others, sometimes violent, are released early.

Evidence shows that imprisonment by itself makes little difference to crime rates. Los Angeles County, for example, has a 70 percent recidivism rate. Looking only at drug offenses, the U.S. Department of Justice says, "of 27,000... sentenced to probation in 32 counties across 17 states in 1986, 49 percent were rearrested for a felony offense within 3 years of sentencing."[76]

University of Minnesota Professor Michael Tonry says, "The clear weight of the evidence in every Western country indicates that tough penalties have little effect on crime rates." Criminologists, the American Bar Association, the Correctional Association of New York, and others agree. In 1993, the National Academy of Sciences after what Tonry describes as, "the most exhaustive and ambitious analysis of the subject ever undertaken" came to the conclusion that "greatly increased use of imprisonment has had little effect on violent crime rates."[77]

A Rutgers University criminologist, Todd R. Clear, explains why "the police and prisons have virtually no effect on the sources of criminal behavior":

> About 70 percent of prisoners in New York State come from eight neighborhoods in New York City. These neighborhoods suffer profound poverty, exclusion, marginalization, and despair. All these things nourish crime. Isn't it a bit much to believe that removing some men from their streets will change the factors that promote law breaking among the many who remain?[78]

Prisons only exacerbate the very problems that lead to crime. Those with criminal records are not prime candidates for employment. An ex-convict expresses how incarceration only increases anger and hostility: "One thing jail does is make you bitter, make you so you don't care, which is why people beat someone over the head when they are being robbed. They don't care if they hurt them." Imprisonment, in fact, had not changed this particular young man's intention to make his living by robbery.[79]

In 1992, federal and state prisons cost taxpayers more than $34 billion.[80] In the same year, Aid to Families with Dependent Children (AFDC), which most people equate with welfare programs, cost $23 billion. Leading politicians frequently say AFDC does not work and advocate spending much less money on this kind of assistance. By the same logic, funding for prisons should be decreased. More is spent on them, and yet crime rates do not change substantially.

Preventing crime makes much more sense than continuing the lock-em-up approach. Many crimes are not reported; most criminals are never caught;

Table 3.3   Incarceration Rates per 100,000, State and Federal Prisons, 1993

White males	398
Black males	2,920
White females	20
Black females	165

Note: International comparisons can be found in Table 1.2.
Source: U.S. Department of Justice, Bureau of Justice Statistics, *Prisoners in 1994* (August 1995), p. 8.

many of those who are arrested never go to prison; and, therefore, even if imprisonment worked, crime would continue at high rates.[81]

There are those benefiting from this country's high imprisonment rates. Prisons are being privatized, and there are direct financial gains to the companies that produce the equipment used by the criminal justice system. Prison-related industries made $26 billion in 1995. Why this is the case can be demonstrated by looking at some of the items displayed at the 1996 American Correctional Association convention in Nashville, which featured over eight hundred booths and five thousand attendees.

A security bus with barred windows and interior cells could be bought for $260,000, and a single high-security cell can cost at least $100,000. A temporary cell, however, only costs $40,000, and razor wire, should the inmates try to break out, goes for $170 a foot. AT&T's Nashville installation featured phone fraud and call monitoring detection systems and the hopeful statement: "How he got in is your business. How he gets out is ours—AT&T the authorized inmate calling service."[82]

In a more indirect fashion, capitalists in the United States, as a class, benefit when the status quo is not challenged, when social protest is at a low level. Those who are oppressed by the system are likely to engage in rebellious activities. Sociologists as well as activists have pointed out that by offering alternative opportunities, crime lessens anger at high unemployment.

Narcotics especially lessen the possibilities of protest in the most deprived communities. Drug dealers fighting with each other for a piece of the action are not likely to be fighting for a more just society. Those caught up in drug use, trafficking, and the prison system are less likely to be engaged in social protest. Nearly two thirds (61 percent) of those in federal prisons are there for drug offenses; in state prisons, it is 21 percent.[83]

African-Americans are about half the prison population, four times their proportion in the general population. Table 3.3 lists the almost unbelievable rate at which African-American men are incarcerated. Imprisonment rates for whites are also higher than in any developed country in the world.

Michael Tabor personally attests to the social-control aspect of narcotics. He began using heroin when he was a thirteen year old living in Harlem.

He was addicted for five years, stopping when he joined the Black Panther Party in the late 1960s. In an antidrug pamphlet, he wrote of "black youths [who] vent their rage, frustrations, and despair at each other rather than deal with the true enemy." He also wrote of the insidious effects of substances that make the user oblivious to the horrors of daily life in ghettos.[84]

At the National Press Club in December 1994, former Surgeon General Joycelyn Elders was asked whether or not legalization of drugs would reduce crime. Her answer is worth a public discussion:

> I do feel that we would markedly reduce our crime rate if drugs were legalized. But I don't know all the ramifications of this. I do feel that we need to do some studies. And some countries that have legalized drugs ... certainly have shown that there has been a reduction in their crime rate and there has been no increase in their drug use rate.[85]

Her rational approach to the problem of drugs and crime may be one of the reasons she is now the *former* surgeon general. She was only asking for a study. The Clinton administration's response was "Basically, it's not going to happen." But we do need to learn more about the approaches of other countries, such as Germany, the Netherlands, and Cuba, where drug trafficking was stopped after the revolution in 1959, and organized crime was kicked out. China also eliminated drug addiction following the revolution.

WAR ON CRIME, WAR ON DEMOCRATIC RIGHTS

Current strategies for dealing with crime are not only counterproductive, they also threaten our civil liberties and democratic rights. Plots on cop shows often imply that ignoring constitutional rights makes the police more effective, and television cops frequently express disdain for constitutional restraints. This reflects real-life attitudes. As a member of Washington, D.C., police's Rapid Deployment Unit said, "This is the jungle ... we rewrite the constitution every day down here."

In Florida, when a young black man allegedly killed a British tourist, sheriff's deputies began rounding up every black male, ages fifteen to twenty-two, with criminal records involving firearms or stolen cars. The sheriff of Jefferson County, the site of the killing, said, "We have not focused on any one person" but admitted "we've got some mothers very upset because we're picking up their children."[86]

Thousands of young people of color have dossiers compiled on them. In Los Angeles, even those not charged with crimes have "their names and addresses entered into the electronic gang roster for future surveillance."[87] Mass military-like raids occur in African-American, and sometimes poor white, communities in which police kick in doors, push people, and sometimes destroy homes. The National Guard has swept through housing projects in Puerto Rico searching for narcotics and weapons.[88]

Terrorized by violent crime, a community may even accept a weakening of their own rights, hoping for personal safety in return. At the crime-ridden Robert Taylor housing project in Chicago, for example, five thousand residents petitioned a judge to allow warrantless searches of their buildings. One tenant, Daisy Bradford, has come to feel that "sometimes you got to sacrifice your rights to save your life."[89]

PRISONS OR SOCIAL PROGRAMS

Repressive policies make people think the problem is being addressed when it is not. Programs that do show some promise of decreasing crime and violence are not funded adequately, and some have been cut altogether. In East Los Angeles, for instance, a program where gang members were hired to work with potentially violent gangs was defunded in spite of its apparent success.[90] Providing funds for prisoners so they can earn college credits has proven to reduce recidivism. The Omnibus Crime Bill passed in 1994, however, prevents such grants, while allotting over $30 billion for repressive measures. The thirty-seven members of the Congressional Black Caucus opposed this bill, calling for social programs instead, but they were not successful.

Politicians and the media rarely discuss real alternatives. A scientific approach to the problems discussed in this chapter would be for the government to target a community that has high unemployment and high crime and to introduce, for a reasonable time period, a massive program of decently paid jobs, recreation, schools, and counseling. This would test whether a support system that helped individuals and families to play a useful role in the society would change behavior. It is necessary to punish those who prey on others, but if this is the only approach, the road goes nowhere. As long as social conditions effectively encourage crime, individuals trapped in communities with few alternatives will risk the punishments.

Notes

1. Rick Bragg, "New York's Bodegas Become Islands Under Siege," *New York Times*, 3 March 1994, pp. 1, 39. In 1994, the most likely to be killed at their job site nationwide were cab drivers. A study by the National Institute for Occupational Safety said the most likely to be killed at work are those who are delivering goods and services to the public. "Cab Driving Termed Riskiest Job in U.S.," *New York Times*, 9 July 1995, p. A14.
2. Mary Taylor Previte, "What Will They Say at My Funeral?" *New York Times*, 7 August 1994, p. 17.

3. U.S. Department of Justice, Bureau of Justice Statistics, *Crime and Neighborhoods*, June 1994, p. 1; Bureau of Justice Statistics, *Criminal Victimization in the United States: 1973–1992 Trends*, Table 4, p. 14.
4. Maria Newman, "Once His Honor, Now the Professor," *New York Times*, 14 September 1994, p. B9.
5. Stephen Steinberg, *The Ethnic Myth: Race, Ethnicity, and Class in America* (Boston: Beacon Press, 1989), p. 116.
6. Quoted in John Higham, *Strangers in the Land: Patterns of American Nativism, 1860–1925* (New Brunswick, NJ: Rutgers University Press, 1966), p. 66.
7. Quoted in Albert Fried, *The Rise and Fall of the Jewish Gangster in America* (New York: Holt, Rinehart and Winston, 1980), pp. 90, 111.
8. Jeffrey Fagan, "Interactions Among Drugs, Alcohol and Violence," *Health Affairs* 12 no. 4 (1993), p. 71.
9. Albert Fried, pp. 36–37.
10. Polling data reported in Douglas S. Massey, and Nancy A. Denton, *American Apartheid: Segregation and the Making of the Underclass* (Cambridge, Mass.: Harvard University Press, 1993), p. 95; quote from Bob Herbert, "The Soap Opera Machine," *New York Times*, 9 November 1994, p. A27.
11. Joseph Berger, "After Fistfight, Yonkers Officers Invented Tale of Black Assailants," *New York Times*, 24 April 1993, pp. 1, 16; quote from Don Terry, "A Woman's False Accusation Pains Many Blacks," *New York Times*, 6 November 1994, p. 32.
12. Rick Bragg, "Mother of 'CarJacked' Boys Held in Their Death," *New York Times*, 4 November 1994, pp. 1, 30; quotes from Terry.
13. Michael Tonry, *Malign Neglect* (New York: Oxford University Press, 1995), pp. 106–7. A New Jersey public defender, John Schadegg, told me that in his experience young adult whites are more likely to have their own apartments, and drug transactions take place there, often at parties and not in the streets. Black youths of an equivalent age are often outside conducting their business, get arrested, and become his clients.
14. On racial discrimination in the criminal justice system, see Marc Mauer, "A Generation Behind Bars: Black Males and the Criminal Justice System," in *The American Black Male: His Present Status and His Future*, eds. Richard G. Majors and Jacob U. Gordon (Chicago: Nelson-Hall, 1994), pp. 88–89; Michael Tonry, "Sentencing Guidelines, Disadvantaged Offenders, and Racial Disparities," *Report from the Institute for Philosophy and Public Policy* (Summer/Fall 1994), pp. 7–13; Blackwell, pp. 427–28, 456–58. Homicide statistic, U.S. Department of Justice, *SourceBook of Criminal Justice Statistics—1994*, Table 4.11, p. 388.
15. Quoted in Herbert; Delbert Elliot, "Serious Violent Offenders: Onset, Developmental Course, and Termination," 1993 Presidential Address to the American Society of Criminology, *Criminology* 32 (1994): pp. 5, 14.
16. Quoted in Isabel Wilkerson, "The Tallest Fence: Feelings on Race in a White Neighborhood," *New York Times*, 21 June 1992, p. 16.
17. Nathan Glazer, and Daniel Patrick Moynihan, *Beyond the Melting Pot: The Negroes, Puerto Ricans, Jews, Italians and Irish of New York City* (Cambridge, Mass.: M.I.T. Press, 1970), p. 190.
18. Steinberg, pp. 97–99.
19. Nicholas Lemann, *The Promised Land: The Great Black Migration and How It Changed America* (New York: Vintage Books, 1991); Massey and Denton, pp. 29, 43, 45.

20. An unidentified musician's description quoted in Massey and Denton, p. 61.
21. Quoted in Isabel Wilkerson, "Worse Segregation Than Was Expected Is Found in 10 Cities," *New York Times*, 5 August 1989, pp. 1, 6.
22. Quoted in Massey and Denton, p. 54.
23. William W. Goldsmith, and Edward J. Blakely, *Separate Societies: Poverty and Inequality in U.S. Cities* (Philadelphia: Temple University Press, 1992), p. 119.
24. Yale Rabin, "Highways as a Barrier to Equal Access," in *Majority and Minority: The Dynamics of Racial and Ethnic Relations*, eds. Norman R. Yetman and C. Hoy Steele, 2d ed. (Boston: Allyn and Bacon, Inc., 1975), p. 469; 1990–95 figures from *Statistical Abstract of the United States, 1995*, Table 479, p. 302.
25. Jonathan Brown, "Opening the Book on Lending Discrimination," *Multinational Monitor* (November 1992), pp. 8–14.
26. Elliot Currie, *Reckoning: Drugs, the Cities and the American Future* (New York: Hill and Wang, 1993), p. 126.
27. Richard Child Hill, and Cynthia Negry, "Deindustrialization and Racial Minorities in the Great Lakes Region, USA," in *The Reshaping of America: Social Consequences of the Changing Economy*, eds. D. Stanley Eitzen and Maxine Baca Zinn (Englewood Cliffs, N.J.: Prentice-Hall, 1989), p. 174.
28. New Jersey Council of Churches, *The Reshaping of New Jersey: The Growing Separation* (East Orange, N.J.: New Jersey Council of Churches, 1988), pp. 18–19.
29. Judith Goode, "Polishing the Rustbelt: Immigrants Enter a Restructuring Philadelphia," in *Newcomers in the Workplace*, eds. Louise Lamphere, Alex Stepick, and Guillermo Grenier (Philadelphia: Temple University Press, 1994), pp. 205–6.
30. John D. Kasarda, "The Severely Distressed in Economically Transforming Cities," in *Drugs, Crime and Social Isolation: Barriers to Urban Opportunity*, eds. Adele V. Harrell and George E. Peterson (Washington, D.C.: Urban Institute Press, 1992), p. 71.
31. 19 March 1991, pp. A1, D22.
32. Robert Aponte, "Urban Employment and the Mismatch Dilemma: Accounting for the Immigration Exception," *Social Problems* 43 (1996): pp. 268–83.
33. Aponte study cited above.
34. Quoted in Goldsmith and Blakely, p. 114.
35. Quoted in William J. Wilson, "Work," *New York Times Magazine*, 18 August 1996, p. 31.
36. Quoted in Wilson, p. 40.
37. Mary Merva, and Richard Fowles, *Effects of Diminished Economic Opportunities on Social Stress: Heart Attacks, Strokes and Crime* (Washington, D.C.: Economic Policy Institute, n.d.), p. 2. The rates of nonviolent property crimes also increase with unemployment.
38. U.S. Department of Justice, Bureau of Justice Statistics, *Profile of Inmates in the United States and in England and Wales, 1991*, p. 1.
39. Elliot Currie, *Confronting Crime* (New York: Pantheon Books, 1985), p. 119.
40. David Corn, "Ganging Up on Congress," *Nation*, 29 April 1996, pp. 6–7; *City of Quartz: Excavating the Future in Los Angeles* (New York: Vintage, 1990), pp. 300–301.
41. Allan Sheahen, "Poverty in America Is a Serious Problem," in *Poverty: Opposing Viewpoints*, ed. William Dudley (St. Paul: Greenhaven Press, 1988), pp. 21–22; "Help Wanted Ads Don't Add Up," *Dollars and Sense* 93 (January 1984), pp. 13, 17.

42. Quotes from Seth Mydans, "The Young Face of Inner City Unemployment," *New York Times*, 22 March 1992, p. A24; Davis, pp. 305–6, his emphasis.
43. Alison Mitchell, "Where Markets Are Never Super," *New York Times*, 6 June 1992, p. 25; Shawn G. Kennedy, "Supermarket Invests in Harlem, Long Shunned by Chains," *New York Times*, 22 September 1994, p. B3. The absence of supermarkets causes other problems besides adding to the lack of jobs. People have to shop at more expensive small groceries or travel long distances. Charles Strum, "Six Screens, with Melted Butter," *New York Times*, 4 April 1993, p. 40; "Celebrating a Drugstore," *New York Times*, 10 July 1996, p. B1; Housing aspect from Mercer Sullivan, *"Getting Paid": Youth Crime and Work in the Inner City* (Ithaca: Cornell University Press, 1989), p. 148.
44. William E. Geist, "Waiting in Line and Hoping: 296 Jobs and 4,508 Applicants," *New York Times*, 28 September 1982, pp. A1, B8; "10,000 Stand in Rain for $4.50 Cleveland Jobs," *New York Times*, 22 March 1983; "Officials Say 26,200 Applied for 75 Jobs in Baltimore," *New York Times*, 21 September 1980.
45. Jacques Steinberg, "Jobs with No Future Draw Hundreds," *New York Times*, 17 March 1995, p. A12.
46. Quoted in Marvin Harris, *America Now: The Anthropology of a Changing Culture* (New York: Simon and Schuster, 1981), p. 126.
47. James Bennet, "Mere Hint of Jobs Draws Crowd in Detroit," *New York Times*, 12 November 1993, pp. A1, A29.
48. Mercer Sullivan, *"Getting Paid": Youth Crime and Work in the Inner City* (Ithaca: Cornell University Press, 1989).
49. Richard B. Freeman, "Crime and the Employment of Disadvantaged Youths," in *Urban Labor Markets and Job Opportunity*, eds. George Peterson and Wayne Vroman (Washington, D.C.: Urban Institute Press, 1992), p. 229; Jeffrey Fagan, "Drug Selling and Licit Income in Distressed Neighborhoods: The Economic Lives of Street-Level Drug Users and Dealers," in Harrell and Peterson, p. 101.
50. Davis, pp. 307–8, 315. A study of school performance and family structure gives evidence that it is not the number of parents in a household but the involvement of the adult (or adults) with the child that makes a difference. However, school discipline problems are less with two parents in both white and African-American households. Jerold Heiss, "Effects of African-American Family Structure on School Attitudes and Performance," *Social Problems* 43 (1996): pp. 246–67.
51. Quoted in Elliot Currie, *Reckoning: Drugs, the Cities and the American Future* (New York: Hill and Wang, 1993), p. 97. A useful study on neighborhood social controls and crime is Sally Engle Merry, *Urban Danger: Life in a Neighborhood of Strangers* (Philadelphia: Temple University Press, 1981). A large-scale study done in England and Wales also found that crime increased with community disorganization. Robert J. Sampson and W. Byron Groves, "Community Structure and Crime: Testing Social-Disorganization Theory," *American Journal of Sociology* 94 (1989): pp. 774–802.
52. Dirk Johnson, "Move to Suburbs Spurs the Poor to Seek Work," *New York Times*, 1 May 1990.
53. Currie, 1993, pp. 82–88; Tonry, 1995, p. 4; Clarence Lusane, *Pipe Dream Blues: Racism and the War on Drugs* (Boston: South End Press, 1991), pp. 49, 57.
54. Quote and figures from Don Terry, "Flare-up of Gang Gunfire Vexes Gary, Ind.," *New York Times*, 14 September 1996, p. 6.
55. Philippe Bourgois, "Just Another Night on Crack Street," *New York Times Magazine*, 12 November 1989, pp. 61, 66, 94.

56. Felicia R. Lee, "A Drug Dealer's Rapid Rise and Ugly Fall," *New York Times*, 10 September 1994, pp. 1, 22.
57. Quoted in Dennis Hevesi, "Gang Leader Details Crimes of Drug Ring," *New York Times*, 1 March 1995, pp. B1, B4.
58. Bureau of Justice Statistics, *Drugs and Crime Facts, 1994*, p. 9; and *Drugs and Crime Facts, 1993*, pp. 8–9.
59. Fox Butterfield, "Study Discounts the Role of Drug Users in Gun-Related Crime," *New York Times*, 8 October 1995, p. 36.
60. "Violence by Young People: Why the Deadly Nexus," *National Institute of Justice Journal* (August 1995), p. 6.
61. Bourgois, p. 64.
62. Fagan, 1992, pp. 103–4; Davis, p. 270; Fox Butterfield, "Study Discounts the Role of Drug Users in Gun-Related Crime," *New York Times*, 8 October 1995, p. 36.
63. Joan Moore, "Gangs, Drugs, and Violence," in *Gangs: The Origins and Impact of Contemporary Youth Gangs in the United States*, eds. Scott Cummings and Daniel J. Monti (Albany, N.Y.: State University of New York Press, 1993), p. 40.
64. *The Congressional Record*, Vol. 135, No. 62, 16 May 1989, p. 9301.
65. Tim Weiner, "C.I.A. Formed Haitian Unit Later Tied to Narcotics Trade," *New York Times*, 14 November 1993, pp. 1, 12. Elaine Sciolino, "U.S. Urging Afghan Rebels to Limit Opium," *New York Times*, 26 March 1989, p. 4; Alfred W. McCoy, *The Politics of Heroin: CIA Complicity in the Global Drug Trade* (New York: Lawrence Hill Books, 1991).
66. The series called "Dark Alliance" is available on the newspaper's Web site, http://cgi.sjmercury.com/drugs. Reprints can be obtained by calling 408-920-5999. This quote is from "dayone," [sic] 18 August 1996.
67. Webb, Day 2, p. 5 from Web site.
68. Quoted in Webb and Pamela Kramer, "Postscript," published 4 September 1996, from Web site http://cgi.sjmercury.com/drugshock/postscript/htm. CIA spokesperson Mark Mansfield, quoted in this article, called the charges "ludicrous." It is interesting to compare the media's coverage of this story with their quick retelling of a tabloid's allegations that presidential advisor Dick Morris had had assignations with a call girl. This story, which appeared at about the same time as Webb's thoroughly researched and documented account, resulted in Morris's quickly resigning from his position. A month after Webb's well-documented story in a reputable newspaper, there was still little media coverage of it.
69. This letter appeared in the *San Jose Mercury News*, 29 August 1996 and was taken from the Website, http://cgi.sjmercury.com/drugs/boxer829.htm.
70. Malcolm X, *By Any Means Necessary* (New York: Pathfinder Press, Inc., 1970), pp. 51–52.
71. Quoted in Stephen Shalom, *Imperial Alibis: Rationalizing U.S. Intervention after the Cold War* (Boston: South End Press, 1993), p. 191.
72. Quotes from Leslie Maitland Werner, "U.S. Crime Panel Seeks New Laws to Halt the Laundering of Money," *New York Times*, 31 October 1984, pp. A1, A25.
73. Bureau of Justice Statistics, *Prisoners in 1994*, August 1995, pp. 1, 4.
74. Steven A. Holmes, "Inmate Violence Is on Rise as Federal Prisons Change," *New York Times*, 9 February 1995, p. A14.
75. Quoted in Holmes, p. A14.
76. Seth Mydans, "Racial Tensions in Los Angeles Jails Ignite Inmate Violence,"

New York Times, 6 February 1995, p. A13; U.S. Department of Justice, Bureau of Justice Statistics, *Drugs and Crime Facts, 1994*, p. 26.
77. Michael Tonry, *Malign Neglect* (New York: Oxford University Press, 1995), pp. 19, 20. On pages 20–24, he critiques officials who argue the contrary, showing the flaws in their analysis; Steve Whitman, "The Crime of Black Imprisonment," *Z Magazine* (May/June 1992), p. 69.
78. Todd R. Clear, "'Tougher' Is Dumber," *New York Times*, 4 December 1993, p. 21.
79. Quoted in Sally Engle Merry, *Urban Danger: Life in a Neighborhood of Strangers* (Philadelphia: Temple University Press, 1981), p. 172.
80. Editorial, *Nation*, 21 November 1994, pp. 599–600.
81. David C. Anderson, "The Crime Funnel," *New York Times Magazine*, 12 June 1994, pp. 56–58; National Issues Forum, p. 12.
82. Jeff Gerth, and Stephen Labaton, "Jail Business Shows Its Weaknesses," *New York Times*, 24 November 1995, pp. A1, B18; Donatella Lorch, "The Utmost Restraint and How to Exercise It," *New York Times*, 23 August 1996, pp. B1, B7; Editorial, "A World Leader in Prisons," *New York Times*, 2 March 1991.
83. Bureau of Justice Statistics, *Drugs and Crime Facts, 1993*, p. 19.
84. Michael Tabor, "The Plague: Capitalism+Dope=Genocide," in *The Triple Revolution Emerging: Social Problems in Depth*, eds. Robert Perrucci and Mark Pilisuk (Boston: Little Brown and Company, 1971), pp. 241–49, quote from p. 244.
85. Stephen Labaton, "Surgeon General Suggests Study of Legalizing Drugs," *New York Times*, 8 December 1993, p. A23. Useful discussions of the pros and cons of legalization can be found in Currie, 1993, pp. 148–212; Stephen Rosskamm Shalom, "Drug Policy & Program," *Z Papers* (January 1992), pp. 9–17.
86. Washington, D.C., quote from William J. Chambliss, "Policing the Ghetto Underclass: The Politics of Law and Law Enforcement," *Social Problems* 41, no. 2 (May 1994), p. 179; sheriff quoted in Larry Rohter, "Fearful of Tourism Decline, Florida Offers Assurances on Safety," *New York Times*, 16 September 1993, p. A14.
87. Davis, p. 268.
88. "Big Housing Project Is Raided by Troops," *New York Times*, 20 March 1996, p. A15.
89. Don Terry, "Chicago Project in Furor about Guns and the Law," *New York Times*, 8 April 1994, p. A12. A local judge issued an injunction against warrantless searches. A debate on this proposal can be found on the Op-Ed page of the *New York Times*, 7 May 1994, p. 23.
90. Joan Moore, p. 38.

Interpersonal Violence and Race and Gender

In 1992, Shirley Lowry, a fifty-one-year-old bus driver, had left her abusive companion, moved into a secret apartment, and even hired bodyguards. But as she entered a Milwaukee courthouse to seek a restraining order, her ex-partner was waiting with a butcher knife. She died after he stabbed her nineteen times.[1]

Claudia Brenner and her companion Rebecca were hiking the Appalachian Trail in 1988. Unbeknownst to them, Stephen Roy Carr, in the woods with his shotgun, was watching them. He saw them make love, followed them through the forest, and fired eight times, killing Rebecca and wounding Claudia. Carr's lawyer argued the killer had been provoked by seeing a lesbian act.[2]

In 1989, sixteen-year-old African-American Yusuf Hawkins was thought to be dating a white girl in Bensonhurst, Brooklyn. He was actually in that section with some friends, looking for a used car. About twenty neighborhood (white) teenagers formed a mob. Hawkins was shot and killed, and his companions were injured. In anguish, Yusuf Hawkins's father said, "To see my son's life wasted because of some . . . fool with a gun in his hands who saw nothing but a black man is a very, very vile thing to me. Who will pay for this? Who will pay?"[3] White residents, however, expressed no sense of remorse. A white teenage girl asserted, "The black people don't belong here. This is our neighborhood."[4]

Such instances of gender and racial/ethnic interpersonal violence cannot be directly linked to capitalism and class inequality. Instead, the class system creates the conditions that make such violence more explainable. Class also affects the availability of and access to resources that could help lessen some of this violence.

Interpersonal violence is a way to achieve certain ends, including maintaining hierarchy, venting anger and frustration, or asserting one's masculinity. Violence used to maintain inequality may be partly a reaction against attempts by subordinate groups to improve their position. There is obviously still a great deal of inequality, but real gains have been made. Antidiscrimination laws have been expanded, and women now have a legal right to an abortion; gays and lesbians are demanding equal rights as well and in many cases refusing to pretend that heterosexuality is the only acceptable form of sexuality.

These progressive changes have come at the price of some of the accustomed privileges of white males. A sense of loss can be exacerbated by other stresses—such as an economic crisis, which makes people fearful of their own and their children's futures. Right-wing politicians and religious and media figures help transform this frustration into hostility toward women, people of color, immigrants, gays and lesbians, and, lately, even the federal government.

Anger is coupled with a socialization process that teaches everyone, but especially males, that physical force is an acceptable way of dealing with problems. Violence becomes the means to try to re-create traditional gender and ethnic roles and to turn back the clock to a time when, some think, things were better.

GENDER AND INTERPERSONAL VIOLENCE

DOMESTIC VIOLENCE

In June 1993, a shocked but titillated public learned that Lorena Bobbitt had cut off her husband's penis as he slept in a drunken stupor. Her defense argued she was temporarily insane, driven to violence by repeated instances of battering and rape by her spouse. A jury accepted this argument and acquitted her. A year later, ex-football hero turned actor, O. J. Simpson, went on trial, accused of murdering Nicole Brown Simpson, his ex-wife, and Ron Goldman, her friend, in a jealous rage.

These high-profile cases have focused media attention on spousal abuse and share features with less publicized instances. Lorena Bobbitt, for example, had been abused for several years; her husband believed he had a right to dominate her life. Simpson also had a history of attacking his wife, who had made at least eight calls to the police attesting to this. When arrested, after one of these calls in 1989, Simpson was given lenient treatment: small fines and some community service. Like many batterers, O. J. Simpson felt that what went on between him and his wife was not of concern to the police: he reportedly said after one call, "What are you doing here? This is a family matter."[5] The terms domestic violence, intimate violence, spouse abuse, child abuse, and elderly abuse, are all terms used to describe violence within the same household.

Households are miniature power systems, and family values can mean valuing male domination and the right of the more powerful to use violence as a way to control the relationships and maintain household inequality. Family violence experts Richard Gelles and Murray A. Straus point out the connection between household inequality and domestic violence:

> Our statistical evidence shows that the risk of intimate violence is the greatest when all the decision making in a home is concentrated in the hands of one of the partners. Couples who report the most sharing of decisions report the lowest rates of violence. Our evidence goes beyond the statistics. Over and over again, case after case, interview after interview, we [heard] batterers and victims discuss how power and control were at the core of the events that led up to the use of violence.[6]

Home is not always the warm, cozy sanctuary described by many politicians, and a marriage license, as described by Richard Gelles and Murray A. Straus, is often "a hitting license."

Intimate partners are more dangerous for women in general than are strangers in the street. Some statistics will illustrate this. Thirty-seven percent of women murdered in 1992 were killed by an intimate companion, compared with 4 percent of male murder victims.[7] According to the U.S. Department of Justice, based on data from 1987–91: "On average each year, women experienced over 572,000 violent victimizations committed by an intimate compared to approximately 49,000 incidents committed against men."[8] These figures show why even the generally conservative American Medical Association, in 1992, described men as a major health threat to women in this country.[9]

When women do attack or murder their partners, it is typically in self-defense after years of abuse. A study of Kentucky women serving time for murder or manslaughter indicated that 40 percent had killed a male abuser. In several cases, the women had tried to get police protection before finally killing their partner in desperation.[10]

Even pregnancy doesn't guarantee immunity. A 1994 study by the CDC revealed that *minimally* 6 percent of pregnant women are battered by a male partner during their pregnancy, and some of these beatings result in miscarriages or birth defects.[11]

Women do not call the police for a number of reasons. They may fear reprisals; after all, they live with and are often economically dependent on their abuser. Like their male partners, some, too, may feel domestic violence is a personal affair. The police are, in any case, often reluctant to intervene. One badly beaten woman, Tracy Thurman of Torrington, Connecticut, was awarded nearly $2 million from her local police department, who had simply looked on as her husband beat her, inflicting injuries that left her permanently disabled.[12]

There is evidence that police intervention can protect the woman. A study by the National Crime Survey based on data from 1978–82 concluded that women who did call the police were much less likely to be reassaulted than women who did not make such calls. Research in 1981 in Minneapolis indicated that where men are arrested for spouse abuse, they are less likely to repeat the offense. It is not just fear of punishment that causes the change: there is now public disapproval of his acts, as well as a change in the power relationships in the household. By calling the police, the woman has demonstrated some authority and the ability to take some control.[13]

Children are even less powerful in the family hierarchy. Physical punishment for a child's misbehavior is widely accepted and has even been sanctioned in schools by a 1975 Supreme Court decision. In a 1995 poll, 87 percent of the respondents felt spanking was appropriate in some circumstances. However, there is also evidence of changing attitudes: younger parents are more disapproving of corporal punishment than older ones. In many European countries, however, spanking is forbidden by law.[14]

In the United States in 1994, there were 232,061 cases of physical child abuse reported.[15] Children are abused by their mothers, as well as their fathers or mothers' male companions. Yale University studies suggest that women who are at risk from battering are more likely to be child abusers. Abuse of the elderly is also a problem, but there is very little research available. One sociological study, however, estimates that the number of elderly victims is between 700,000 and 1.1 million.[16]

It is widely believed that batterers are most likely to have been physically abused themselves. Children who see their parents engaged in physical violence are more likely to be violent when they establish their own homes. But nonetheless not all abused children grow up to be violent, and not all violent adults were abused children.[17]

Several other factors help account for domestic violence. Cultural beliefs can play a role. The American emphasis on individualism can lead a troubled person to feel they must take care of their own problems rather than seek help from others—help that could, in some cases, possibly prevent violence. It is also the case that in many facets of American life, violence, especially for males, is believed to be an appropriate way to deal with a problem. The availability of firearms makes it even more likely that any kind of violent encounter will turn deadly. In 1992, nearly two-thirds of domestic homicides involved a gun.[18]

Stress is an important variable in explaining domestic violence. If stress

Table 4.1 Physical Abuse of Women by Household Annual Income Level

	Rate per 1,000 Women
Incomes below $10,000	11
Incomes above $30,000	2

Source: U.S. Department of Justice, Bureau of Justice Statistics, *Violence between Intimates*, November 1994, p. 2. Data are for the years 1987–91.

is coupled with social isolation and a lack of emotional and material support, then the likelihood of violence occurring in the household rises further. Isolation also means social standards are less of a control on behavior.

Certain variables counteract others, however. Gelles and Straus found no difference between whites and African-Americans in rates of child abuse, even though blacks can be expected to have higher rates of stress. These researchers reasoned that African-Americans are more likely to be involved in community and church groups and to have relatives to help with child care and financial difficulties.[19]

Domestic violence occurs in all social classes, but it seems to be higher among lower-income groups, which are likely to have more problems. This is shown in Table 4.1.

Less income usually means more problems and fewer possibilities for solving them. There are fewer resources for getting away from the household for a while if the situation there seems overwhelming. Therapy for troubled family members is less of an option in lower-income households.

One cause of both stress and lower incomes is unemployment. During the 1979–82 recession, the American Humane Association, which monitors child abuse, reported a 120 percent national increase in child abuse cases. Thirty-nine states also reported increases in child abuse during this period. For example, in Youngstown, Ohio, as unemployment rose to 21 percent in this period, domestic violence cases increased by over 400 percent.[20]

We expect our homes to make us happy. Major holidays such as Christmas and Easter are times when the family is supposed to be especially joyful and when gifts are to be given, however unaffordable. These are also the times when violence is most likely. This helps explain why admissions to hospitals for child abuse rise during the holidays.[21]

Families are private places, and the sanctions against violence are relatively few. Anger that can't be released elsewhere after all may be safely expressed at home. There are serious repercussions if a man beats up his boss, an employee, or an annoying customer, but if he smacks his wife or kids, he has an easier time getting away with it. The same holds true if the woman abuses a child. You hear suspicious noises from a neighbor's apartment, what should you do? Ignore it, intervene, or should you call the police?

There are no clear norms or guidelines, but the general sense is that you are not supposed to interfere with other people's households. Although important, the cultural value of privacy can have a negative impact on household safety.

If an abusive man won't change his behavior, the woman must choose between accepting the abuse or leaving. Minimally, about 50 percent do leave. The choice is a difficult one: a woman has to find and pay for a new home and arrange care for her dependent children, usually on low earnings. She will have court costs if she files for divorce and if there are custody battles. If her job doesn't provide health care, that will be another economic burden. Even obtaining insurance can be difficult as a number of companies refuse to provide life, medical, or mortgage insurance to women they think have been physically abused.[22] In short, there are few social supports for an abused woman wanting to make a new life.

An economically needy woman who moves to another state, in an attempt to evade her abuser, may find she is either ineligible for welfare or able to get only very small payments, because she doesn't meet the new state's residency requirements. The welfare "reforms," currently in effect will make life harder for women desperate to leave a violent home, by imposing restrictions on how long a woman can get benefits, for example.

With affordable housing hard to find, violence is one cause of homelessness for women. There are only about one thousand four hundred shelters for abused women in the entire country, and even the best shelters offer only temporary refuge. Pennsylvania, with a relatively good system of shelters, has to turn away eleven thousand women a year. Studies in that state show from one-third to two-fifths of families at homeless shelters were fleeing intimate violence.[23]

When the woman asserts herself and moves out, she becomes especially vulnerable: about three-quarters of the murders of battered women occur when they try to gain control over their lives.[24] Many batterers take their companion's leaving as a devastating repudiation of a man's ability to control "his" woman.

The women's movement has helped make domestic violence a public issue and women's groups have provided services to victims of this violence. Often operating on shoestring budgets, with inadequate or no public funding, women have established shelters, hot lines, and support groups. In the 1970s, there were fewer than ten shelters for abused women in the whole country, now there are over a thousand although this is still inadequate to meet the demand. Changes in laws and police behavior are a result of the efforts of women's organizations. Nearly half of all police departments now have domestic violence units, and fourteen states and Washington, D.C., have mandatory arrest policies. This means the police can arrest a suspected batterer even if the victim does not make a personal complaint. In some areas, services are available for men who are trying to change their violent behavior.[25]

RAPE AND SEXUAL ASSAULT

In a middle-class suburb of Los Angeles, twenty to thirty male high school students in the early 1990s formed a group called the "Spur Posse." Members got "points" for each sexual encounter, consensual or otherwise. Eight of the gang members were arrested, charged with raping and molesting girls, some as young as ten. At least one father proudly exclaimed, "Aren't they virile specimens?" Echoing the sentiments expressed in the Glen Ridge, New Jersey, sexual assault case mentioned in chapter 1, some community residents excused these attacks with the cliché, "Boys will be boys."[26]

Rape occurs in most societies but is more likely in those where gender inequality is high. In the United States, the combination of gender inequality and a wide acceptance of violence in many contexts helps explain why the United States has the highest rape rate of any comparable society, as indicated in Table 1.2. Add to this the fact that official statistics are likely to be underestimates, because rape is an underreported crime. New methods of data collection indicate the rate may even be as high as 700 rapes per 100,000 women. One of the most underreported types of rape is marital rape: in some states it is not even a crime unless the couple is separated. This fact caused California state senator Bob Wilson to ask plaintively, "If you can't rape your wife who can you rape?"[27]

Economic inequality increases the risks of sexual assault for lower-income women, as Table 4.2 shows. In lower-income communities, women use public transportation and walk more frequently than women who can afford cars. The streets they use are likely to be poorly lit, and abandoned buildings, where assaults can take place, are numerous as well. A woman's own building may be dangerous, with poorly lit hallways and dark

Table 4.2 Average Annual Rape Rate, per 100,000 Females, Age 12 or Older, and Income, 1987–91

Family Income of Victim	Rape Rate
Less than $9,999	240
$10,000–$19,999	140
$20,000–$29,999	100
$30,000–$49,999	100
$50,000 or more	50

Source: U.S. Department of Justice, Bureau of Justice Statistics, *Violence against Women: A National Crime Victimization Survey Report*, calculated from Table 3, p. 3.

stairwells. These conditions could be addressed if there was sufficient political interest.

Both economic and gender inequality help explain rape rates. Diane Scully, a sociologist who has studied rape, summarizes the cross-cultural findings of anthropologists on this issue:

> ... sexual violence is related to cultural attitudes, the power relationship between women and men, the social and economic status of women relative to the men of their group and the amount of other forms of violence in the society.[28]

Her statement is confirmed for the United States by the findings of Larry Baron and Murray A. Straus, who are with the University of New Hampshire's Family Violence Research Program. They wanted to explain why rape rates differ dramatically by states. Over a nearly twenty-year period, Alaska's rate has been the highest. The lowest has varied between North Dakota and Iowa. In 1992, Alaska's rate was 99 rapes for every 100,000 people, and Iowa's was 19 per 100,000. Baron and Straus found that "the more economic inequality, unemployment, and urbanization in a state, the higher the rape rate." They also found that when the general status of women was lower, rape rates were higher.[29]

Male socialization contributes to the occurrence of rape. Males are often taught that a woman wants a male to be dominant, whereas women learn to be less overt in expressing their sexual desires. Furthermore, males, in all social classes and racial/ethnic groups, may feel they are entitled to sex from their wives or if a woman appears "provocative." In 1987, following a "Take back the night" march at Princeton University where participants sought to publicize the problem, a group of male students had their own demonstration. Their slogan was "We can rape anyone we want." After a woman was raped and severely beaten in Central Park, a man told a reporter that he didn't understand the beating, "They should've just raped her."[30]

Some people think that males have uncontrollable sexual impulses and that it is a woman's responsibility not to provoke a man sexually. In 1989, a Florida jury acquitted three men accused of raping a woman at knifepoint in a parking lot. The jury focused on the fact that the twenty-two-year-old victim was wearing a tank top with a short lace skirt and no underwear. One male juror defended the decision, explaining, "She asked for it."[31]

Male peer groups sometimes use sexual assault as a way for members to demonstrate their masculinity to one another, and to reinforce male bonding. A gang rapist interviewed by Diane Scully reported that

> We felt powerful, we were in control. I wanted sex and there was peer pressure. She wasn't like a person, no personality, just domination on my part. Just to show I could do it—you know, macho.[32]

Gang rapists are sometimes caught, because they are overheard bragging about their actions.

Interviews by *New York Times* journalists with fifty teenagers in the New York metropolitan area found teenage boys wanting to impress their friends. They feared being thought "soft" and sought "to demonstrate their manhood by abusing or showing disrespect to girls." This attitude was "repeated time and again." These findings were corroborated by a national study of junior high and high school students that found some form of sexual harassment common in junior highs and high schools.[33]

Rape can be a way of asserting a sense of power and control. This is illustrated by comments from convicted rapists:

After a rape, I always felt like I had just conquered something.

Rape was a feeling of total dominance. . . . I would degrade women so that I could feel there was a person of less worth than me.

I decided to rape her to prove I had guts. She was just there.[34]

Rapists may feel temporarily empowered by sexual assaults, but rape victims suffer for a long time. Some rape victims still experience fear and anxiety even years after the attack. Victims often feel humiliated, fearful, depressed, and their own sexual relationships are affected. Some even blame themselves for being attacked, a reflection of the societal definitions mentioned above.

The women's movement has helped victims by creating rape crisis centers and hot lines and by changing the way law enforcement deals with rapes. Policewomen are now more available to question rape victims. Interrogating a victim about her sexual history, which used to be a common practice in courts, is usually not permitted. Some states have adopted laws providing that victims need not show bruises proving they resisted the attack. Corroborating witnesses are also not as imperative as they once were to establish a woman's credibility.

FORCED MOTHERHOOD OR ACCESS TO SAFE, LEGAL ABORTIONS

One of the great victories of the women's movement was the 1973 Supreme Court decision, *Roe v. Wade*, which legalized the right to an abortion. Without this right, in effect women were forced to be mothers if they were raped, if their contraceptive methods failed, or if they didn't use contraception.

The right to terminate an unwanted pregnancy is not so much a point of contention for capitalists as for conservative Christian groups. It makes political sense for the Republican Party to be more antichoice as fundamentalist Christians, valuing a patriarchal family, provide about a third of Republican votes. Robert J. Billings, who founded the Moral Majority in 1979 and served in Reagan's Department of Education, successfully persuaded the

Republicans to use the abortion issue as a way to win traditionally Democratic Catholics over to the Republicans.[35]

When abortions were illegal, some women sought them anyway, with dangerous consequences. No one is sure exactly how many deaths resulted from illegal abortions. In 1961, there were 320 recorded deaths as a result of complications from illegal procedures. Since 1974, or since *Roe* v. *Wade*, there have been less than five a year.[36] Abortion, performed properly, is actually safer than childbirth. Approximately 1 woman in every 160,000 dies as a result of an abortion. For white women, as of 1992, death in childbirth was 5 per 100,000 births; for African-American women, it was 21 per 100,000.[37]

Some doctors willing to perform abortions are motivated by the horrors they witnessed when abortion was illegal. Dr. David McDowell remembers "seeing vaginal lacerations from hangers, and wards full of women with infections from criminal abortions. I remember a gal who had a piece of a wood packing crate in her."[38]

New horror stories are appearing about anguished women such as twenty-three-year-old West Virginian Mary Jiveden who became pregnant as a result of date rape. Unemployed, divorced, and with a two-year-old, she felt she could not afford another child. Each clinic she went to said her pregnancy was too advanced for them to give her an abortion, and as she continued her search, her pregnancy kept advancing. When finally she discovered she could have an abortion in Wichita, Kansas for a whopping $2,500, she just gave up, saying, "I don't know how I'm going to make a life for myself and these kids."[39] How many other women are effectively coerced into becoming mothers? How many are making major financial sacrifices that may damage their own and their families' health in the long run? How many women are staying in unhappy, possibly abusive relationships because they are trapped by an unwanted pregnancy? How many unwanted babies have become abandoned, abused, or even killed?

The right to an abortion is already limited by income, age of the potential mother, geographic locality, and by the number of abortion providers. There is no medical procedure that men are entitled to that is so restricted. Since 1976, the Hyde Amendment has prohibited the use of Medicaid funds for abortions unless a woman's life is in danger, or, since 1993, if the pregnancy results from rape or incest. At least six states are even openly disobeying the law by refusing Medicaid assistance for abortions resulting from rape or incest, and Clinton administration officials have said there would be no penalties for their stance. The states that should have forfeited Federal Medicaid funding, apparently will not.

Teenagers in many states have to get parental consent for abortions. Sometimes both parents' consent is needed even if the person lives with only one. This places at least some teens at risk of punishment from an angry mother, father, or both.

Finding abortion providers has become more and more difficult. In 84 percent of all counties containing 31 percent of the country's women of child-bearing age, there are none. Fewer hospitals are providing abortions, and less than 15 percent of medical schools mandate abortion training.[40]

Why are doctors so reluctant to provide a legal medical procedure? One answer may be that it has become life-threatening for doctors to perform abortions. A Pensacola, Florida, provider, Dr. David Gunn, was killed in March 1993. A year later in the same town, Dr. John Bayard Britton and clinic escort James H. Barrett were murdered. Mr. Barrett's wife was also wounded when she was providing escort services. Two clinic workers, Shannon Lowney and Leanne Nichols, were shot to death in a Boston suburb in 1995. In 1994, there were at least four hundred death threats to choice advocates. In 1993, Wichita, Kansas abortion provider Dr. George Tiller was wounded outside the clinic where he worked, and a Southern California doctor was assaulted outside his home by antichoice demonstrators who held rallies there weekly.

Some of the most zealous antichoice forces are even forming alliances with racist and paramilitary organizations and are engaging in terrorism against abortion facilities. Operation Rescue, headed by Randall Terry, one of the most vocal antiabortion organizations, is known to have such ties.

Fanatical forced-motherhood groups have published manuals that give advice to would-be assassins, bombers, and arsonists, and their manuals have been put to use. Tom Burghardt, a researcher and reproductive rights activist, compiled the following grim tally, using 1982–94 data from the Bureau of Alcohol, Tobacco, and Firearms: "37 bombings in 33 states; 123 cases of arson; 1,500 cases of assault, stalking, sabotage and burglary; and some $13 million in property damage."[41] To deal with these tactics, clinics have to divert already scarce funds to security measures.

Antichoice groups defend their actions, physically violent or otherwise, by arguing that they are saving the lives of "babies." In 1995, a supporter of John Salvi, who murdered Shannon Lowney and Leanne Nichols, the Boston suburb clinic workers, said, "When people are involved in killing babies, then it's justified to save the babies. Babies deserve to be defended at any cost."[42]

The argument that abortion is murder is based on the assumption that human life begins at conception and that the developing fetus is already a baby. To accept such arguments is to accept that religious beliefs of some should be the basis of preventing all women from having access to safe, legal means of ending unwanted pregnancies.

SOCIALIZATION FOR MASCULINITY AND HOMOPHOBIC VIOLENCE

Most acts of violence are committed by men; their socialization helps account for this. Males, for example, are raised to be more active, competitive, achieving, and dominant but less emotional and empathetic. Women, on the other hand, are supposed to be more passive, supportive, emotional, and nurturant. Men, more than women, some assume, should be able to handle stress, shoulder burdens, and be responsible supporters of women and children. A sort of militant heterosexuality, in the form of risk-taking behavior and use of weaponry, can be part of the conception of maleness.

Militant heterosexuality is sometimes associated with extreme homophobic violence. Allen R. Schindler was a twenty-two-year-old navy radio operator who was tired of hiding his "true self." He decided that it was time to let people know he was gay. In 1992, shortly before his ship reached Japan, he came out to his commanding officer. A month later he was beaten to death in a public restroom by two fellow sailors. His face was so disfigured by the battering that his mother had to use his tattooed arms to identify him.[43]

Gays and lesbians do not have the same freedom of movement as heterosexuals. "Gay bashers" sometimes go to known or presumed gay and lesbian gathering places looking for victims. Several studies of homophobic violence show a minimum of 20 percent of gay respondents experiencing at least one physical assault at some time in their lives. Even larger numbers have been threatened. Men are more likely to be attacked than women—their behavior is more violating of gender norms. In some cases the attackers accused their victims of being responsible for AIDS.[44]

Attacks on gays and lesbians have been increasing, from 425 reported incidents in 1991 to 832 in 1993. Survey data on gays and lesbians indicate a wide experience of physical violence. A study of homicides sponsored by the New York City Gay and Lesbian Anti-Violence Project, covering the period between 1992 and 1994, labeled the violence "gruesome." Violence was heightened for victims who were people of color.[45] Like victims of rape, victims of homophobic attacks experience a variety of symptoms for a long time afterward. They may change their behavior, become surreptitious about expressing their feelings, and avoid locations they think are dangerous.

Homophobia partly stems from gender inequality as a way males can distance themselves from "feminine" qualities within themselves. A man insults another by comparing him to a woman; a nondominant husband is "hen-pecked" or, more crudely, "pussy-whipped." There are no comparable terms that females use toward one another. It is not an insult, for example, for a young girl to be called a "tomboy." It is acceptable for girls and women to wear clothing associated with males, but the reverse would most likely subject a man to ridicule or worse. The epithets "fag" and "fairy" connote weakness: "real men" are strong and tough and show their maleness by sexual prowess with women. "Real women" are sexually attracted to men and should not be "tough" or "butch."

For decades in the United States, homosexuality was widely considered to be a shameful perversion. To be identified as such was to jeopardize one's physical safety, one's livelihood, and social ties. Many gay men and women internalized the stigma that they were unhealthy, damaged people. There have been important changes, however, many dating from the 1969 "Stonewall Rebellion" in New York's Greenwich Village, when gays and lesbians fought the police during a raid on the Stonewall bar.

Gays and lesbians have struggled for the right to be open about who they are and to have equal access to jobs and a family life. They have challenged the stereotypes that label them as dangerous and "perverted." Many have refused to be ashamed and have created organizations to fight for their rights. But there is still much prejudice, discrimination, and violence against homosexuals. Conservative politicians and religious leaders, who oppose gay and lesbian rights, help legitimize homophobic feelings. The courts, too, sometimes validate homophobia: some lesbian mothers have lost their rights to their own (biological) children, not because they were deemed bad caretakers but simply because of their sexual orientation.

In some states and counties where gay rights laws have been passed, right-wing organizations have organized to overturn them. They have also campaigned against textbooks and library books that present homosexuality as a legitimate lifestyle. One argument right-wingers use against federal funding for public television has been that it shows homosexuality in a positive light. In September 1996, Congress passed a "Defense of Marriage Act," which denies federal recognition to same-sex marriages. Arguing against passage of the bill, Democratic Senator Edward Kennedy from Massachusetts pointed out that "this bill is designed to divide Americans, to drive a wedge between one group of citizens and the rest of the country solely for partisan advantage." Defending the bill, West Virginia Democrat Robert Byrd alleged that "the drive for same-sex marriage is, in effect, an effort to make a sneak attack on society by encoding this aberrant behavior in legal form."[46] These ideas and efforts to make homosexual behavior illegitimate help maintain a climate where only heterosexuality is acceptable. If gays and lesbians are such a threat then, for some, it makes sense to use violence against them.

Racial and Ethnic Interpersonal Violence

An act of violence can be the way an individual or group tries to maintain traditional gender hierarchies. Violence can also become an outlet for the stress caused by corporate and political decisions that lead to such problems as unemployment. Many of the most serious problems in people's lives cannot be solved by their own efforts and consequently seem overwhelming.

Using violence against others, weaker than oneself is, therefore, a low-risk way of feeling a sense of control and a reminder to both assailant and victim of who is more powerful. Some interpersonal violence can take the form of *bias crimes*. The homophobic attacks we have just discussed fall into this category as does much racial/ethnic violence.

BIAS CRIMES

Bias crimes, also called hate crimes or *ethnoviolence*, occur against a person who is identified as a member of a group toward which there is some socially approved hostility. These despised targets are seen as violating the attackers' property, self-conception, and/or their values. The ideas that justify such violent crimes are legitimated by prominent figures in our society; popular culture, films, television, and advertising also perpetuate stereotypes with slanted portrayals.

Hate crimes have two characteristics that distinguish them from other crimes. First, the attacks are astonishingly vicious, especially considering the victims did nothing to their attackers. In street assaults, only about 7 percent of the victims have injuries that warrant hospital treatment, whereas 30 percent of hate crime attacks send the person to the hospital.[47]

Second, hate crimes are often committed by groups of four or more assailants. This fact helps explain the brutality of the assaults. The larger the group, the less any single individual need feel responsible for his or (less often) her actions. The members of the group effectively give each other support for their behavior and create an atmosphere in which people are allowed to suspend their normal moral judgments.

Those committing hate crimes are generally young males. In racially motivated bias crimes, young men feel they are protecting their neighborhood and families. White teenagers interviewed in Brooklyn express unequivocally why they attack African-Americans:

> You go on missions to impress your friends. You get a name as a tough guy who is down with the neighborhood and down with his people.

> I have a reputation as a tough guy who defends the neighborhood and I want to keep it. People know when you've taken care of people who don't belong in the neighborhood. You get respect. Especially if it is some of the blacks.[48]

FINDING SCAPEGOATS

Howard Beach in Queens, New York, is a largely Italian-American enclave. One sixteen year old bragged, "We own the turf of this neighborhood. If

Whoopi Goldberg came into this neighborhood she'd be killed." The actress never came to Howard Beach, but on 10 December 1986, three black men did. Their car had broken down, and they went into a local pizza parlor to eat. Upon leaving, they were chased down by youths armed with bats, golf clubs, and tree limbs. One escaped with minor injuries, another was badly beaten, while the third, Michael Griffith, twenty-three, ran into traffic and was killed by an oncoming car.[49] Four people were indicted, three were convicted of manslaughter, and the fourth was acquitted on all counts. The community, however, supported the attackers, denying charges of racism and jeering the interracial march of two thousand held to protest this killing and other racial violence. A similar response greeted marchers protesting Yusuf Hawkins's death in Bensonhurst, also a mostly white working-class community.

Economic downturns have hurt many in the United States. With high levels of unemployment, even those with jobs can become anxious and fearful. A job today, after all, is no guarantee of a job tomorrow. People seek to understand these problems. Why doesn't the system they believe in work for them? Feeling unjustly treated, they turn their anger against scapegoats, especially African-Americans who they think are getting special treatment.

A study of attitudes in two white working-class areas with histories of racial incidents illustrates the anger white teenagers have about unemployment. Many felt that they were losing jobs to African-Americans. One said, "You know I been lookin' for work for awhile but I can't get a job 'cause they're givin' them all to the black people." They described blacks as dangerous criminals who get away with their crimes. A black comes to your neighborhood for one thing, to "look for trouble," and the violence against African-Americans was justified as a form of community defense.[50]

Scapegoats are not chosen at random. They are groups who are (1) socially approved targets of hostility; (2) vulnerable, less protected against physical attacks; and (3) visibly different from the majority with some characteristic such as skin color or an accent that allows them to be singled out.

It is almost a reflex for some to blame people of color for their problems. In the early 1980s, northern New Jersey towns with overbuilding and inadequate drainage experienced damage following heavy rains and subsequent floods. A woman pondered her losses including

> two cars, my son's motorcycle, the French provincial in the living room . . . my husband's worked all his life for this. Everyone talks about the poor people. What about the middle class? *We're paying for those people in Newark to sit around so they don't have to work.*

She is blaming the largely black and Latino population of Newark for her plight. She then finds another group to accuse:

> I used to work nights. Right now I have to get a job to put my house in order, but I'm not qualified to do anything. I tell you it's not right. *How long are you going to be able to hold a job when they're letting in people from other places?*

She understands the government isn't always on her side:

> I got five kids living at home. Four of them are older and work. The Government lets me claim only one on my income tax. Is that fair? No one is giving us the answers.[51]

She has answers, however. Immigrants, blacks on welfare, they are all somehow implicated in her lack of qualifications, her inability to find work, and her high taxes. Politicians encourage this kind of thinking, a substitute for rational analysis of social conditions. Over and over one hears that "they" are responsible for the problems of the good, hard-working (white implicitly understood) people, and the media very rarely correct the misrepresentations.

As with the Willie Horton ads mentioned earlier, politicians take advantage of white fears. For example, in the 1990 North Carolina senatorial campaign, an ad for Jesse Helms depicted the white hands of a job seeker crushing and flinging away a letter of rejection. The commentary blamed affirmative action for having cost the white man his chance.

Ex-Klansman David Duke, changing his sheets for a respectable dark suit, was elected to the Louisiana state legislature in 1989 and almost became Republican governor of that state in 1991. He changed his clothes but not his basic message. In his campaign, Duke, founder of the National Association for the Advancement of White People, attacked an allegedly growing welfare system, asking, "Why should your tax dollars go to people to buy lottery tickets?"[52]

Former Republican senator and 1996 presidential candidate Robert Dole encouraged whites to feel they are the victims of affirmative action by alleging:

> the people in America are paying a price for things that were done before they were born. We did discriminate. We did suppress people. It was wrong. Slavery was wrong. But should future generations have to pay for that?[53]

Bias crimes have increased throughout the United States. Los Angeles, for example, reported an 11 percent increase in hate crimes between 1991 and 1992, with the attacks more brutal in 1992. The director of Los Angeles County's Human Relations Commission explained: "People are more angry, more hostile, there's more bitterness.... There are many people out there who are threatened by the changes in their personal economic circumstances, and they use this occasion to stereotype and scapegoat others."[54]

The FBI issues national hate crime statistics and claimed there were minimally 4,755 incidents in 1991 and 7,684 in 1993. According to a March 1994 report by the Southern Poverty Law Center, which monitors bias crimes and the hate groups discussed later, 1993 "began and ended with some of the most brutal hate crimes Klanwatch has ever documented." African-Americans are the most frequent targets. In 1993, in Los Angeles 37 percent of the victims were African-Americans, whereas they are only 12 percent of the city's population.[55]

One case laid bare the economic motivations behind such attacks. Vincent Chin, a twenty-seven-year-old Chinese American, was celebrating his upcoming marriage in a Detroit bar when he was confronted by two laid-off autoworkers, Ronald Ebens and Michael Nitz. They mistook him for a Japanese and yelled, "It's because of you we're out of work." Later they followed him out of the bar and beat him to death with a baseball bat. A judge fined the two men $3,780 and gave them three years' probation. Following protests by outraged Asian-Americans, the U.S. Department of Justice filed civil rights charges against the assailants. Nitz was acquitted, Ebens sentenced to 25 years. On appeal this sentence was overturned, and in a subsequent retrial in 1987, Nitz was acquitted. Ten years later, in California, a Japanese real estate consultant was killed after being harassed by two men who also blamed the Japanese for their unemployment.[56]

In Jersey City, New Jersey, in 1987, Dr. Karushal Sharan, an Indian doctor, was severely beaten with an iron pipe by three men in their early twenties, one of them an off-duty police officer. In the same year, in the nearby city of Hoboken, four teenagers were involved in killing Navroze Mody, also an Asian Indian. They assaulted Mody with bricks and repeatedly kicked him but left his white companion alone. The feelings expressed by some of the white residents reveal deep-seated racial resentment; Jersey City and Hoboken were once thriving blue collar communities, but the factories are gone, and the future for working-class white kids without college educations is bleak.

One Jersey City youth complained, "They're not clean, they smell, they take our jobs." His father was a construction worker, but the son can't find decent paying work and is trying to become a boxer. His mother is bitter. "I have no future here," she lamented, "my kids have no future here, we're lost." She resents the fact that she's lived in Jersey City all her life but can barely afford her rent, much less buy a house, while Indians come and buy property.[57]

Each hate-crime attack is a statement to all people of color that their freedom is restricted. They cannot freely live where they want, go where they want, or conduct the ordinary business of life, such as buying a car, eating a slice of pizza, going to a bar, walking down the street.

Interpersonal Violence and Race and Gender   93

African-American anger and resentment can also lead to bias crimes. These are also on the increase, although African-Americans are still much more likely to be victims than assailants. Some of these incidents were well publicized. There was the severe beating of Reginald Denny, a white truck driver pulled from his van during the uprising following the verdict in the police beating of Rodney King, discussed below. Colin Ferguson's shooting rampage on the Long Island Railroad (LIRR) is another example.

Jews and Koreans have also been targets of black rage. In Crown Heights, Brooklyn, African-Americans and Jews live in close proximity. Some blacks believe Jews have been given preferential treatment in housing and seem to be more affluent. In the summer of 1991, a car driven by a member of a Jewish sect, the Hasidim, struck and killed a seven-year-old black boy. Many African-Americans believed that the boy had been callously ignored by a Hasidic ambulance driver. There was rioting, and some days later, a twenty-nine-year-old Australian rabbinical student was stabbed to death by a black assailant.[58]

Koreans, who have economic advantages and educational backgrounds that many United States blacks lack, frequently set up stores in African-American neighborhoods where rents are lower, and there are few large supermarkets. In 1991, in Los Angeles, Soon Ja Du, a Korean-American grocer, got into a fight with fifteen-year-old Latasha Harlins, accusing her of shoplifting a $1.79 bottle of orange juice. Although she gave Du the money, the Korean woman killed her anyway with a shot to the back of her head as she was leaving the store. The African-American community was outraged when a court sentenced Du to a fine of only $500 and some community service. During the next year's uprisings, nearly two thousand Korean businesses were looted and burned.[59]

INTERETHNIC VIOLENCE—ORGANIZED HATE GROUPS

Following the April 1995 bombing of an Oklahoma City federal building, the media spotlight turned to organized armed hate groups. The attention was overdue: groups with explicitly racist agendas have long been a feature of American society. They are indicative of the anger and suspicion that exist among some whites, and their readiness for violence makes them very dangerous.

There have been no reports of organized racist groups among nonwhites, although there is not much analysis of why this is the case. One reason could be that such groups are unlikely to be tolerated by authorities and would be quickly detected and repressed at an early stage. In the past, even nonviolent expressions of black pride have been viewed in the larger community with hostility and fear. This was the case with the "black power" movement in the 1960s and 1970s. Black power was a call for African-

American communities to run their own economic and political institutions and an affirmation of the worth of an African heritage. Whites, however, felt it was a racist attack on themselves.

There are over three hundred organized hate groups, collectively referred to as Neo-Nazis because of the similarity between their agendas and that of the German fascists, whom they openly admire. These groups are antiliberal, antiblack, anti-immigrant, antigovernment, prowhite Christian supremacists, and they are often heavily armed. White opponents of their ideas are labeled "race traitors" and become potential victims of violence.

Experts on these organizations claim their membership is growing, attributing this to tensions caused by the economic downturn. Such groups offer support, advice, companionship, excitement, and hope to lonely, bored, and pessimistic white people. Their activist program seems an alternative to the empty promises of traditional politicians.

There are no firm figures on how large these organizations are. Their active membership is estimated from 10,000 to 20,000 with at least 200,000 supporters.[60] It is believed that they are directly responsible for about 15 percent of violent racial incidents. However, their messages may incite actions by those not directly involved in their organizations. They have rock bands, computer networks, and cable TV shows. Ex-Klanner and founder of the White Aryan Resistance (WAR), Tom Metzger has a cable show based in San Diego called *Race and Reason*. Among other things, the show tells interested viewers how to contact the "Aryan Update" hot line.

WAR racism isn't limited to American blacks. The organization was held responsible for the beating death of an Ethiopian student in Portland, Oregon. In 1988, Mulugeta Seraw and two friends were attacked by skinheads armed with baseball bats and steel-plated shoes. Mulugeta Seraw died of a fractured skull, and his friends had lesser injuries. One assailant was eventually sentenced to life imprisonment and the two others to twenty-year sentences. The attackers were found to be closely connected to Metzger's group.

Alan Berg was a talk show radio host at station KOA in Denver, Colorado, and unusually liberal for his profession. He often got into arguments with white supremacist listeners, challenging their claims that the Holocaust never happened, that Jews run the government and the banks. One evening in June 1984, he drove into his driveway and was killed as he left his car. Thirteen shots were fired at him from a submachine gun. The murder weapon was eventually found in Idaho, where a number of white supremacist groups are headquartered, and two men, members of The Order, were found guilty of violating his civil rights.[61]

In addition to the killings mentioned here, there have been numerous other murders, beatings, and shoot-outs with the police. There have also been robberies of stores and armored cars for money that was subsequently

Interpersonal Violence and Race and Gender 95

used to buy weapons and land on which paramilitary training camps have been set up.

REPRESSIVE POLICE VIOLENCE: KEEPING A LID ON

In March 1991, George Holliday awoke a little after midnight, disturbed by noises from the street below. Looking out of his window, he saw a helicopter and six police cars. On the ground, an African-American man, Rodney King, was trying to evade police blows and kicks. Holliday used his new video camera to record one of the most famous incidents of police brutality in recent history. His 90-second video showed four cops hitting King 56 times as he lay on the ground while 14 others, 10 from the L.A.P.D., the rest from other agencies, watched.

Holliday's videotape of the incident seemed clear enough evidence that the police engaged in excessive force. Nonetheless, there were whites who claimed that only reasonable force had been used. The police were tried and acquitted in Simi Valley, a virtually all-white community, and their acquittal was followed by what has been repeatedly described as the costliest riot in U.S. history: at least thirty-eight people died and there was over $1 billion worth of property damage. The protests resulted in federal charges being brought against several officers. Two were found guilty by a Los Angeles jury, yet the judge sentenced them to two-and-a-half-year prison terms out of the possible ten years they could have received. These were the two who, after beating King, admitted the seriousness of their attack. One radio conversation went: "I haven't beaten anyone this bad in a long time." The response from a second car was "Oh not again. . . . Thought you agreed to chill out for a while."[62]

The King case was a dramatic example of a pattern of racism in the L.A.P.D. Three years after this incident, veteran L.A.P.D. officer Mark Fuhrman's racism was exposed during the O. J. Simpson trial. During his years on the force, Fuhrman had openly expressed contempt for people of color, as well as for women, including his own colleagues. He had used racial epithets, planted evidence, and may even have tortured suspects. Yet in an example of denying responsibility for the behavior of individual officers, L.A.P.D. Chief Williams claimed that Fuhrman's behavior was atypical of his police force. Williams said, "The few bad apples that came out in the trial such as Mark Fuhrman, are not reflective of the L.A.P.D."[63] Although his beliefs and behavior were known to the department, Fuhrman remained on the force until he voluntarily retired.

Fuhrman was not just one "bad apple" in a nonracist "barrel." In 1990, alone, Los Angeles paid over $11 million in suits against the department. African-Americans filed 41 percent of the 4,400 misconduct charges made against the L.A.P.D. between 1987 and 1990. In 1982, ten years prior to King's beating, Los Angeles's long-time Police Chief Darryl Gates offered a defense of the chokehold, a method of restraint favored by the L.A.P.D. that had resulted in numerous fatalities: "In some blacks when it is applied, the veins or arteries do not open up as fast as they do in normal people."[64]

Los Angeles is not the only city with racist police incidents. African-Americans throughout the country frequently experience beatings, shovings, and humiliating searches from the police. In 1996, Amnesty International issued a report on police brutality in New York City, which has the nation's largest urban police department. The human rights organization documented the disproportionate number of people of color physically abused and sometimes killed, often by shots in the back, in situations that, according to Amnesty, "did not warrant the use of lethal force" and were "in violation of police guidelines and international standards."[65] Pulitzer prize-winning writer David K. Shipler, who has done research on police racism throughout the United States, said about two years of data collection, "I have encountered very few black men who have not been hassled by white cops."[66]

Even African-American officers are in danger from their own colleagues. Don Jackson, a Long Beach, California cop, was investigating police racism for a local TV station. He was stopped, and his head was shoved through a window. In Philadelphia a black female officer was beaten with fists and flashlights by fellow police who mistook her for a suspect. She identified herself as a police officer, but they kept hitting her. She said, "It was like Rodney King—only I'm a cop. Even if I wasn't a cop, they had no right to beat somebody like that. Not in the head. You hit in places you're taught to hit." Minority cops attest to the extra dangers they face when out of uniform. The chairwoman of the National Black Police Association claims, "Police who are not in uniform and who are black are subject to being attacked much quicker than white officers who are not in uniform."[67]

Not all cops are racists, but police departments in many parts of the United States tolerate the attacks described above. A professor who beats up nonwhite students or a bank teller who makes racist remarks to his/her customers would unlikely be able to keep his/her job, but police officers with racist assault records often stay on the force.

Institutional racism has resulted in appalling social conditions for many minorities and is largely responsible for high rates of street crime. Into this situation come the police, with an impossible and frustrating job. They are supposed to prevent crime, yet they are unable to remedy the conditions that cause crime. Nevertheless, there is pressure to make arrests, to show the public that city government is fighting crime, which many whites—including police—view as a natural product of communities of color. The police are as likely as anyone else to hold the stereotype that sees African-

American and Latino males as violent criminals. These factors help explain police violence toward blacks and Latinos.

The structure of police forces heightens the likelihood of the police committing acts of violence against the very people they are supposed to be protecting. Police departments are organized in a quasi-militaristic way, with the police trained to go out to fight "wars."[68] Furthermore, a sense of "us" against "them" heightens the solidarity of the police and their willingness to protect each other, which sometimes includes concealing acts of brutality. The Amnesty report mentioned above refers to "The 'code of silence' in which police officers refuse to testify against their colleagues."[69]

The bureaucratic tactics discussed in chapter 2 come into play in police departments. In New York, a committee that was supposed to review police shootings of colleagues was disbanded without issuing any recommendations. Former Chief of Patrol William R. Bracey, who sat on the short-lived committee, explained: "The Police Department just didn't want to touch the race issue because it was too politically explosive. So they just stopped having meetings, and if they ever issued a final report they never told us committee members about it." Bureaucratic doublespeak veils the violence. In New York, the police department refers to reacting on the basis of stereotypes as "symbolic opponent syndrome."[70]

Minority communities don't see the police protecting them from their real victimizers, exploitative landlords and indifferent politicians. In fact, the only representatives of city government who are consistently in their neighborhoods are the armed police.

James Baldwin graphically described ghettos as "occupied territory" where police keep an eye on the inhabitants, making sure they stay in their place, in effect, playing the role of a colonial army.[71] The term occupying army is still used by those in the ghettos, and the police themselves see this as a valid description. A police station in the Bronx called itself Fort Apache after the Western fort used to control that group of Indians.

In *New York Times* Op-Ed pieces, two police veterans expressed eloquently the untenable situation existing between police and ghetto residents. Ira Socol, former New York City cop, writes:

> We send our police out to fight a ... war on crime. ... trained for "combat" and with no political support for efforts to win the hearts and minds of the inner-city population. ... Do the police become racist? Certainly. Do they become violent? It happens.

Edmund Stubbing had worked six years in Harlem when he wrote of his experiences on one block there.

> I am a police officer. To me the block is a graveyard in a sea of the drowned and the drowning ... the whole scene is disturbing and

frustrating. I believe that the problem of West 127th Street has its root in international and domestic economic and political policies. *I also believe that what I do does absolutely no good.* . . . My frustration, ironically spills onto the other victim in this absurdity—the "enemy."

He also describes how his job causes him to becomes more callous.

I don't really like what I do, what I am. I resist it somewhat but as time goes on, as the condition grows stronger, I resist less.[72]

Suspicious police killings have continued. On 4 July 1996, a twenty-five-year-old African-American man named Nathaniel Levi Gaines Jr., unarmed, was shot in the back by New York City police officer Paolo Colecchia who already had several complaints made against him. In 1994, Colecchia had been briefly suspended for giving false information during an investigation of some of these charges. Nathaniel Gaines Sr. expressed his feelings about his son's death:

We are not oblivious to the history of the criminal justice system. We didn't want to say that his life was taken because he was born with his skin dark. But there is no other explanation.[73]

Another example comes from Paterson, New Jersey, where in February of 1995 an officer shot an unarmed sixteen year old who was allegedly dealing drugs. The youth died several days later, and young people rampaged through the streets in rage. One twenty-five year old, who refused to give his name, said, "You can't put a lid on boiling water."[74] Yet that is what the police are expected to do.

THE POT BOILS OVER: URBAN REBELLIONS

Police violence has been the spark igniting the anger that has set off urban upheavals since at least 1935, the year of the Harlem uprising. The investigating commission at that time wrote: "The insecurity of the individual in Harlem against police aggression is one of the most potent causes for the existing hostility to authority." In 1968, a year after 164 urban disturbances, the National Advisory Commission on Civil Disorders reported that "Negroes firmly believe that police brutality and harassment occur repeatedly in Negro neighborhoods."[75]

The rebellions resulted from the conditions described previously: unemployment, bad schools, poor housing, and so forth. Police violence, however, seems to be an especially provocative indication of the callousness of the larger society toward people of color. It is somewhat ironic then that the immediate response to disorders is usually large amounts of force.

In May 1993, then president George Bush, visiting Los Angeles to speak "about our course as a nation," attacked federally funded social programs and welfare which, he claimed, robbed people of "their sense of responsibility." On the programmatic side, he said the police needed more money, and government policies toward the poor must "foster personal responsibility." Vice President Dan Quayle explained that the L.A. disorders resulted from a "poverty of values."

Two onlookers at the 1992 L.A. rebellion offer deeper insights. As he stood watching the burning buildings, Ervin Mitchell Jr., a thirty-one-year-old African-American engineer, reflected:

> Almost everybody I know has been harassed and much worse by the police. Young blacks and Hispanics have been persecuted, beaten, and pulled out of our cars because of stereotypes. We're tired of being treated like garbage. We're tired of living in a society that denies us the right to be considered as a human being.

His companion, Michael Ming, a twenty-three-year-old student, agreed, adding:

> The way the whole entire system is structured, the rich get richer, the poor get poorer. It provides almost no hope for most folks, especially black folks.[76]

Notes

1. Don Terry, "Killing of Woman Waiting for Justice Sounds Alert on Domestic Violence," *New York Times*, 17 March 1992, p. A14.
2. Claudia Brenner, "Survivor's Story," in *Hate Crimes: Confronting Violence against Lesbians and Gay Men*, eds. Gregory M. Herek and Kevin T. Berrill (Newbury Park, Calif.: Sage Publications, 1992), pp. 11–15.
3. Father quoted in Ralph Blumenthal, "Black Youth Is Killed in Brooklyn by Whites in Attack Called Racial," *New York Times*, 25 August 1989, p. B2; Nick Ravo, "Marchers and Brooklyn Youths Trade Racial Jeers," *New York Times*, 27 August 1989, p. 32.
4. Teenager quoted in Don Terry, "On Slain Youth's Block Sorrow and Bitterness," *New York Times*, 25 August 1989, p. B2.
5. Quoted in Tamar Lewin, "Case Might Fit Pattern of Abuse, Experts Say," *New York Times*, 19 June 1994, p. 21.
6. *Intimate Violence: The Causes and Consequences of Abuse in the American Family* (New York: Simon and Schuster, 1988), p. 92.
7. Author's calculations of percentages killed from U.S. Department of Justice, Bureau of Justice Statistics, *Violence between Intimates* (November 1994), pp. 3, 9; and *SourceBook of Criminal Justice Statistics—1994*, Table 3.113, p. 338.
8. Bureau of Justice Statistics, *Violence between Intimates* (November 1994), p. 2.
9. Nancy Gibbs, "Till Death Do Us Part," in *Crisis in American Institutions*, 9th ed., eds. Jerome H. Skolnick and Elliott Currie (New York: HarperCollins, 1994), p. 233.

10. Ronald M. Holmes, and Stephen T. Holmes, *Murder in America* (Thousand Oaks, Calif.: Sage Publications, 1994), p. 20.
11. Philip J. Hilts, "6% of Women Admit Beatings While Pregnant," *New York Times*, 4 March 1994, p. A23.
12. Kathleen J. Ferraro, "Cops, Courts, and Woman Battering," in *Violence against Women: The Bloody Footprints*, eds. Pauline B. Bart and Eileen Geil Morgan (Newbury Park, Calif.: Sage, 1993), p. 167. She has a useful overview of the variations in police response.
13. Lisa G. Lerman, "Prosecution of Wife Beaters: Institutional Obstacles and Innovations," in *Violence in the Home: Interdisciplinary Perspectives*, ed. Mary Lystad (New York: Brunner/Mazel, 1986), pp. 262–65; Demie Kurz, "Battering and the Criminal Justice System: A Feminist View," *Domestic Violence: The Changing Criminal Justice Response*, eds. Eve S. Buzawa and Carl G. Buzawa (Westport, Conn.: Auburn House, 1992), p. 30; Lawrence W. Sherman, and Richard A. Berk, "The Specific Deterrent Effects of Arrest for Domestic Assault," *American Sociological Review* 49 (1984): pp. 261–72.
14. Clare Collins, "Spanking Is Becoming the New Don't," *New York Times*, 11 May 1995, p. C8. On European laws, Sarah Lyall, "European Rights Court to Hear Case of British Boy's Caning," *New York Times*, 10 October 1996, p. A11.
15. Bureau of the Census, *Statistical Abstract of the United States, 1995*, Table 346, p. 215.
16. American Public Health Association, Position Paper, 9211, Domestic Violence, pp. 3–4; Evan Stark, and Anne H. Flitcraft, "Women and Children at Risk: A Feminist Perspective on Child Abuse," in *Women's Health, Politics and Power: Essays on Sex/Gender, Medicine, and Public Health*, eds. Elizabeth Fee and Nancy Krieger (Amityville, N.Y.: Baywood Publishing Co., Inc., 1994), pp. 313–19; Richard J. Gelles, and Murray A. Straus, *Intimate Violence: The Causes and Consequences of Abuse in the American Family* (New York: Simon and Schuster, 1988), p. 63.
17. For a critique of the idea that battered children necessarily become battering adults, see Stark and Flitcraft, p. 132. There is some evidence that children who have been abused are more likely to become violent criminals. Cathy Spatz Widon, *The Cycle of Violence* (Washington, D.C.: U.S. Department of Justice, 1992).
18. Bureau of Justice Statistics, p. 4.
19. Gelles and Straus, pp. 85–87.
20. Child abuse data, Anne Crittendon, "Recession Vs. Babies," *New York Times*, 23 May 1984; Youngstown data, "Private Violence," *Time Magazine*, 5 September 1983, p. 24.
21. Gelles and Straus, pp. 94–96.
22. "State Officials Move to Aid Abused Women on Insurance," *New York Times*, 19 March 1995, p. 30.
23. Patricia Horn, "Beating Back the Revolution," *Dollars & Sense* (December 1992), pp. 13, 22.
24. Ibid., p. 13.
25. Ibid., pp. 13, 22
26. Quoted in Jane Gross, "Where 'Boys Will Be Boys' and Adults Are Befuddled," *New York Times*, 29 March 1993, p. A13; Seth Mydans, "High School Gang Accused of Raping for 'Points,'" *New York Times*, 20 March 1993, p. 6.
27. Jay Livingston, *Crime & Criminology*, 2d ed. (Englewood Cliffs, N.J.: Prentice-Hall, 1994), pp. 184–89, quote p. 185.

28. Diane Scully, *Understanding Sexual Violence: A Study of Convicted Rapists* (Boston: Unwin Hyman, 1992), p. 48.
29. Larry Baron, and Murray A. Straus, *Four Theories of Rape in American Society: A State-Level Analysis* (New Haven, Conn.: Yale University Press, 1989), p. 185. Availability of pornography was also related to higher rape rates, although they downplay this association and are very concerned about the censorship issue. The evidence on pornography is controversial, with no clear nonlaboratory relationship proven. However, minimally, we can say that pornography illustrates the objectification of women and helps strengthen myths regarding women's sexual desires.
30. Quotes from Editorial, *Nation*, 29 May 1989, cover.
31. "Defendant Acquitted of Rape," *New York Times*, 7 October 1989.
32. Quote, p. 156.
33. Melinda Henneberger, and Michel Marriot, "For Some, Rituals of Abuse Replace Youthful Courtship," *New York Times*, 11 July 1993, pp. 1, 33.
34. Quotes from Craig Wolf, "5 Youths Arrested in Rape of Coney Island Jogger," *New York Times*, 14 April 1994, p. B1; Ian Fisher, "Court Asked to Reinstate Rape Counts," *New York Times*, 16 April 1994, p. 27; Melinda Henneberger, and Michel Marriot, "For Some Rituals of Abuse Replace Youthful Courtship," *New York Times*, 11 July 1993, pp. 1, 33; Diane Scully, *Understanding Sexual Violence: A Study of Convicted Rapists* (Boston: Unwin Hyman, 1992), pp. 158, 141, 142.
35. "Robert J. Billings Is Dead at 68, Helped Form the Moral Majority," *New York Times*, 1 June 1995, p. D21. In his 1996 platform, however, Dole did not have an antiabortion plank, because he feared losing some of his female support.
36. Frederick S. Jaffe, Barbara L. Lindheim, and Philip R. Lee, "Legal Abortion Improves Public Health," in *Abortion: Opposing Viewpoints*, ed. Bonnie Szumski (St. Paul, Minn.: Greenhaven Press, 1986), p. 148.
37. Abortion deaths from Patricia Lunneborg, *Abortion: A Positive Decision* (New York: Bergin & Garvey, 1992), p. 67; maternal deaths from U.S. Bureau of the Census, *Statistical Abstract of the United States, 1995*, Table 120, p. 90.
38. Tamar Lewin, "Hurdles Increase for Many Women Seeking Abortions," *New York Times*, 15 March 1992, pp. 1, 18. Quote from p. 18.
39. Lewin, p. 18.
40. Marlene Gerber Fried, "Reproductive Wrongs," *Women's Review of Books* 11 (July 1994), p. 7; "Shrinking Choice," *Nation*, 29 May 1995, pp. 743–44; Lewin, p. 18.
41. Tom Burghardt, "Neo-Nazis Salute the Anti-Abortion Zealots," *CovertAction Quarterly* (Spring 1995), p. 26.
42. Quoted in Robert Pear, "Authorities Trying to Find the Reason for Clinic Attacks," *New York Times*, 2 January 1994, p. 10.
43. James Sterngold, "Death of a Gay Sailor: A Lethal Beating Overseas Brings Questions and Fear," *New York Times*, 31 January 1993, p. 22.
44. Figures from Bureau of Justice Statistics, *SourceBook of Criminal Justice Statistics—1993*, Table 3.118, p. 375; Kevin T. Berrill, "Anti-Gay Violence and Victimization in the United States: An Overview," in Herek and Berrill, pp. 19–45.
45. U.S. Department of Justice, Bureau of Justice Statistics, *SourceBook of Criminal Justice Statistics—1993*, Table 3.118, p. 375, and *SourceBook of Criminal Justice Statistics—1994*, Table 3.105, p. 330; quote from David W. Dunlap, "Survey Details Gay Slayings Around U.S.," *New York Times*, 21 December 1994, p. D21.

46. Eric Schmitt, "Senators Reject Both Job-Bias Ban and Gay Marriage," *New York Times*, 11 September 1996, pp. A1, A16, quotes from A16. The Senate vote was 85–14. Another bill banning workplace discrimination against gays and lesbians was also defeated but by only one vote.
47. Daniel Goleman, "As Bias Crime Seems to Rise, Scientists Study Roots of Racism," *New York Times*, 29 May 1990, p. C5.
48. Quoted in Howard Pinderhughes, "The Anatomy of Racially Motivated Violence in New York City: A Case Study of Youth in Southern Brooklyn," *Social Problems* 40 (1993): p. 488.
49. Quote from "Mean Streets in Howard Beach," *Newsweek*, 5 January 1987, p. 24.
50. Quotes from Pinderhughes, pp. 478–91; see also Pinderhughes, "'Down with the Program': Racial Attitude and Group Violence among Youth in Bensonhurst and Gravesend," in *Gangs: The Origin and Impact of Contemporary Youth Gangs*, eds. Scott Cummings and Daniel J. Monti (Albany, N.Y.: SUNY Press, 1993), pp. 82, 87.
51. Quoted in Michael Norman, "Our Towns: Flood Victims, Perplexed, Angry and Plucky," *New York Times*, 19 April 1984, p. B2, emphasis added.
52. Helms quoted in Jack Levin and Jack McDevitt, *Hate Crimes: The Rising Tide of Bigotry and Backlash* (New York: Plenum Press, 1993), p. 38. Duke quoted in Don Terry, "In Louisiana, Duke Divides Old Loyalties," *New York Times*, 31 October 1991, pp. A1, B9.
53. Dole quoted in Steven A. Holmes, "Backlash Against Affirmative Action Troubles Advocates," *New York Times*, 7 February 1995, p. B9.
54. Quoted in Somini Sengupta, "Hate Crimes Hit Record High in 1992," *Los Angeles Times*, 23 March 1993, pp. B1, B8.
55. Southern Poverty Law Center, *Intelligence Report* (March 1994), p. 4; "Pulse: Bias Crime," *New York Times*, 11 July 1994, p. B1; "U.S. Had More Than 7,000 Hate Crimes in '93, F.B.I. Head Says," *New York Times*, 29 June 1994, p. A16. Because of the way they are gathered, the FBI's statistics are believed by experts to underestimate the incidence of hate crimes.
56. Quotes in Levin and McDevitt, p. 58; U.S. Commission on Civil Rights, *Civil Rights Issues Facing Asian Americans in the 1990's* (February 1992), pp. 25–26; Seth Mydans, "Killing Alarms Japanese-Americans," *New York Times*, 26 February 1992.
57. Quotes from the video *Pockets of Hate*, 1988.
58. This and several other anti-Semitic incidents involving African-Americans are discussed by Richard Goldstein, "The New Anti-Semitism: A *Geshrei*," in *Blacks and Jews: Alliances and Arguments*, ed. Paul Berman (New York: Delta, 1994), pp. 204–16.
59. A discussion of minority bias crimes can be found in Levin and McDevitt, pp. 137–48; the Latasha Harlins incident is discussed by Wanda Coleman, "Remembering Latasha: Blacks, Immigrants and America," *Nation*, 15 February 1993, pp. 187–91.
60. Elinor Langer, "The American Neo-Nazi Movement Today," *Nation*, 16/23 July 1990, p. 85.
61. This may seem a strange charge given that Berg was murdered. However, this is the way in which the federal government is able to prosecute racially motivated murderers. There are federal civil rights laws, but only a very few types of homicide are federal crimes, and bias killings are not among them.

62. Quotes from Seth Mydans, "In Messages, Officers Banter after Beating in Los Angeles," *New York Times*, 19 March 1991, pp. A1, A18.
63. Kenneth B. Noble, "Police Department Reeling after Verdict," *New York Times*, 15 October 1995, p. B8.
64. Jerome H. Skolnick, and James J. Fyfe, *Above the Law: Police and the Excessive Use of Force* (New York: The Free Press, 1993), p. 3; Gates quote from "Coast Police Chief Accused of Racism," *New York Times*, 13 May 1982, p. A24.
65. Amnesty International, *United States of America: Police Brutality and Excessive Force in the New York City Police Department* (New York: Amnesty International, June 1996), p. 11.
66. David K. Shipler, "Khaki, Blue and Blacks," *New York Times*, 26 May 1992, p. A17.
67. Quotes from "Black Plainclothes Officer Says the Police Beat Her," *New York Times*, 13 January 1995, p. A14.
68. Skolnick and Fyfe, pp. 113–33.
69. Amnesty International, p. 2.
70. Quotes from David Kocieniewski, "Officers Confronting Officers: Old Rules Still in Place," *New York Times*, 28 March 1996, p. B3. In the same article, Bracey, a former head of the black police organization The Guardians Association, notes that no African-American "cop has . . . shot another officer while on duty or in civilian clothes or killed him. Black officers know that there's another side."
71. James Baldwin, "A Report from Occupied Territory," *Nation*, 11 July 1966, pp. 39–43.
72. Ira Socol, "Trained to Do Our Dirty Work for Us," *New York Times*, 2 May 1992, p. 23; Edmund Stubbing, "The Performance Becomes the Reality," *New York Times*, 4 August 1980, emphasis added.
73. Bob Herbert, "Grief and Justice," *New York Times*, 19 July 1996, p. A27.
74. Robert Hanley, "Unrest Follows a Police Shooting in Paterson," *New York Times*, 25 February 1994, p. B5.
75. Quotes from Skolnick and Fyfe, p. 78; U.S. Riot Commission, *Report of the National Advisory Commission on Civil Disorders* (New York: Bantam Books, 1968), p. 302.
76. "Excerpts from Speech by Bush in Los Angeles," *New York Times*, 9 May 1992, p. 10; Quayle quoted in Andrew Rosenthal, "Quayle Says Riots Sprang from Lack of Family Values," *New York Times*, 20 May 1992, p. A1; onlookers quoted in Don Terry, "Decades of Rage Created Crucible of Violence," *New York Times*, 31 May 1992, p. 24.

5 / Structural Violence for Workers and the Unemployed

The previous chapters discussed how corporate and political decision making plays a major role in creating the conditions that cause street crime and other forms of interpersonal violence. In this chapter, we will examine how structural violence results from the dynamics of capitalism. The structural violence experienced by working people results from decisions made by corporate executives, not because they are malicious, but because they are doing their jobs and looking after their own interests.

STRUCTURAL VIOLENCE AND THE PROFIT MOTIVE

In chapter 1, we noted that inequality leads to structural violence by denying resources for a healthy life and environment to the less privileged. The more privileged use their resources and social positions to maintain or improve their own positions—an unintended consequence of this is structural violence.

Criminologists Marshall B. Clinard and Peter C. Yeager summarize the violence emanating from corporations:

> It includes losses due to sickness and even death resulting from air and water pollution, and the sale of unsafe foods and drugs, defective autos, tires, and appliances and hazardous clothing and other products. It also includes the numerous disabilities that result from injuries to plant workers, including contamination by chemicals that could have been used with adequate safeguards and the potentially dangerous effects of other work related exposures.[1]

Social scientists who study corporate and other forms of crime agree the crimes committed by those occupying executive suites actually cost the public more and lead to more physical harm than do the crimes of those in the streets.[2] For much of its early history, American criminology looked exclusively at the crimes of ordinary people, usually termed street crime. Pioneering work by Edwin Sutherland, starting in the late 1930s, helped focus attention on "white collar" crime as well. Sutherland pointed out that no one debates the crookedness of the nineteenth-century robber barons, the founders of many of today's corporations and banks. In 1890, J. P. Morgan told a gathering of railroad presidents, "I have the utmost respect for you gentlemen individually, but as railroad presidents I wouldn't trust you with my watch out of sight." The gangster, Al Capone, Sutherland remarked, referred to businesses as "the legitimate rackets," and folk balladeer Woody Guthrie sang, "Some will rob you with a six-gun and some with a fountain pen."[3]

There is a large literature on corporate crime, but not all company actions that endanger lives are against the law. Corporations are able to use their political power, discussed in chapter 2 and further discussed below, to prevent the passage of laws that would make illegal certain of their acts. In the words of Russell Mokhiber, editor of the newsletter *Corporate Crime Reporter*,

> corporate lawbreakers double as corporate lawmakers. Corporate America has saturated the legislatures with dollars in order to promote laws making legal or non-criminal what by any common standard of justice would be considered illegal and criminal, and to obstruct legislation that would outlaw the violent activity.[4]

Street criminals are not able to affect the legislative process in this way.

The media, as mentioned in chapter 2, does not dramatize tales of corporate misdoing to viewers and readers. Corporate executives may express concern about street crime but not about their own illegal behavior. In October 1994 at the annual meeting of the Business Council, an organization of the country's largest businesses, the CEO of Pepsico said, "I think most of us feel that violence and crime is a real issue for the country, if not the number 1 issue." The gathering listened to a number of presentations on crime from professors and the police commissioner of New York City. No experts on corporate crime seem to have been invited.[5]

In this chapter, we are interested in decisions leading to injury or death regardless of whether or not they are technically illegal. These violent consequences are related to the goals and organization of economic enterprises.

Executives and managers are evaluated and compensated in terms of how well they are helping the corporation to achieve its primary goal, that is, maximizing profits. Thus their own financial worth is tied to the profitability of their companies. Sociologist Michael Useem studied seven of the nation's largest corporations. "More managerial income," he concluded, "was made contingent upon company or division performance in all of the companies" with performance judged by stock value. His findings are confirmed by former Harvard president Derek Bok, who also studied executive compensation. Bok noted that "the ten-, twenty-, and fifty-million-dollar incomes that a few CEOs received in recent years were chiefly the result of stock options designed to motivate them to exert every effort on behalf of their shareholders."[6]

The need of executives to protect their companies' profits is linked to the fostering of unhealthy working conditions for those with jobs and helps to create unemployment, which, itself, has implications for violence.

STRUCTURAL VIOLENCE ON THE JOB

In 1986, the president, plant manager, and a foreman at the Film Recovery Systems company were convicted of murder, reckless conduct, and involuntary manslaughter when an employee died of cyanide poisoning in a plant the prosecutors likened to a "huge gas chamber." This was probably the first case of its kind, and the defendants were sentenced to twenty-five years in prison. None, however, spent any time in jail, and the convictions were overturned when an appeals court ruled in a complex argument that the defendants' states of mind did not warrant the convictions.[7]

Workers at a thermometer factory in Brooklyn were inhaling dangerous fumes as they extracted mercury from old thermometers in an unventilated cellar; some suffered brain damage. Brought before a jury in 1987, the factory owners were found guilty of criminal charges, the first time in New York State that such charges had even been brought. Fortunately for William and Edward Pymm, the owners of Pymm Thermometer Corporation, a State Supreme Court judge immediately overturned the verdict, claiming New York State had no jurisdiction in the case. Disappointed New York State Attorney General Robert Abrams said that the brothers had engaged in "a criminal assault. Mercury was the weapon."[8]

The Pymm case is not exceptional. State courts have been ruling that state prosecutors do not have the authority to bring criminal charges against executives or their companies in cases of worker exposure to hazardous substances. The rationale of the state courts is that federal law forbids this. Prosecutors who want to protect workers are indignant. Ken Ogden, a county attorney from Texas, said, "Murder is murder: it should be punished as such whether it occurs in the workplace or anywhere else."[9] Many potential cases never get to court because regulatory agencies are so inadequately staffed that they do not catch violaters.

It isn't rational for an employer to shoot his workers, but it makes economic sense to keep production costs as low as possible. As criminologist Joel Swartz states, in a capitalist society,

the general functioning of the system is at the heart of the problem....
The tremendous toll in occupational illnesses results from the oppression of one class by another. The people who own corporations try to exact as much wealth as they can from the workers. Improvements in working conditions to eliminate health hazards would eat into the profits that could be exacted.[10]

The weaker workers are in relation to their employer and the more probusiness government is, the more dangerous workplaces are likely to be. It should not be surprising then that, according to the National Safety Workplace Institute, the United States holds the developed world's worst job safety record. United States workers are thirty-six times more likely to be killed on the job than workers in Sweden and nine times more likely to be killed than British laborers.[11]

Some people die on the job from injuries, but more eventually succumb from illnesses contracted at work. It is easier to get statistics on the violence caused by street crime than on this kind of violence. A 1986 congressional subcommittee noted that "the United States is the only large developed country without a national system for reporting occupational disease."[12]

The estimates of those who die from occupationally induced illness varies from 50,000 to about 100,000. The most commonly cited figure is the larger one, but we will use the smaller number so as not to overstate our case. For 1992, the government gives a figure of 8,500 workers killed at work. A number of experts consider this too low also, but we shall accept it here. In 1992, then, indirectly and directly, a minimum of 58,500 died because of the work they had been doing. The number of people who were murdered that year is 24,500. Put another way, there were more than twice as many deaths among workers as a result of their employment than as a result of actions by those most likely to be called criminals.[13]

Table 5.1 shows that the most dangerous occupations are those held by blue collar workers.

Table 5.1 Occupational Injury and Illness Rate, per 100 Full-Time Workers in 1993

TYPE OF WORKER	RATE
Food plant workers	18
Lumber workers	16
Construction workers	12
Engineering and management services	3
Insurance agents and brokers	2
Security and commodity brokers	1

Source: U.S. Bureau of the Census, *Statistical Abstract of the United States, 1995*, Table 691, p. 441.

How Do They Get Away with It?

If the corporations themselves aren't behaving in a responsible way, if they are causing great harm, why aren't they punished by the government? After all, one of the functions of the federal government is, according to the Constitution, "to promote the general welfare." Chapter 2 suggested the answer to this question: government officials frequently follow corporate wishes, finding it in their own interest to do so and/or sharing a business worldview.

Still, business is not free to do whatever it wishes. Largely due to public pressures, legislation has been passed to protect workers, consumers, and the environment. Although these laws do make a difference, companies are often able to weaken or circumvent them or avoid serious consequences from breaking them. For example, in the 1960s "when Congress passed the auto safety law . . . industry lobbyists defeated an effort to add criminal sanctions to the bill for knowing or willful violations."[14] About thirty years later, when the Justice Department was considering larger fines for corporate law-breakers, business successfully lobbied to prevent this.[15] The Omnibus Crime Bill passed in 1994 says nothing about corporate crime and allots no money for fighting this law-breaking.[16]

Federal and state prosecutors have the option of taking a corporate lawbreaker to civil or criminal court, and the former is usually the choice. This means that much of the time there is no jury of ordinary people judging the companies. The device of "consent decrees" is used in which the corporation does not have to admit or deny any wrongdoing but agrees to pay a fine. By doing so, they avoid negative publicity and are not branded criminals.[17]

As a result of corporate America's privileged position vis-à-vis the law, Thomas R. Donahue, secretary-treasurer of the AFL-CIO, noted that "since 1970 . . . only one person has served time in jail for a willful violation that resulted in the death of a worker. In contrast, seven people have been jailed for violations of a Federal statute that protects wild burros and horses."[18]

Workers' Victory: OSHA

Business is not omnipotent, and there has been some government attention paid to improving safety in the workplace. Coal miners led the drive for safer workplaces in the 1960s. Faced with horrifying working conditions, with many miners succumbing to black lung disease after years of inhaling coal dust, they engaged in wildcat strikes, marches, and lobbying. When seventy-eight Virginia miners were killed in a 1968 mine explosion, Congress finally passed a Coal Mine Health and Safety Act. This became the model for a coalition of union, consumer, and environmental activists, health professionals, and members of progressive religious organizations that organized grassroots actions to focus attention on occupational health and safety.

In 1970, the Occupational Safety and Health Act (OSH Act) was passed, and a year later the Occupational Safety and Health Administration (OSHA) was created in the Department of Labor. The act proclaims that its purpose is "to assure safe and healthful working conditions for working men and women." This legislation recognized the right of workers to know what hazards they face on their jobs, the right to participate in inspections of the plants, and it offered them protection against reprisals for exercising their rights.

This acknowledgment of on-the-job rights opened the doors for further reforms. The act provides penalties for violations, fines of $1,000 to $5,000 for first violations, timetables to remedy the problems, and an agency within the Health and Welfare Department to engage in research and to develop standards. Some states have even passed their own OSHA bills.

BUSINESS VICTORIES: OSHA WEAKENED

Since 1970, however, as unions have become weaker and business more powerful, OSHA's potential effectiveness has been undermined. As of 1995, OSHA had only 2,000 inspectors responsible for monitoring about 6 million workplaces. The consequences of this can be seen by looking at figures from January 1994 to April 1995. During this time, there were 4,830 workplaces where workers died or experienced serious injuries. Only 25 percent of these sites had been inspected in the period from 1990 to 1995.

Crime in the streets is given many more resources than is workplace health and safety. In 1990, there was about 1 police officer for every 325 persons in the United States. If we assume that there are as many state OSHA inspectors as federal ones, we would get 2,600 inspectors for 6 million work sites, or 1 inspector for 2,307 workplaces.[19] To date, no mainstream politicians have called for more policing of the workplace.

Although the OSH Act provides for higher fines, between 1973 and 1985, employers had to pay only $263 on the average. When an explosion occurred in a mine owned by the Pittston Coal Company, killing seven miners in 1983, the company was fined $47,000. In contrast, six years later, the United Mine Workers of America was fined over $22 million for activities connected with a strike against Pittston.[20]

Compared with some other federal agencies, OSHA is underfunded and understaffed. With a budget of about $300 million, and a staff of 2,300, OSHA has the responsibility of policing the nation's approximately 5 to 7 million workplaces. The Fish and Wildlife Protection Service receives $1.1 billion, the CIA about $28 billion, and the Defense Department in 1984 spent over $3 billion just on ammunition.[21] OSHA is supposed to be defending the nation's workers against their own employers. It isn't given half of what goes to agencies who are allegedly protecting us against the more problematic threats discussed in chapter 7.

For at least fifteen years, OSHA staff have unsuccessfully advocated setting up guidelines for such workplaces as tunnels, sewers, chemical tanks, and grain elevators. Without adequate regulation, there are many gruesome deaths in the American workplace. About 3 percent of job deaths a year come from people working in small spaces, where, without proper ventilation, they breathe in toxic fumes; some perish trying to rescue their fellow workers. This happened in an Auburn, Indiana, factory. One man was felled by hydrogen cyanide gas while cleaning a tank, two coworkers died trying to save him. Two others also died during this incident.[22]

Cancer is an occupational hazard for numerous workers. According to the American Cancer Society, there are from 8,000 to 25,000 preventable deaths a year, resulting from occupational exposure to toxic chemicals. At least 26,000 toxic substances are used in industry, with about a thousand new ones coming on the market annually. OSHA was supposed to set standards for exposure to hazardous substances, but out of 2,000 likely carcinogens used in businesses, OSHA's exposure limits in the 1980s covered fewer than 24.[23]

Early detection and treatment increases a cancer victim's survival rate. But in 1988, a bill that would have provided notification to and monitoring of high-risk workers was opposed by large corporations and business organizations such as Procter and Gamble, Goodyear, Uniroyal, the National Association of Manufacturers, and the U.S. Chamber of Commerce. Their allies in the Senate, Republicans Dan Quayle and Orrin Hatch, were able to prevent the bill from coming to a vote.[24]

The Reagan administration was zealous in its attempts to roll back earlier worker gains. In the first two years of Reagan's administration, OSHA's budget was cut 8 percent, inspections were reduced by 21 percent, and fines by 48 percent. Standards for exposure to noise and lead were reduced. In addition to reducing OSHA funding, the administration limited workers' access to information.

The textile industry provides a useful case. Byssinosis, or "brown lung," is an occupational risk facing these workers in which breathing becomes a torment. As the disease progresses, lung tissue is destroyed. An ex-textile worker describes his suffering:

> Since I've had this brown lung, I have come to the point where I can't do much of anything... changing clothes, shaving or taking a bath. Even talking I can't do sometimes. I had to leave the mill at the age of fifty-four. I tried to keep working but I just couldn't.[25]

In 1982, OSHA published a booklet warning workers on the hazards of cotton dust. OSHA head Thorne Auchter found the booklets "offensive." He charged that the cover showing the gaunt face of Louis Harrell "makes a statement that is obviously favorable to one side." He ordered over 100,000 copies destroyed. He also ordered that three industrial films and two slide shows dealing with workers' rights and the danger of cotton dust be pulled from distribution.[26]

More recently the Clinton administration has claimed to support OSHA's goals, and Labor Secretary Robert Reich has presented useful data on occupational health and safety to Congress, but OSHA finds itself with no more staff or money than before. Business has continued its vigorous campaign to weaken OSHA, with no apparent resistance from the Clinton administration.

Business publicly takes the position that laws are not needed and that voluntary efforts will do the job. A spokesperson for Inland Steel Company told a Congressional Hearing on expanding OSHA's provisions that employers would use OSHA's educational services, but they should be able to do so "without fear of being penalized. The objective should be to collaborate in pursuit of workplace safety and health and not to catch an employer in a violation."[27] In fact, for decades before OSHA's creation, business could have joined with their workers to create safer places of employment. Their seeming indifference to workers' health and safety, however, is what led to a movement demanding stronger government protections.

Where workers have more powerful organizations representing them and a political party that is responsive to their needs, working conditions are safer and healthier. Sweden, for example, meets these conditions more than any other capitalist nation. Swedish workers have a number of rights that U.S. workers lack. They can refuse to work in dangerous situations, they supervise the health services that their employers are required to establish in the workplace, and they even have the right to temporarily close a factory if the workers are in immediate danger.[28]

RACE AND OCCUPATIONAL JEOPARDY

Many whites do hazardous work. Coal mining, for example, is mostly done by white men. People of color, however, hold a disparate proportion of the most dangerous jobs, a result of the inequality that prevents them from having the same occupational choices as many whites. Robert Davis, a sociologist specializing in health issues, notes: "Historically, Blacks have been more likely than Whites to be employed in less skilled jobs, where exposures to hazardous substances tend to be greater." This has been the case in the chemical, rubber, and steel industries. A 1978 study found that African-Americans were 50 percent more likely to have serious occupational illnesses or injuries than whites.[29]

In the South, poultry processors are likely to be African-American women. In 1991, a fire swept through an Imperial Food Products chicken processing plant in North Carolina. Twenty-five workers died, and forty were injured by the blaze. The fire had started in a frying machine where chicken parts were prepared for delivery to restaurants. The plant's doors were locked because management feared workers might steal chicken parts.

Sam Breeden, passing by, heard trapped workers screaming, "Let me out!" Brenda MacDougal, a survivor, described the plant: "That fryer was dangerous and there were no fire alarms in there ... those doors in the back stayed shut." Daisy Ratliff, a former employee, described seeing her friends injured and dead: "It was pitiful, it was sad, it was terrible. I used to work on the line breading chickens and it was awfully dangerous in there." Sharing this view, a former worker, David Covington, claimed fires frequently occurred in the plant when "grease or the wasted parts would fall out and hit the flames." These fires were extinguished by workers before a disaster occurred. The plant's manager tried to defend himself by saying "there were plenty of doors that were open. Certain doors are locked at certain times. I can't tell you which doors were locked, if any were locked." Imperial had not been inspected in its eleven years of operation by either state or federal officials.[30]

Latino factory workers sometimes experience higher rates of occupational hazards than do white or black workers in similar jobs. One explanation could be that their knowledge of English may be poor, and employers often do not bother to instruct them in Spanish. A study in New Jersey found that Latino workers had higher rates of finger amputations and fatalities at construction sites. A California study found higher concentrations of lead in Latino workers. Of all ethnic groups, Latinos are also the most likely to be without health insurance.[31]

Racist attitudes are often part of the indifference to Latino workers' problems. Francisco Calito, from Guatemala, can no longer work because of shoulder injuries sustained while he was assembling golf clubs at the Chicago factory where he'd worked for ten years, making 2,300 golf clubs a day, for $5.50 an hour.

> I told them about the pain. They said if "you don't work, you'll be fired." My supervisor would shake his finger at me. He would kick me. He would tell me, "I don't like you because you're a Latino." I worked for two years with the pain.[32]

Agricultural work is among the most dangerous in the United States. Thirty-eight percent of farm workers are Latino, although this group is only about 9 percent of the labor force.[33] Agricultural workers are frequently exposed to high levels of pesticides which leads to nerve damage, cancer, sterility, and birth defects. The United Farm Workers claim that a study in the *American Journal of Public Health* shows that "in California agricultural counties where pesticide use is high [there is] almost double the normal risk of having babies with birth defects." Children have been born without arms and legs and even seemingly healthy children are at risk. If they are not actually working beside their parents, they may still be brought into the fields, because there is no place to leave them. Home is often not a refuge from the contaminants, because pesticide residues cling to the workers' clothes.[34]

It was not until 1987 that agricultural enterprises were required to provide toilets and fresh drinking water for agricultural workers, and the rules are frequently ignored. Dangerous pesticides are used in the fields, and often there are no places for workers to wash. According to the Environmental Protection Agency (EPA), there are three hundred thousand illnesses each year among farm workers from pesticides.[35]

GENDER AND OCCUPATIONAL JEOPARDY

The percent of women who are part of the paid labor force has increased since the 1950s, with especially large increases since the 1970s. Not only gender but class and race affect a woman's job opportunities. For example, affluent mothers who can afford child care have more choice of where to work than women who must organize their time *around* child care.

Primarily female occupations are lower paid and, if not as physically intensive as the manual labor jobs that usually go to men, carry their own physical risks. Working-class and underclass women are less likely to have the credentials for professional or management positions and are therefore more likely than affluent women to accept physically risky jobs. These less advantaged women are also likely to be women of color.

We described the fire at Imperial. Less dramatic health threats are more routine. Poultry processors must keep their hands in almost constant (and repetitive) motion. Betty Harpe has had three operations on her hand and can't sleep well because of the pain she feels "the whole time at work and at home."

Journalist Laura Allen, summarizing a report in the *Occupational Health and Safety Journal*, wrote:

> Poultry workers experience the highest risk of debilitating skin diseases of any group of American workers, and there is a whole class of muscular and nervous system disorders endemic to the poultry industry caused by poorly designed tools, the constant rapid, repetitive motion required on the assembly line, and the demanding production pace.[36]

The women at Perdue, for instance, process ninety birds a minute. Janie Knights, who works at a Perdue plant in North Carolina, explains why people continue to stay at these jobs:

People have to feed their kids; people have to work. Nine of 10 of these people are poor, black, uneducated. Many of them are single parents. They're too scared to complain and you can't blame them.[37]

In 1989, OSHA reported two-thirds of the workers in these plants had injuries and were "knowingly and willfully exposed" to health risks by their employers. The plants are cold and noisy, leading to additional health problems. An investigation by Bob Hall, research director of the Institute for Southern Studies, found that Perdue regularly misinformed OSHA about workers' injuries. He quotes an internal memo from a personnel manager who wrote that it is "normal procedure for about 60 percent of our workforce" to get daily doses of "Advil, the vitamin B6 and hand wraps" from the company nurse.[38]

Poultry processing and office work give rise to similar repetitive motion disorders, such as carpal tunnel syndrome, incidences of which are increasing in U.S. workplaces. Blue and white collar workers, who repeat the same motion for hours in a day, are likely to suffer the tissue damage that comes from this process. In 1987, for every 10,000 full-time workers, there were 10 cases of repetitive motion ailments; by 1993, the figure had risen to 38 per 10,000.[39]

Women are more likely to do office jobs requiring repetitive keyboard work. Many companies measure clerical productivity by tracking the speed of the employees' keystrokes. In addition to repetitive motion disorders, clerical workers are susceptible to neck and back pain, and cardiovascular and respiratory problems resulting from exposure to toxic substances, such as those used in photocopying machines.

The electronics industry, which also employs many women at lower level jobs, exposes them to toxic chemicals. When used without proper ventilation, these chemicals are suspected of causing cancer, nerve damage, reproductive problems, blood diseases, and so on. There is little regulation of these industries, and, to date, there are few studies of the hazards of the high-tech workplace.

Unemployment as Structural Violence

As part of its goal of high profits, capitalism strives to keep down the costs of labor. Unemployment is one of the ways this is done. The creation of what Marx termed the "reserve army of labor" has been a feature of capitalism for hundreds of years.[40] Full employment is very rare in capitalist economies.

Profits can only be made if workers are paid less than the value of the goods they produce. Inevitably, workers are unable to buy all that has been manufactured, stocks pile up, and people are laid off. As unemployment rises, there is increasing competition for jobs, and in the absence of successful collective actions on the part of the working class, a lowering of wages and a worsening of working conditions occurs.

Government policies can strengthen or mitigate the tendency to unemployment and also affect the impact of joblessness on households. The more social supports there are in the form of unemployment insurance, family allowances, subsidized health care, and so on, the more those in the working class can withstand pressures to take low-paying and unhealthy jobs. Corporations are able to use their already discussed political power to influence both fiscal and welfare (broadly defined) policies.[41]

When employment rises, mainstream economists worry. *New York Times* business reporter Louis Uchitelle noted that in early 1994, with the "economy growing strongly and the unemployment rate falling, the Federal Reserve has responded by raising interest rates three times since early February." Raising interest rates makes borrowing more expensive; this becomes a way of slowing down economic growth that would be likely to increase employment. In November 1994, interest rates climbed to their highest level since 1981, against the expressed wishes of unions.[42]

Unemployment is increased not only because of federal fiscal policies but because of the great flexibility that capital has in deciding where and how to operate. In 1992 alone, over half the job losses in the United States were due to plants or companies shutting down or moving.[43] Because of advances in communication and transportation, operations can be moved from one region to another within a country or out of the country altogether if this is rational from a profit-making perspective, a phenomenon known as "capital flight." Since the Second World War, U.S corporations have steadily increased their overseas investments. As the chief financial officer at Colgate-Palmolive said, "There is no mind-set that puts this country first." Presently about 17 percent of total corporate assets are overseas, up from 14 percent in 1984. This is greater than for other industrial countries, for example, it is three times the rate for Japan.[44]

Laws can discourage or encourage the movement of jobs. For example, between 1921 and 1996, Section 936 of the U.S. Tax Code encouraged companies to move operations to Puerto Rico. They paid no federal income tax on the profits earned there, which in recent years meant an annual loss in tax revenues of about $3 billion. Because Puerto Rico is exempt from minimum wage laws and some environmental protections, there were additional incentives for relocation. Union-backed proposals to prevent companies from moving if this would have a negative impact on mainland jobs were not enacted by Congress. Between 1980 and 1993, 23,644 jobs were transferred to the U.S.–controlled island. Footwear, chemical, pharmaceutical, and electronic industries were the prime beneficiaries of these policies but not the workers.[45] Foreign policy can help create conditions abroad that encourage investment overseas. This will be further discussed in chapter 7.

Corporations also decide, without input from affected workers or communities, how they will invest their profits. They could decide to reinvest, upgrading their plants and equipment and developing new product lines by paying for research and development. Instead, in many instances, companies are diversifying through acquisition of other enterprises.[46] This process is in turn accompanied by large-scale dismissals euphemistically called "downsizing."

Companies can decide to fire workers to improve their profitability even if they are doing well. They justify this by appealing to the higher value, for them, of increasing their competitive edge. When Procter and Gamble decided it would fire at least four thousand workers in the United States between 1993 and 1995, Edwin L. Artz, CEO, explained:

> We have today a healthy, growing business, a strong balance sheet, positive cash flow, state-of-the-art products and a well-stocked technology pipeline with plenty of opportunities for growth. However, we must slim down to stay competitive.[47]

Charles R. Lee, CEO of the telecommunication company GTE, announced that seventeen thousand jobs would be cut in 1994. He justified the decision by saying, "This is a defining moment for the company. We intend to be the market leader. . . . But to do that you have got to have competitive costs."[48] When Allied Signal Inc. announced its plan to fire one thousand workers, about half of its labor force, in its Stratford, Connecticut, plant, a company spokesman said, "While we regret that employment levels in Stratford must be reduced to meet today's demanding market requirements, the result will be a more competitive organization."[49] Similarly, the *New York Times* reported that despite its profitability Xerox was cutting about 10 percent of its workforce, ten thousand workers, over the next three years. "Xerox," the article pointed out, "takes its place among financially sound companies seeking higher profits through mass layoffs," and they quoted the CEO of Xerox, Paul A. Allarite, who said, "To compete effectively we must have a lean and flexible organization." Following the announcement, the value of Xerox shares rose.[50] Similarly, Whirlpool's stock rose when it announced a shutdown of two factories in the United States and Canada and a cut in its workforce worldwide.[51]

Downsizing is often followed by an increase in a company's stock value. Surveying this trend, journalist George Russell notes that in the 1980s there was an

> avalanche of corporate mergers and acquisitions. More than 4,000 of those unions, worth a record $190 billion took place [in 1986]. After most of the buyouts, the merged company eliminates staff duplications

and unprofitable divisions. In the past six years [1981–87], for example, General Electric spent $11.1 billion to buy 338 businesses, including RCA, a $6.3 billion acquisition. During the same period, GE shed 232 businesses worth $5.9 billion and closed 73 plants and offices.[52]

Mergers, buyouts, and layoffs have continued in the 1990s. The CEOs who have presided over massive firings have themselves been well rewarded, and the improved stock values meant the personal wealth of CEOs has increased.[53]

Costs are lowered when workers are laid off, that is, costs to the company, and investors reward the corporation for its leanness and flexibility, but workers and communities pay a high price. The companies' suppliers are hurt as well as the fired employees. According to economists Barry Bluestone and Bennett Harrison, the Department of Labor estimates that "for every 100 jobs [lost] in the motor vehicle industry, 105 jobs are wiped out in the direct supplier network."[54]

Local business loses customers. In chapter 3 we cited William J. Wilson's research in Chicago on how the loss of jobs was connected to a rise in crime. He and his research team also found a loss of small businesses as large companies moved elsewhere. On Chicago's South Side, in 1950, there were over eight hundred enterprises. In 1996, there were about one hundred. Researcher Loïc Waiquant described the now bleak neighborhood:

> The once-lively streets—residents remember a time, not so long ago, when crowds were so dense at rush hour that one had to elbow one's way to the train station—now have the appearance of an empty, bombed-out war zone. The commercial strip has been reduced to a long tunnel of charred stores, vacant lots littered with broken glass and garbage, and dilapidated buildings left to rot in the shadow of the elevated train line. . . . The only enterprises that seem to be thriving are liquor stores and currency exchanges, those "banks of the poor" where one can cash checks, pay bills and buy money orders for a fee.[55]

Unemployed workers do not buy coffee or food from the local restaurant, coffee shop, or lunch wagon; they stop having a beer at the local tavern on their way home from work. Their families have less money to go to the movies and to buy clothes and appliances. In effect, when the plant shuts down, the lights go out on Main Street.

UNEMPLOYMENT CAN BE A KILLER

Unemployment has a number of consequences relevant to structural violence. Individuals and households experience economic stress, which, in turn, is associated with violence. At the very time that there is an increased need for services, the tax base of communities is reduced.

Studies have shown a relationship between recession and mental and physical illnesses. In the 1970s, social psychologists Ramsey Liam and Paula Rayman matched two groups of forty families: in one set the men had all lost their jobs, in the other they hadn't. During the two-year period of the study, the unemployed husbands were found to have "higher levels of psychiatric symptoms," including depression, anxiety, and hostility.

M. Harvey Brenner, professor of Health Policy and Management at The Johns Hopkins University, has been studying the relationship between unemployment and physical and mental health since the 1970s. He has found that an approximate 1.3 percent increase in unemployment is correlated with about twenty-one thousand additional deaths a year over what would be the case if the unemployment rate had not risen. Admissions to mental hospitals rise by about 1.8 percent. There are also increases in the interpersonal violence previously discussed.[56]

Suicide rates have been found to increase as unemployment goes up. Brenner estimates that each 1.3 percent rise in unemployment is matched by the same rise in suicide rates. As one laid-off manager explained, "Working is breathing. It's something you don't think about; you just do it and it keeps you alive. When you stop you die." A year after making this statement he shot himself.[57]

Of course only a small percentage of unemployed people kill themselves: suicide is the most extreme expression of despair. Less dramatic indicators also exist such as hypertension, higher cholesterol levels, and elevated bloodsugar—all conditions found among unemployed workers after their factories closed.

Some laid-off workers increase unhealthy behaviors such as smoking and drinking. These can give rise to incidences of cardiovascular diseases, cirrhosis of the liver, and kidney disease. Sickness is exacerbated during unemployment as households are forced to cut back on medical care for family members. This will especially be a problem for those families with the fewest assets to fall back on. Dr. Lewis Ferman of the University of Michigan's Institute of Labor and Industrial Relations feels that "the relationship between unemployment and physiological or psychological stress is so strong that every pink slip should carry a Surgeon General's warning that it may be hazardous to your health."[58]

In addition to these potential problems, unemployment disrupts accustomed social ties and roles. Studies in Sweden, Finland, and the United States indicate that social isolation, anxiety, and stress, all of which can increase when a job is lost, are associated with deteriorating health.

Unemployment can put pressure on the employed to accept onerous working conditions, which, in turn, affect their health. With jobs scarce and unions weak, workers may feel they must choose between a job and a healthy life. In Connecticut, for instance, autoworkers in their late forties and older were getting up before dawn, preparing to drive nearly one hundred miles to their jobs at a General Motors assembly plant in New York State. Their former G.M. plant had closed and, unless they were willing to commute and train for new jobs, they would have no work. Tens of thousands of other G.M. workers are in similar straits. The auto industry even has a term for workers like this, "G.M. gypsies." The commuting Connecticut workers, however, will no longer have to continue their long drives as the New York plant closed in July 1996.[59]

With massive downsizing eliminating jobs from blue collar to managerial and professional jobs, more workers are forced to accept part-time work. This means lower wages, on the average about 60 percent of full-time pay, and no benefits. Some of the problems resulting from an involuntary pay-cut are summed up by a laid-off accountant who is doing the best he can as a "temp."

> I need brakes on my car, but I'll push it as far as I can on the old brakes. My wife needs dental work ... because her teeth are rotting. I eat one meal a day because it ... helps put food on the table for the kids.[60]

This chapter has shown how working people's health and even their lives are jeopardized by an economic system that puts profit first. The political power of the capitalist class allows them, too often, to sacrifice their workers to the bottom line. In the next chapter, we will see how this same system threatens consumers and communities.

Notes

1. Clinard and Yeager, *Corporate Crime* (New York: Free Press, 1980), p. 9.
2. Clinard and Yeager, pp. 8–11; Clinard, *Corporate Corruption: The Abuse of Power* (New York: Praeger, 1990), p. 15; James W. Coleman, *The Criminal Elite: The Sociology of White-Collar Crime*, 3d ed. (New York: St. Martin's Press, 1994), pp. 8–10; David R. Simon, *Elite Deviance*, 5th ed. (Boston: Allyn and Bacon, 1996), p. 39; Russell Mokhiber, *Corporate Crime and Violence: Big Business Power and the Abuse of Public Trust* (San Francisco: Sierra Club Books, 1989), pp. 4, 14–17.
3. Edwin H. Sutherland, "White Collar Criminality," in *Crime and Delinquency: A Reader*, ed. Carl Bersani (Toronto: MacMillan, 1970), p. 26.
4. Mokhiber, 1989, p. 5.
5. Steven A. Holmes, "A Business Gathering Focuses on Crime," *New York Times*, 8 October 1994, p. 30.
6. Michael Useem, *Executive Defense: Shareholder Power and Corporate Reorganization* (Cambridge, Mass.: Harvard University Press, 1993), p. 102; Derek Bok, *The Cost of Talent: How Executives and Professionals Are Paid and How It Affects America* (New York: Free Press, 1993), p. 4. Sociologists David James and Michael Soref in their study of firings of top executives found that "profit criteria appear to be the most important standard by which corporate chiefs are judged and

dismissal is the ultimate sanction that conditions their behavior." "Managerial Theory: Unmaking of the Corporation President," *American Sociological Review* 46 (1981): p. 16.
7. "Job-Related Murder Convictions of 3 Executives Are Overturned," *New York Times*, 20 January 1990, p. 10.
8. Quoted in "Factory Owners Guilty; Judge Sets Aside Verdict," *New York Times*, 14 November 1987.
9. Quoted in William Glaberson, "States Are Toppling Workplace-Injury Convictions," *New York Times*, 19 September 1988, pp. A1, D5.
10. Quoted in David R. Simon, *Elite Deviance*, 5th ed. (Boston: Allyn and Bacon, 1996), pp. 143–44.
11. "U.S. Job Death Rate Still Relatively High," *New York Times*, 4 September 1989.
12. Quoted in Jeffrey Reiman, *The Rich Get Richer and the Poor Get Prison*, 3rd ed. (New York: MacMillan, 1990), p. 63. He has a useful discussion of statistics of occupational hazards versus street crime on pp. 58–62.
13. Hearings, p. 72; U.S. Bureau of the Census, *Statistical Abstract of the United States, 1994*, Table 676, p. 436; Daniel Berman, *Death on the Job: Occupational Health and Safety Struggles in the United States* (New York: Monthly Review Press, 1978), pp. 38–53; Reiman, pp. 57–62. Of the eight thousand five hundred deaths, seventeen were homicides at work; double counting of these has no mathematical effect.
14. Mokhiber, 1988, p. 5.
15. Jay Livingston, *Crime & Delinquency* (Englewood Cliffs, N.J.: Prentice-Hall, 1992), p. 315.
16. Russell Mokhiber, "The 10 Worst Corporations of 1993," *Multinational Monitor* 14, no. 12 (December 1993), p. 9.
17. Mokhiber, 1988, pp. 8–10.
18. U.S. Congress, House Committee on Education and Labor, *Hearings on H.R. 1280, Comprehensive Occupational Safety and Health Reform Act*, 103rd Cong., 1st sess., 28 April, 29 July 1993, p. 73.
19. Editorial, "Workplace Body Bags," *Multinational Monitor* 16, no. 10 (October 1995): p. 5; "More Muscle for the Same Money," *New York Times*, 23 January 1994, Section 3, p. 25; Hearings, p. 58. For number of workplaces, see William Serrin, "The Wages of Work," *Nation*, 28 January 1994, p. 81; Police figures from Bureau of Justice, *SourceBook of Criminal Justice Statistics—1993*, p. 31.
20. Phill Kwik, "Pittston Power," *Nation*, 16 October 1989, p. 409.
21. OSHA figures, "More Muscle for the Same Money," *New York Times*, 23 January 1994, Section 3, p. 25. For number of workplaces, *Hearings on H.R. 1280*, pp. 58, 72; CIA budget from Tim Weiner, "The Worst-Kept Secret in the Capital," *New York Times*, 21 July 1994, p. B10; DOD figures, Elliot Currie and Jerome Skolnick, *America's Problems: Social Issues and Public Policy*, 2d ed. (Glenview Ill.: Scott, Foresman and Company, 1988), p. 304.
22. William Robbins, "Grieving Relatives Gird for Federal Hearing...," *New York Times*, 30 January 1990, p. A17.
23. Charles Noble, *Liberalism at Work: The Rise and Fall of OSHA* (Philadelphia: Temple University Press, 1986), pp. 179–80.
24. David Shernoff, "Workers at Risk," *Multinational Monitor* 9, no. 10 (October 1988), p. 21.
25. Quoted in Joan Claybrook, *Retreat from Safety: Reagan's Attack on America's Health* (New York: Pantheon, 1984), p. 83.

26. "Safety and Health Director Orders Purging of Booklet He Calls Unfair," *New York Times*, 27 March 1982; "Recalled by OSHA," *NJSFT Action*, April–May 1982.
27. Hearings, p. 233.
28. Noble, p. 233.
29. "Racial Differences in Mortality: Current Trends and Perspectives," in *Race and Ethnicity in America: Meeting the Challenge in the 21st Century*, ed. Gail Thomas (Washington, D.C.: Taylor & Francis, 1995), p. 123; "Theory on Black's Disease Rate," *New York Times*, 27 October 1980.
30. Quotes from Ronald Smothers, "25 Die, Many Reported Trapped as Blaze Engulfs Carolina Plant," *New York Times*, 4 September 1991, pp. A1, B7; Peter T. Kilborn, "Once-Tamed Disease Fells Workers on Pork Packing Plant's Killing Floor," *New York Times*, 27 September 1993, p. A12.
31. Lawrence K. Altman, "Many Hispanic Americans Reported in Ill Health and Lacking Insurance," *New York Times*, 9 January 1991, p. A16.
32. Peter T. Kilborn, "For Hispanic Immigrants, a Higher Job Injury Risk," *New York Times*, 18 February 1992, pp. A1, A15.
33. U.S. Bureau of the Census, *Statistical Abstract of the United States, 1995*, Table 649, pp. 411–13.
34. Marion Moses, "Farmworkers and Pesticides," in *Confronting Environmental Racism*, ed. Robert Bullard (Boston: South End Press, 1994), pp. 161–78; "New Research on Pesticide-Birth Defect Link," *Food and Justice* (December 1988), pp. 8–9.
35. "Federal Laws Found Lacking in Guarding Farm Worker Rights," *New York Times*, 25 February 1992, p. A18; a United Farmworkers' video, *The Wrath of Grapes*, shows what these pesticides do to children and adults.
36. Laura Allen, "Women Workers at Perdue: A Chicken in Every Pot, Health Hazards in Every Shop," *Resist Newsletter*, October 1988, p. 5.
37. Peter Applebome, "Worker Injuries Rise in Poultry Industry as Business Booms," *New York Times*, 6 November 1989, p. A20.
38. Bob Hall, "Perdue Farms: Poultry and Profits," *Multinational Monitor* 10, no. 9 (September 1989), p. 20.
39. Steve Lohr, "Waving Goodbye to Ergonomics," *New York Times*, 16 April 1995, Section 3, p. 1.
40. Karl Marx, *Capital*, Vol. 1 (Moscow: Foreign Languages Publishing House, n.d., originally published, 1887), pp. 640–44, has a discussion of the types of surplus labor; useful summaries of Marx's ideas can be found in Paul Sweezy, *Theory of Capitalist Development* (New York: Monthly Review Press, 1942), pp. 87–92; and Harry Braverman, *Labor and Monopoly Capital: The Degradation of Work in the Twentieth Century* (New York: Monthly Review Press, 1974), pp. 386–89. For more discussion of the processes and consequences of creating a surplus labor force, see E. P. Thompson, *The Making of the English Working Class* (New York: Vintage, 1963); and Richard L. Rubenstein, *The Age of Triage: Fear and Hope in an Overcrowded World* (Boston: Beacon Press, 1983), pp. 34–81.
41. Edward S. Herman, "The Natural Rate of Unemployment," *Z Magazine* (November 1994), pp. 62–65; Louis Uchitelle, "A Debate on the Greater Evil: Inflation or Chill of Pink Slips," *New York Times*, 16 November 1994, pp. A1, D6; Keith Bradsher, "Federal Reserve Increases Interest Rates by 3/4 Point: Jump Is Largest Since 1981," *New York Times*, 16 November 1994, pp. A1, D6; Theresa

Amott, *Caught in the Crisis: Women and the U.S. Economy Today* (New York: Monthly Review Press, 1993), pp. 44–45; Frances Fox Piven, and Richard Cloward, *Regulating the Poor: The Functions of Public Welfare*, Updated ed. (New York: Vintage Books, 1993).

42. Louis Uchitelle, "Growth of Jobs May Be Casualty in Inflation Fight," *New York Times*, 24 April 1994, p. 1; and Uchitelle, "A Debate on the Greater Evil: Inflation or Chill of Pink Slips," *New York Times*, 16 November 1994, pp. A1, D6; Keith Bradsher, "Federal Reserve Increases Interest Rates by 3/4 Point: Jump Is Largest Since 1981," *New York Times*, 16 November 1994, pp. A1, D6.
43. U.S. Bureau of the Census, *Statistical Abstract of the United States, 1994*, Table 645, p. 415.
44. Louis Uchitelle, "U.S. Businesses Loosen Link to Mother Country," *New York Times*, 21 May 1989, pp. 1, 30.
45. Katherine Isaac, "Losing Jobs to 936," *Multinational Monitor* 14, no. 7 (July/August 1993), pp. 6–7. The law was changed in September 1996. No provisions were made for softening the effect on Puerto Rico itself where NAFTA has made it advantageous for companies to move to Mexico. Even before the change, official unemployment on the island was 14 percent. Doreen A. Hemlock, "Puerto Rico Loses Its Edge," *New York Times*, 21 September 1996, pp. 31, 43.
46. George Russell, "Corporate Restructuring," in *The Reshaping of America: Social Consequences of the Changing Economy*, eds. D. Stanley Eitzen and Maxine Baca Zinn (Englewood Cliffs, N.J.: Prentice-Hall, 1989), pp. 33–36.
47. Quoted in Michael Janofsky, "Procter & Gamble in 12% Job Cut as Brand Names Lose Attraction," *New York Times*, 16 July 1993, p. D2.
48. Anthony Ramirez, "GTE Says It Will Cut 17,000 Jobs," *New York Times*, 14 January 1994, p. D1.
49. "Allied Signal Plans to Eliminate 1,000 Jobs at Plant in Stratford," *New York Times*, 29 November 1994, p. B5.
50. John Holusha, "A Profitable Xerox Plans to Cut Staff by 10,000," *New York Times*, 9 December 1993.
51. Barnaby J. Feder, "Whirlpool to Shut 2 Plants and Cut Work Force," *New York Times*, 16 November 1994, p. D5.
52. Quoted in Russell, p. 35.
53. "In Fact," *Nation*, 27 May 1996, p. 7.
54. Barry Bluestone, and Bennett Harrison, *The Deindustrialization of America: Plant Closings, Community Abandonment and the Dismantling of Basic Industry* (New York: Basic Books, 1982), p. 71.
55. Quoted in William Julius Wilson, "Work," *New York Times Magazine*, 18 August 1996, p. 28.
56. Ramsey Liam, and Paula Rayman, "Health and Social Costs of Unemployment," *American Psychologist* 37 (October 1982): pp. 1116–23; M. Harvey Brenner, *Economy, Society and Health* (Washington, D.C.: Economic Policy Institute, 1992), pp. 4–5.
57. Quoted in Thomas Cottle, "When You Stop, You Die: The Human Toll of Unemployment," in *Crisis in American Institutions*, 9th ed., eds. Jerome Skolnick and Elliot Currie (New York: HarperCollins, 1994), p. 77.
58. Quoted in Maya Pines, "Recession Is Linked to Far-Reaching Psychological Harm," *New York Times*, 6 June 1982.
59. Kirk Johnson, "Aging Auto Workers Travel Long Roads to Stay in Place," *New*

York Times, 16 January 1995, pp. A1, B4; Thomas J. Lueck, "Auto Plant Closes and Developers See Opportunity," New York Times, 27 June 1996, pp. B1, B6.
60. Quoted by Charles Derber in The Wilding of America: How Greed and Violence Are Eroding Our Nation's Character (New York: St. Martin's Press, 1996), p. 69. He claims there are now 30 million temporary workers, one-fourth of the labor force (p. 68).

6 / Structural Violence Outside the Workplace

Inequality between workers and corporate owners leads to the violence discussed in chapter 5. In this chapter, we will look at how economic and political inequality is associated with structural violence in the form of health risks to the disadvantaged, consumers, and communities. The harm described in this chapter results from the routine workings of the economy and the political system. People's lives are damaged because most of the time the general welfare of the public is not the first priority of either business or government. Those with higher incomes can protect themselves, to a large extent, from this indifference; the less affluent cannot, as we shall discuss below.

POVERTY, RACISM, AND HEALTH

Infant mortality has been shown to rise as poverty increases. Summarizing the results of a recent government study, Dr. John Kiely, chief of the Infant and Child Health Studies Branch of the National Center for Health Statistics, claimed the relationship was "stronger than we expected it to be," with infant mortality rates 60 percent higher for poor women than for those above the poverty line. Because of poverty, twelve thousand infant deaths needlessly occur annually in the United States.[1]

If they survive infancy, poor children still face greater threats than their more affluent peers. A study in Boston found low-income children, white and black, to be at greater risk from fire deaths. This is because older deteriorated buildings in low-income neighborhoods are more likely to experience fires. Adults may be using relatively inexpensive, but dangerous space heaters to cut fuel costs.

Life is also more hazardous outside the home for poorer children. They are less likely to have safe places to play and less likely to be supervised by responsible adults. In chapter 1, we gave the example of the three-year-old Harlem girl who was run over while playing in the water from a fire hydrant.

Inadequate nutrition is another health-threatening problem for poorer children whose parents are forced to make difficult choices. A study done between 1989 and 1992 concluded that in the coldest months of the year, parents could not afford both adequate heat and food. They often chose heat, resulting in a 30 percent increase in underweight children visiting emergency rooms after a cold spell. Homeless families have special difficulties in caring adequately for their children. Children in New York City shelters for the homeless, for example, show signs of malnutrition, such as iron deficiency. Without access to kitchens and affordable nutritious food, their mothers are unable to feed their families properly.[2]

With current ruthless cutbacks in social services, including food programs, heating assistance, and Aid to Families with Dependent Children (AFDC), the conditions described here are only likely to get worse.

INFANTS AND CHILDREN OF COLOR AT GREATER RISK

The daily death toll occurring among infants and children of color as a result of structural violence does not receive the media attention given a murdered child. Table 6.1 gives the death rates for fetuses and infants by ethnicity. Fetal death rates for African-Americans are twice as high as for whites, and infant mortality rates are more than twice as high.

As was mentioned in chapter 1, the U.S infant mortality rate (IMR) is high relative to other developed countries. Even if the rate for only white infants is used, the United States ranks below ten other countries. The African-American IMR, on the other hand, is higher than the IMR of *thirty-eight* other countries, including several in the Third World.

Greater rates of poverty mean more women of color turn to public health services that are frequently overcrowded and understaffed and may be far from the woman's home. By the time a low-income woman gets to see a doctor, her pregnancy is often more advanced than that of a woman who can afford a private physician. Pregnant African-American women are also

Table 6.1 Fetal and Infant Death Rates by Race

	AFRICAN-AMERICAN	WHITE
Fetal death rate (1991)	11	6
Infant mortality rate (1992)	17	7

Source: U.S. Bureau of the Census, *Statistical Abstract of the United States, 1995*, Table 120, p. 90. Rates are per 1,000. Fetal death rate is for blacks and other.

less likely to be warned by doctors of the dangers of smoking and drinking. Doctors at the National Center for Health Statistics in a study of pregnant women reported that 29 percent of the white women surveyed were not given these warnings compared with about 40 percent of black women.[3] Politicians do not demand more prenatal care for the poor with the same zeal they have for demanding the building of more prisons.

Minority children are also less likely to be protected against preventable diseases than white children and more likely to be exposed to unhealthy conditions. For example, African-American children are less likely than white children to have been vaccinated by age three for diphtheria-tetanus, polio, and measles. African-American children are more at risk from lead poisoning than white children.

Lead poisoning is a threat to the healthy physical and mental development of children and can lessen academic achievement because of its impact on the nervous system. In 1994, the *Journal of the American Medical Association* (*JAMA*) published findings showing that 9 percent of all children aged one to five have blood-lead levels high enough to cause brain damage. Two years later, another *JAMA* article claimed to find a link between elevated levels of lead and aggressive behavior in children, even when other factors, such as the presence of a father in the household, were controlled for. About 22 percent of African-American children aged one to two had these dangerous levels. Latino children also have higher levels of lead in their blood than do white children.[4]

Elevated levels of lead can come from water leaching through old pipes, paint, hazardous waste sites, automobile oil, and oil refineries. Lead is also used in smelting, in battery manufacture, and in some other industries that have higher rates of minority workers; and lead particles may be carried home by the workers. A major source of this toxic substance is leaded indoor paint, now illegal, but still present in older housing.

The poor often cannot afford routine dental care, and although no one looks forward to visiting the dentist, it is still preferable to living with the suffering associated with diseased teeth and gums. Addressing this subject, the Public Health Service claims, "Millions of Americans have been left behind, resulting in needless pain, increased cost, decreased health and loss of self-esteem." The report noted that 80 percent of children eligible for Medicaid are not getting dental care. Dental checkups are the best way to detect oral cancer, which strikes about 30,000 victims each year and kills 9,400 in the same period.[5]

The officially poor are eligible for Medicaid, but they still must find money for transportation to a health care facility, a place to leave a child, and a doctor willing to accept Medicaid reimbursements. Medicaid does not reach over half those below the official federal poverty line. There are also many in the United States whose incomes are too high to qualify for Medicaid but too low for them to afford health insurance.

Many doctors refuse to practice in areas where they would be dependent on the low Medicaid reimbursements. A 1990 survey in New York City by the Community Service Society found that for a total of 1.7 million people living in low-income, largely minority neighborhoods in Manhattan, Brooklyn, and the Bronx, there were only twenty-eight qualified doctors. Three years later, David R. Jones, president of the organization, described this picture as "bleak," pointing out that when the study was done "there was a concentration of older physicians who were nearing retirement, so we have every expectation that the situation has gotten worse." With primary care difficulties, problems that are relatively minor are ignored until they become serious enough to send the sufferer to a hospital.[6]

As yet there is no program in the United States that guarantees people quality health care at affordable costs. Insurance plans help, but at least 37 million people, 17 percent of whom are under 65 years of age, have no health insurance, and the number has been growing.

In 1996, about 40 million people were without health insurance for some period of time. Over 80 percent of the uninsured are workers or dependents of workers whose jobs do not provide coverage. Death rates are higher for the uninsured. A study published by *JAMA* controlled for sex, income, tobacco use, and other factors that might effect death rates. The authors found that for every 100 deaths among the insured there were 125 for those without insurance.[7]

Other industrial countries provide health care for all, but in the United States, medical insurance is linked to one's job. Given the high unemployment rates, the kinds of jobs available, and the lower incomes of certain segments of the population, it is not surprising that racial inequality extends into medical insurance coverage. In 1993, 21 percent of African-Americans had no insurance, compared with 14 percent of whites. Between 1990 and 1992, 77 percent of whites had private insurance for the whole period, compared with 64 percent of African-Americans.[8]

BEING A NONWHITE ADULT IS DANGEROUS TO YOUR HEALTH

Because African-Americans are disproportionately poor, they have all the problems of low-income groups, as well as some additional problems. Where doctors are available, and income is not a factor, as in veterans' hospitals, African-Americans still receive a lower quality of care than do whites. A study done by the Health Care Financing Administration, the federal agencies overseeing Medicare coverage, found that in 1993 African-Americans were receiving less care than whites regardless of income. Researchers at

Table 6.2 Life Expectancy and Race, 1993

	AFRICAN-AMERICAN	WHITE
Females	74	80
Males	65	73

Source: Bureau of the Census, *Statistical Abstract of the United States, 1995*, Table 114, p. 86.

Table 6.3 Age-Adjusted Death Rates per 100,000 by Race, 1987

	AFRICAN-AMERICAN	WHITE
Cancer	172	130
Diabetes	20	9
Liver disease	19	12
Nephritis, nephrosis	11	4
Heart disease	227	165

Source: Rose Weitz, "Health and Illness: Sex, Class and Race," *Race, Sex & Class* 2, no. 1 (1994), p. 138.

the Harvard Medical School found that black patients were less likely to have bypass surgery in the V.A. facilities and were less likely to have catheters inserted in their hearts so that doctors could look for damaged arteries.[9]

As Table 6.2 shows, African-Americans have a several year lower life expectancy than whites. In Harlem, which is 96 percent African-American, researchers found a lower life expectancy than for men in Bangladesh, one of the world's poorest countries.[10]

African-American and white death rates can also be compared by disease, as illustrated in Table 6.3.

Differences in cancer rates may be partially explained by the environmental and occupational factors discussed earlier, as well as by inequalities in medical care. African-Americans are more at risk from diabetes associated with diet even if genetics does play some role. Latinos and Native Americans also have a higher death rate from diabetes. Diabetes is a more serious disease for African-Americans than for whites even aside from the higher mortality rates. Lack of adequate care in the disease's early stages leads to complications which, in turn, create an amputation rate double that of whites; the rate of blindness is three times that for whites.[11]

African-Americans and Latinos experience higher rates of AIDS than do whites. In 1993, people of color accounted for 55 percent of the 106,949 known cases of AIDS.[12] About a third of AIDS cases result from drug users using contaminated needles or having sex with an infected addict.

Social policy directly impacts on the incidence of disease. A study of AIDS and other health problems in poor communities of color in The Bronx,

New York, indicates that a reduction in fire-protections service increased the number of fires. As housing was destroyed, people moved, and social organizations, such as churches, youth groups, and block associations, lost their members. The remaining buildings became overcrowded. With increased community disorganization came a rise in alcoholism and associated diseases, drug use, and AIDS. Tuberculosis, a disease associated with substandard living conditions, has also increased.[13]

RACIAL INEQUALITY, STRESS, AND DISEASE

Not all individuals faced with the same conditions will respond in the same way. Not all heavy smokers will get lung cancer, not all drunk drivers will kill someone, not all babies born to agricultural workers will have birth defects. Social conditions, however, heighten individual susceptibility to health problems.

Heart disease, for instance, is partially a result of stress. Although some medical experts claim the higher African-American rate is best explained by genetics, this is unlikely. Blacks in Africa do not show any rapid heightening of blood pressure as they get older. Yet in the United States, African-Americans start having rapid increases after age twenty-four. A common heart problem among this group is heart enlargement, which is thought to be a consequence of hypertension and high blood pressure.[14]

James Baldwin once said, "To be a Negro in this country and to be relatively conscious is to be in a rage all the time."[15] One example will show why. Al Tatum, aged twenty-six, seemed fortunate when in 1988, following the closing of the airline maintenance firm he had been working for, he found a blue collar job paying $12 an hour at Cooper Power, an electrical transformer manufacturer, outside of Milwaukee. This job lasted only four years because conditions were so bad he had to quit.

Soon after Al Tatum started working for Cooper Power, insulting graffiti about him appeared on the men's room walls. His supervisor told him his fellow workers were just "having fun." Then a fake application form appeared on his desk. Among the items was "Yo Prior Experience: Govt worker. Evangelist. Dope dealer. Postmaster. Pimp." At the bottom was a statement "No photo is necessary since yo all look alike anyway."

He brought charges of discrimination to the Milwaukee Office of the Equal Employment Opportunity Commission. The case dragged on for two and a half years until a finding was reached in his favor. Eventually there will be a hearing to see if his civil rights were violated. In the meantime, Al Tatum used all the family's savings to open a restaurant that failed. The Tatums then lost the home they had been buying and moved to Kansas City where he found a job for $5.25 an hour as a baggage handler. He did receive $10,000 in workers' compensation based on his doctor's diagnosis of extreme job-related stress which impaired his ability to continue working.[16]

Ernest Johnson, a University of Houston psychologist, studied the relationship between anger, suppression, and blood pressure among 1,000 tenth-grade students in Florida. He found "that the black kids were angrier than the whites, but... they suppressed their hostility more. The higher the level of suppressed hostility, the higher is their blood pressure." In interviewing African-American "men about the sources of stress in their lives, the most frequently cited is trouble at work, which they believe is due to racism. Their blood pressure rises when they are talking about it."[17]

Strokes and kidney problems are also linked to stress. Death rates from stroke for African-Americans are twice the rate for whites. Although homicide rates add to the mortality rates in places like Harlem, the leading cause of excessive death there is cardiovascular problems. Hypertension, by damaging blood vessels in the kidneys, exacerbates the rate of kidney failure. In the age group twenty-five to forty-four, black males are twenty times more likely than white men to have kidney failure. African-American men, however, are half as likely as white males to receive kidney transplants.[18]

Anger may be transmuted into physical symptoms. It also may be turned into rage loosed on one's fellows, domestic companions, and/or oneself in the form of suicide. Suicide is often clinically analyzed as an inward-directed aggression. Rates among African-American males have been rising in the last thirty years; some analysts attribute this to their continued and seemingly enduring problems of racism.

Alcoholism and illegal drug use are ways of coping with anger and stress. Both can become health risks; for example, liver ailments are associated with greater alcohol use. Alcohol is often implicated in cases of interpersonal violence, and although alcoholics, like drug users, can be found in any socioeconomic group, experts "see the inner city as a noxious stressful environment that encourages many residents to drink as an escape."[19]

HEALTH ON THE RESERVATION

The economic abandonment of communities, coupled with a lack of social support, results in poverty rates higher than anywhere in the developed capitalist world. Racial discrimination means the highest rates of poverty are experienced by people of color, especially Native Americans, African-Americans, and Latinos.

Native-American reservations and inner-city ghettos share a number of characteristics. They are places of low employment and poverty that lack social services. There are high rates of violence, both structural and interpersonal, and they are separate from the larger society. Except for an occasional television documentary, most people in the United States never see the conditions that the residents of these communities experience daily.

Native Americans comprise only about 1 percent of the total U.S. population now, but their situation is especially instructive for thinking about the nature of our government. They are the only ethnic group with whom the government has specific treaty obligations, as well as an official agency with responsibility for their well-being, the Bureau of Indian Affairs (BIA). Yet Native Americans are among the poorest of all peoples in the United States; they live in some of the worst conditions, reflecting their political powerlessness.

On average, about half of the total Native-American population lives on reservations. If you drive through a typical reservation in the Southwest or in South Dakota, you will see landscapes that are often spectacularly beautiful but barren. Men, women, and children lounge idly outside the "trading post" or general store. Inside there is little variety—sacks of flour, cans of lard, hot dogs, components of an unhealthy but inexpensive diet. Broken-down vehicles are in front of shacks. There are few places of employment.

The poorest county in the United States in 1992 was Shannon County, South Dakota. Shannon County is the site of Pine Ridge, the Oglala Sioux reservation. A journalist's description of Pine Ridge conveys the deprivation of its residents: "There is no train, bus, bank, theater, clothing store, drug store, barbershop, restaurant, place to get a car fixed or home delivery of mail."[20] With less than 30 percent of the adults holding jobs, the Pine Ridge poverty rate is 63.1 percent, over five times the national rate.

A government report summarizing the health status of Native Americans notes that "on almost every health indictor, Indian health remains poorer than that of the U.S. population in general."[21] The Pima Indians of Arizona are an instructive example. The Pima have the highest incidence of diabetes in the world, and a rate of the disease that is 8.5 times that of the general U.S. population. As a consequence of this disease, they have an amputation rate of legs and feet that is ten times that of the general population and a dialysis rate twenty-five times higher than for others in this country.

There was no diabetes among the Pima, until settlers diverted the Gila River's waters decades ago. The Pima were dependent on this once quarter mile wide river for their farming. It is now dry. When the Pima lost their water, the federal government stepped in, not to protect their resources but to provide an alternative diet.

The diet provided by the government, high in fat, salt, and sugar, is one doctors say is almost certain to produce diabetes. The National Institutes of Health have been studying the Pima for thirty years. The research, according to Dr. James Reed, who helped oversee a federal diabetes program, has increased doctors' understanding of diabetes, but the data have not been used to help the Pima.[22]

Death rates from motor vehicle accidents, suicide, and homicide are also higher for Native Americans, as Table 6.4 shows.

Table 6.4 Age-Adjusted Death Rates, per 100,000 for Native Americans and Others, 1988

	NATIVE AMERICANS	ALL RACES	OTHER THAN WHITE
Motor vehicle accidents	44	20	19
Suicide	15	11	7
Homicide	14	9	28

Source: Indian Health Service, *Trends in Indian Health*, 1991, pp. 42, 45, 47.

The high accident rate is caused in part by alcohol but also by poor roads and overcrowded vehicles in poor condition, a reflection of low incomes. People, stores, clinics, and so on, are scattered throughout the reservation, and the long distances necessary to reach a destination also contribute to the accident rate.[23]

The Indian Health Service (IHS), part of the Department of Health and Human Services, is responsible for the health care of over a million Native Americans. Native-American health is not a federal budget priority. There are about 200 doctors for every 100,000 persons in the general population, but only 96 physicians for every 100,000 Indians.[24] In the late 1980s, throughout the United States, per capita spending on health care was $1,800; the IHS was spending half that amount for health care, water, sewer, and sanitation services combined.[25] Funding for the IHS was cut by the Reagan administration, and President Clinton proposed an additional 13 percent cut.[26]

GENDER AND HEALTH

Women and men face gender-specific health problems caused by gender stereotyping and the never-ending search for profits. Gender roles, for example, partially account for the fact that men have shorter life expectancies than women; they are more likely to drive recklessly, to engage in interpersonal violence, and to be given more stressful and dangerous jobs. Women, on the other hand, are brought up to be caretakers and also bear most of the responsibility for contraception.

WOMEN AND BIRTH CONTROL: THE DALKON SHIELD

Women are generally responsible for the consequences of sexual intercourse. According to a recent poll, both men and women agree that males "are not responsible enough" to be trusted to provide for birth control.[27] Virtually all the research and marketing of birth control devices, with the exception of condoms, is aimed at women, who consequently bear whatever health risks are associated with contraception.

The emphasis on female birth control devices and the goal of profit have sometimes combined in a lethal way, as in the case of the Dalkon Shield marketed in 1971 by A. H. Robins Co. This intrauterine device had not been adequately tested, but it was very profitable: it cost about twenty-five cents to produce, and it sold for $4.35. The Dalkon Shield led to pelvic infections, sterility, miscarriages, and birth defects. At least eighteen women died in the United States from its use. The company ignored warnings from its employees, from doctors with infected patients, and from the Food and Drug Administration (FDA). When Wayne Crowder, a quality control supervisor at Robins, expressed concern about the Shield's safety, his supervisor responded by saying, "Your conscience doesn't pay your salary" and warned him to be quiet.[28]

With the encouragement of the National Women's Health Network, over ten thousand women sued the company for hundreds of millions of dollars. The company's defense claimed that the women's own sexual practices had caused their problems. One company lawyer even asserted, "There is not a damn thing wrong with the Dalkon Shield."

> Ninety percent of these gals, Christ, you ought to read their histories.... It's unreal. The number of men they screw would knock you off your feet.[29]

Distribution in the United States stopped in 1975, but the health problems associated with this product continue. The Dalkon Shield was also distributed in at least seventy-eight other countries. Even after marketing ceased here, it continued overseas. This is an example of the "corporate dumping" that is discussed in chapter 7.

BREAST CANCER

Diseases such as breast cancer that are specific to women have not been studied as thoroughly as male disorders, for example, prostate cancer. Breast cancer is responsible for over forty thousand deaths annually. The incidence of this disease has been increasing, and it is one of the leading causes of death for women. Women are advised to do routine breast examinations, and older women are encouraged to have periodic mammograms to find early signs of potential breast cancer: as with other diseases, prevention is the most effective way of reducing the incidence.

A number of chemicals with carcinogenic properties may be particularly dangerous to women. These chemicals, found in many pesticides, dissolve in fat, and women's breasts contain much fatty tissue. The incidence of breast cancer can be linked to environmental toxins, but a strategy to reduce pollution is resisted by industry.

Although white women experience a greater incidence of breast cancer,

African-American women are more at risk of dying from the disease, usually because they see doctors at a later stage of the cancer's development. For the period 1983–89, the five-year survival rate for white women diagnosed with breast cancer was 81 percent, compared with 64 percent for African-American women. The tumors in black women appear to be more aggressive; the tumorous cells divide and spread more quickly. Some cancer researchers attribute this to environmental and dietary factors.[30]

WOMEN AND AIDS

The importance of gender, race, and class-based inequality in lessening well-being can be seen by a look at AIDS. We mentioned earlier how women are held responsible for birth control. If the male partner loathes the use of a condom, then the woman must be assertive, which may be difficult given societal expectations of a woman's subservient role. In addition to being responsible for birth control, the woman now becomes responsible for protection against HIV. Presently AIDS cases among women are growing by about 17 percent annually, whereas among the whole population the rate of growth is about 3 percent.[31]

Women's experience with AIDS was neglected for many years. Dr. Judith Cohen, at the School of Public Health at Berkeley, found it futile in 1983 to interest her male colleagues in women with AIDS. Other women researchers found the same indifference from funding agencies such as the National Institutes of Health. It is women practitioners and researchers, as well as women activists, who have taken the lead in raising awareness about women and AIDS.

A number of characteristics, such as gender, can influence how AIDS manifests itself. For years, diseases specific to women, such as cervical cancer, chronic yeast infections, and pelvic inflammatory disease, were not used in diagnosing AIDS. Because of pressure from AIDS activists that definition has now been expanded. Without an appropriate diagnosis, women are less likely to receive the disability benefits associated with being HIV positive. They are also more likely to die in the earlier stages of the disease.

Poor HIV-positive women are less likely to have the resources for medical treatment. They may be so burdened by child care responsibilities that seeking help is difficult. Child care facilities at public health services could alleviate this problem. Additionally, mothers who are addicts fear they will be punished by having their children taken away from them if their addiction is exposed by a medical worker.

Women with AIDS are more likely to be women of color. In 1993, 50 percent were African-American, 25 percent were white, and 20 percent were Latino. Poverty is a likely explanation for these figures, because desperation influences women to engage in behaviors that make them more vulnerable to HIV infection, such as prostitution and IV drug use.[32]

WOMEN AND MEDICAL RESEARCH

For years, women's health has been secondary to men's, although this is beginning to change. The neglect is a result of the medical profession's history of being largely a white male profession. As more women enter the medical field, there may be greater concern for their specific health problems, but women still make up only 22 percent of physicians, and white males dominate the medical schools as presidents, deans, and chairs of departments.

Typically white males are the population that is used to determine medical standards and practices for everyone. Excluding women and minorities from clinical trials of pharmaceutical products has meant that potential adverse drug reactions in these groups were not known. Conversely, possible benefits from medical practices for women were also studied less. For example, in 1981, a study of the effect of aspirin on heart attacks was begun. All twenty-two thousand people in the study were male doctors, because the researchers believed they were the group that could be most trusted to follow the researchers' instructions. "Various medical boards reviewing the design of this and other studies excluding women noticed nothing amiss."[33]

The effect of aspirin on heart attacks experienced by African-American women, Latinas, and white women, as well as nonwhite males, was thereby assumed to be exactly the same as that of white men. Other studies have been similarly conducted; AIDS, cardiovascular diseases, and many cancers that afflict both men and women have largely been studied only in men. Serious problems may even receive different diagnoses depending on the patient's gender. For example, according to Dr. Joann E. Manson of the Harvard Medical School, who has conducted studies in women's health, heart disease symptoms such as chest pains are more often overlooked in women, who usually receive less thorough treatment for heart disease. A study of thirty-six thousand Medicare patients indicated that men were 18 percent more likely than women to receive the most effective type of pacemaker.[34]

CONSUMERS AS VICTIMS OF STRUCTURAL VIOLENCE

The same structural forces that lead to an indifference to worker health and safety also affect consumers. Because penalties for business crimes are not very great in terms of the potential drain on an organization's resources, it often is profitable to break the law. Corporate lawbreakers rarely go to jail; instead they may have to give a speech or do community service of some sort—these options are not given to street criminals.[35]

In 1985, SmithKline, the pharmaceutical company, pleaded guilty to thirty-four charges that resulted from deaths connected to their marketing of a blood-pressure drug that could damage a user's kidneys and liver. The company was aware of the side effects but did not report them to the FDA, nor did they label the drug to warn potential users. Company personnel—doctors—who were involved could have gone to jail for fourteen years and been fined $14,000 each. Instead the company itself was ordered by a Pennsylvania judge to give $100,000 to a child abuse program and to perform 500 hours of community service.[36] Imagine if Colin Ferguson, who killed six people on the LIRR, was allowed to pay a fine and perform community service.

SICKENING "HEALTH" PRODUCTS

This example shows that health care companies can be a risk to sick people. C. R. Bard, Inc., a medical devices manufacturer with over $1 billion a year in sales, pleaded guilty in 1993 to over 390 counts of fraud and human experimentation in the marketing and production of a heart catheter that resulted in at least one death and twenty-two emergency operations. The catheters had been tested on unknowing patients while they were on the operating table. The company also knew that the catheters caused injury to animals, but this information was concealed from the FDA.

It is not unusual for companies to deceive the FDA. Businesses argue that they must protect trade secrets. The FDA apparently accepts that rationale and so do the courts. Disaster can result. Until 1986, Shiley Inc., a division of the large pharmaceutical company Pfizer, sold faulty heart valves that resulted in over three hundred deaths. The valves had a tendency to crack when implanted, but company documents showing this information were withheld from the FDA.

The FDA is supposed to check on medical devices, pharmaceuticals, and food products. Yet the agency does not even know how many manufacturers of medical devices they should be inspecting. In past inspections, the investigations revealed problems in at least 16 percent of the cases, but action was taken in only half of these instances.[37]

Many mothers rely on infant formula and prepared baby foods to nourish their children. Even these have caused problems. For example, Syntex Laboratories in California marketed Neo-Mul-Soy, which had only one-fifth of the necessary choline content. As inadequate amounts of choline can result in learning disabilities, the product was eventually recalled, but not before it had been fed to tens of thousands of babies. A positive result was that the FDA, which had not had the authority to regulate infant formula, was given this responsibility in 1980. When the Reagan administration came into office, however, new procedures, largely suggested by the infant-formula industry, were instituted and effectively turned back the regulation clock. The analysis justifying the more company-friendly rules was done by Dr. Dennis L. Heuring who worked for eight years for one of the largest infant-formula manufacturers, Mead Johnson. Following this, several more deficient infant formulas went on the market.[38]

WATCH WHAT YOU EAT

People have been shot in fast-food restaurants, but they have also been killed or gotten sick from eating tainted hamburgers. Four customers of Jack in the Box restaurants died in this manner in 1993. The CDC estimates that five hundred deaths a year are caused by eating tainted meat. Beef that contains *e. coli* bacteria, for example, can cause kidney and heart damage. The Reagan administration weakened the food inspection process and allowed violaters of the law to keep selling their products. One instance involved Cattle-King, which was selling hamburger meat to school lunch programs in spite of its record of diseased meat and unclean plants. Canada, in contrast, has banned its products.[39]

In 1996, federal rules for meat inspection were strengthened for the first time since 1906. The so-called "sniff and poke" method has been replaced by more scientific procedures. These are the result of a compromise between consumer advocates and the meat industry by which the industry will do at least some of its own inspecting.[40]

The way agribusiness grows food poses risks to consumers and the environment. About 1.5 billion pounds of pesticides are used in agriculture, on food and industrial crops. There are also tons of herbicides to control weeds and fungicides. Some of the most dangerous, such as DDT, are now banned from use in the United States but are sold by U.S. companies to the Third World. Unsuspecting consumers abroad may be harmed, and these products can also come back to the shopper in the United States by means of what has been called "the circle of poison."

DRIVING MAY BE HAZARDOUS TO YOUR HEALTH

One of the most dangerous consumer products has been the automobile. In 1929, then General Motors president Alfred Sloane explained why he wasn't having safety glass installed in GM's Chevrolets:

> I would very much rather spend the same amount of money in improving our car in other ways because I think from the standpoint of selfish business, it would be a very much better investment. You can say, perhaps, that I am selfish, but business is selfish. We are not a charitable institution—we are trying to make a profit for our stockholders.[41]

That attitude has not changed; people are still being killed and injured, because companies decide that profits are a higher priority than the well-being of their customers.

The automobile companies as well as federal, local, and state governments, have made decisions where the cumulative effect has been to create a dependence on privately owned cars. People drive cars because they have been presented as symbols of freedom, happiness, sexual pleasure, and the like. But cars are also driven because alternative means of transportation are not readily available; many people are dependent on cars to get to work and to shop.

The federal government has allowed automobile companies to manufacture vehicles with few serious penalties if safety laws are violated. When the Motor Vehicle Safety Act was passed in 1966, the industry prevented provisions of the act that would have made it a criminal offense to market a dangerous vehicle knowingly; at most the company could be fined. Few street criminals can influence legislation in this way.

Exposés such as Ralph Nader's 1966 book *Unsafe at Any Speed* and an aroused public led to the creation of the Department of Transportation and, within it, the National Highway Traffic Safety Administration. Standards for making less harmful cars were established, and automobiles in general became less dangerous. The industry fought, of course, as it still fights today against making the safest possible cars. For example, auto manufacturers were able to get the Reagan administration to delay the installation of air bags or automatic seat belts. This likely has contributed to around nine thousand deaths and sixty-five thousand injuries annually.[42]

The automobile industry uses cost-benefit analyses to decide if it is profitable to cut corners on safety. This is what Ford did in the 1970s with its infamous Pinto. Because of the Pinto's design, the gas tank ruptured in rear-end collisions, and fire enveloped the vehicle. At least five hundred people burned to death this way. Ford engineers were aware of this problem, and Ford actually had a patent on a safer tank. But executives, especially President Lee Iacocca, were anxious to come out with a small car that could compete with the then popular Volkswagen Beetle. In such a cut-throat atmosphere, engineers feared bringing up safety issues. One engineer even said that "with Lee [Iacocca] it was taboo."

Using the 1972 National Highway Traffic Safety Administration's decision that a life was worth $200,725, Ford concluded that spending $11.00 a vehicle for a safer fuel system would cost the company more than any payments it would have to make from potential lawsuits.[43]

The "Pinto of the '90's" is how auto-safety experts describe General Motors pickup trucks manufactured between 1973 and 1987. Because of the outside placement of the gasoline tanks, the trucks burst into flames if struck from the side. Passengers have burned to death or suffered permanent-scarring

Table 6.5 Motor Vehicle Deaths versus Firearms Deaths, 1991

NUMBER OF MOTOR VEHICLE DEATHS	NUMBER OF FIREARMS DEATHS
43,536	38,317

Source: "Guns Gaining on Cars as Leading U.S. Killer," *New York Times,* 28 January 1994, p. A12.

injuries. Company documents proved that GM was aware of the problem as early as 1983 yet continued making the trucks for five more years. Pondering GM's actions, burn victim Douglas Wharton asked:

> What is America? Is it the corporation GM or am I America, . . . the people that are going to be burned that are kind of faceless, are they America? This decision seems to be saying, "go ahead and burn . . . Americans can burn."

In 1993, a Georgia jury awarded millions of dollars to a family whose seventeen-year-old son died of burns in a GM pick-up truck.[44]

So far, from one hundred fifty to three hundred people have died because of the truck's faulty design. The government releases the low figure, critics the higher one. General Motors won a victory when the Clinton administration decided not to order a recall of these lethal vehicles. It would have cost GM about $1 billion to recall and fix the trucks, and a recall would have strengthened lawsuits against the company. In exchange for not having to recall their trucks, General Motors agreed to contribute $51.3 million to safety programs, including educational ones regarding drunk driving and the use of seat belts. The amount may seem large, but it is equivalent to only 2 percent of the company's profits for 1993.[45] None of the money is earmarked for teaching auto makers about the value of human lives, a lesson they badly need.

Automobiles are a dangerous form of transportation. Although firearm deaths are catching up, more people are still killed annually in auto accidents, as shown in Table 6.5. For all teenagers between fifteen and nineteen, car accidents are the leading cause of death.[46]

THE ENVIRONMENT AND STRUCTURAL VIOLENCE: DON'T DRINK THE WATER, DON'T BREATHE THE AIR

We can try to be careful consumers and still become victims of structural violence. The air we breathe, the water we drink, the food we eat may all be laced with toxins. As a result of a widespread grassroots environmental movement, there is heightened concern. In recent years, however, business has mounted an effective attack on environmentalists by portraying them

Table 6.6 Deaths and Death Rates from Cancer

	NUMBERS OF DEATHS	DEATH RATE PER 100,000
1970	330,700	163
1993	531,300	206

Source: Bureau of the Census, *Statistical Abstract of the United States, 1995*, Table 125, p. 92.

as enemies of economic growth and as elitists who care more about spotted owls than working people. Environmental activists are justifiably concerned about the preservation of threatened species, but many more are also concerned with the threats to our health that modern corporations have created.

A recent study by the American Lung Association, for example, estimated that close to 24 million people are breathing dangerously polluted air. Airborne contaminants are believed to be responsible for fifty thousand deaths each year. A study of air quality in six cities found that death rates from lung cancer, other lung diseases, and heart diseases were higher in the more polluted urban areas. Emissions from factories, power plants, oil and gas plants, and automobiles were the source of the pollution.[47]

"I'm sorry to tell you, you have cancer." This is one of the most dreaded outcomes of a medical examination. As Table 6.6 shows, there has been a large increase of death from cancerous malignancies. The death rate has increased by 20 percent in a little over twenty years.

A number of health experts link this death rate to the increased number of manufactured chemicals. In addition to pesticides, there are about fifty thousand chemicals in industrial use. Chemicals often interact with one another, and the synergistic effects are not completely known. The estimate is that from 60 to 90 percent of cancer is caused by environmental factors, including occupational and consumer exposure to toxins, as well as from smoking. All told there are thousands of preventable cancer deaths per year.[48]

A 1983 study by the University of Medicine and Dentistry of New Jersey found that in twenty towns with toxic waste disposal sites, the rate of cancer deaths was at least 50 percent more than the national average. The prognosis for New Jersey, my home state, is bleak. In 1994, during her first term in office, Republican Governor Christine Todd Whitman abolished the state's position of environmental prosecutor. According to the Newark *Star Ledger*, the creation of this post, the first such office in the country, "had sent a chill through the business community."[49]

Besides cancer, industrial toxins are associated with birth defects, miscarriages, lowered fertility, and damage to the immune system. The numbers of pollutants stagger the imagination. Each year, for example, 225 million tons of hazardous waste are created, 4 million tons of chemicals enter the water, and 160 million tons of pollutants contaminate the air.[50]

In 1994, a citizens' organization, the Environmental Working Group, analyzed Midwestern water and discovered that over 3.5 million people in that region alone were drinking water laced with the same chemicals used to kill weeds. An EPA spokesperson called this study "another in a series of wake-up calls that tells us we can no longer take for granted that our drinking water is safe all the time." But the Clinton administration was unable to defeat pesticide industry efforts against strengthening the Safe Drinking Water Act, which is currently being weakened by new congressional legislation.[51]

Thinking ecologically means taking a long-term view, that is, viewing the earth and its resources as belonging to future generations. Capitalism, on the other hand, generally takes a short-term view: *What is profitable now?* Corporations make money only when their products are bought, used, and bought again, so there is a vested interest in creating and maintaining markets for materials even (and often) at the expense of the environment.[52] Cost-benefit analysis operates here as well. In 1989, at Senate hearings, the inspector general of the Environmental Protection Agency was questioned by a senator:

> Is it your testimony that EPA's enforcement policies are so weak that it frequently pays polluters to keep polluting and pay EPA's small fines rather than clean up their act?

The inspector general replied: "Absolutely.... We have found that over and over again."[53] The costs businesses refuse to pay to engage in cleaner, healthier production then become social costs the public must bear, one way or another.

The EPA estimates that more than seven hundred thousand tons of hazardous waste are produced each day, which is the equivalent of about one ton each year per U.S. citizen. Communities are used as sinks, places to dump hazardous waste into the streams, rivers, or the ground. Working-class communities are usually chosen as dumping sites, because politicians and corporate executives expect they will be the communities least likely to resist. In 1984, the government of California went so far as to hire a consulting company, Cerrell Associates, to figure out how they could build garbage incinerators without meeting resistance. Cerrell Associates advised placing them in blue collar communities:

> All socio-economic groupings ... resent the nearby siting of major facilities, but the middle and upper socio-economic strata possess better resources to effectuate their opposition.[54]

Some towns, in fact, have been so contaminated that they have been closed down, and their residents relocated; Times Beach, Missouri, was contaminated with dioxin from a road contractor. Love Canal, in New York

State, was fouled by the Occidental Petroleum subsidiary, Hooker Chemical Company.

Herbicides made with dioxin have been on the market for thirty years. Dow Chemical Company knew of the potential hazards of this chemical as early as 1965 and still successfully opposed an effort by the Carter administration to ban its use. The Reagan administration then curtailed further research efforts.[55]

Lois Gibbs, a former housewife from Love Canal who created and heads the Citizens' Clearinghouse for Hazardous Wastes, spoke of Dow's freedom to poison communities:

> Would you let me shoot into a crowd of one hundred thousand people and kill one of them? . . . It's okay for the corporations to do it, but the little guy with a gun goes to jail. . . . I look at the issue of people being poisoned and it makes me mad.[56]

In 1980, faced with the dramatic catastrophes at Times Beach and Love Canal, and under pressure from angry citizens, Congress passed the Superfund law. Revenues were to be generated from a special tax on oil and chemical companies to clean up hazardous waste sites. Industrial polluters would also pay fines. But, as *Time* magazine journalist Bruce Van Voorst reported, firms often bring their own lawsuits to hold up any settlement that would make them actually clean up the mess they have created: "Companies readily acknowledge that it is worth spending millions of dollars on lawyers to put off spending hundreds of millions of dollars on cleanups." Van Voorst notes that only "180 of the 1,202 sites now on the list have been officially cleaned up." And new toxic waste dumps are being created.[57]

ENVIRONMENTAL RACISM

"Environmental racism" describes an all-too-common phenomenon by which minority communities disproportionately become the destination for toxic wastes. Residents become the victims of unseen assailants, people in positions of power, who have no particular desire to harm them but find it expedient to use their neighborhoods as sinkholes for toxic industrial and military wastes or as relatively cheap production sites. Housing discrimination, as discussed in chapter 3, creates concentrations of minorities in areas that are less politically powerful and therefore more exploitable than white neighborhoods. Some people have less choice about where to settle than others: they can't simply move because they don't want to live next to a dump or a noxious factory.

On Evelina Street in Tucson, Arizona, there are thirty houses. In twenty-nine of them, residents have cancer. In this Chicano neighborhood, the water contains TCE, or trichloroethylene, a carcinogen that came from the operations of Hughes Aircraft, a manufacturer of missiles. Community activists have created a map of Tucson, with colored pins showing the location of cases of leukemia, epilepsy, birth defects, and so on. Looking at this map, with the pins concentrated in Latino neighborhoods, Rose Augustine, a local activist, says, "This is what we mean by environmental racism." Many residents have no health insurance. The federal government had given Hughes military contracts and later hired Hughes to clean up the water. The government has the actual responsibility for protecting the environment. Neither the government nor Hughes, however, has done much, and there is little government interest in this community's problems.[58]

The ecological problems of the poor are often a direct result of the greed of the wealthy. Along the U.S.-Mexico border, for example, are Chicano communities, *colonias*, that are among the very poorest in the United States. Whereas the three hundred forty thousand *colonia* residents are poor, the owners of their shanties are wealthy. Purchasing land for only a few hundred dollars, the "developers" in turn sell it to Mexican immigrants who pay some money down and then make monthly payments of approximately $50 to $200. With thousands of people making these payments, the profit margins are high. Profits are especially high, because the developers do not invest in any infrastructure, such as sewers, water lines, or proper garbage disposal facilities. *Colonia* residents have been forced to build outdoor latrines that overflow when there are heavy rains. Uncollected garbage attracts disease-spreading rats, and there is a high incidence of tuberculosis, dysentery, and hepatitis. Children have skin rashes and diarrhea. The developers do not pay for dealing with the consequences of their actions, and some have even managed to avoid paying any income tax for many years.[59]

African-American communities are also too often victims of environmental racism. In 1982, the state government of North Carolina made plans to dump more than six thousand truckloads of PCB-contaminated soil into a Warren County landfill. PCBs, or polychlorinated biphenyls, are a carcinogenic form of hydrocarbon. Now banned, PCBs were a widely used, commercially produced substance that contained dioxin and other hazardous substances. There are still tons of PCB-contaminated soil awaiting disposal. One method has been to put the soil into landfills, but then the chemicals are likely to leak into the groundwater.

Poor and minority communities are frequently seen as the solution to the problem of where to put industrial wastes. Warren County is the poorest county in North Carolina, and it has a 65 percent African-American population. The residents were not willing to allow their lives and families to be threatened. Concerned citizens mobilized to stop the dumping, and over five hundred people wound up in jail as a result of their protests. Their efforts failed, and the dump was built. But they had provided a model and had focused attention on a problem that the environmental movement in general had neglected.[60]

In 1983, the General Accounting Office of the government reported that in the South hazardous landfills were located in predominately black and poor communities. The pattern holds throughout the United States. In 1987, the United Church of Christ issued a report titled *Toxic Waste and Race in the United States*, which concluded that race was the most important factor in the placement of commercial hazardous waste sites, outweighing all other factors including income, property values, and rate of home ownership. Six years later, the EPA also admitted that people of color are more likely to live in polluted communities.[61]

Cleanup at hazardous waste sites in minority communities tends to begin later and is done less effectively than in white communities. Penalties for breaking toxic waste laws are usually less. According to a study done for the *National Law Journal* in 1992, the average fine for violating a hazardous waste law was over $335,000 in white areas and about $55,000 in minority communities.[62]

The town of Emelle, Alabama, is the location of the largest hazardous waste site in the United States; it is used by forty-five states and several other countries. It is also 79 percent African-American. Farther north, the largest single concentration of hazardous waste dumps is on the South Side of Chicago, where almost all the residents are African-American or Latino.[63]

President of the Northeast Community Action Group Charles Streadit, a Houston resident, said of a landfill being built in his neighborhood:

> A silent war is being waged against black neighborhoods. Slowly, we are being picked off by the industries that don't give a damn about polluting our neighborhood, contaminating our water, fouling our air. . . . It's hard enough for blacks to scrape and save enough to buy a home, then you see your dreams shattered by a garbage dump. That's a dirty trick.[64]

It takes higher incomes to live near the ocean or up on a hill, where breezes blow pollutants away. Poorer people live in congested neighborhoods with fewer trees and little grass but with more sources of pollution: traffic, garages, auto repair shops, and small factories.

In Los Angeles, 34 percent of whites live in areas with heavily polluted air, which may seem unacceptably high, but *71 percent* of African-Americans and 50 percent of Latinos are breathing unhealthy air. South Central Los Angeles, for example, has the distinction of being the "dirtiest" zip code in California, 90058. The population there is 59 percent African-American and 38 percent Latino. In 1989, over sixteen thousand tons of pollutants, including cleaning and industrial solvents, lead, and ammonia, were discharged into an area measuring less than one square mile.[65]

Scientists at the University of Southern California performed autopsies on one hundred young men aged fifteen to twenty-five who had come from this area. Their deaths had resulted from accidents or acts of violence, not from any disease, but the study concluded, had they reached the age of forty, they all would have had serious respiratory problems. Four-fifths of the young men had lung abnormalities beyond anything that could be explained by their smoking. The cause was judged to be breathing the smoggy Los Angeles air. Things are only likely to get worse as budget cuts have led to a lessening of enforcement of air-quality standards, and industry has successfully fought regulations, for example, by having clean-air advocates fired from the Air Resources Board.[66]

Businesses clearly cannot be expected to care about the environment, and they use their political power to weaken what environmental protections the government has offered. It was only through sustained public—not business—pressure that sewage and garbage disposal, for example, became public services during the late nineteenth and early twentieth centuries; cities were made healthier and cleaner because of progressive movements.

THERE ARE HEROES

The current struggles for a safer environment date from the 1960s. As awareness of the dangers facing our habitat grew, a movement for protecting the planet developed. There were victories for environmentalists: the EPA was created in 1970, and acts were passed to clean up the air and water. Membership in environmental organizations grew along with public consciousness.

Corporations have feared the consequences of an aroused public opinion and have gone to great lengths to silence environmental activists. Procter and Gamble (P&G), for instance, built a paper mill in Taylor County, Florida, a move initially welcomed for the jobs it provided. P&G was permitted by the state to use the local river as a dump for the plant's wastes, which included dioxin. Local activists began a campaign against the company they nicknamed "Profit & Greed." Their phones were tapped, anonymous threatening phone calls were received, family pets were poisoned, and one of the women leaders was beaten and raped. The activists were the ones threatened with criminal charges by the sheriff's department. P&G has enjoyed a history of close ties with local officials.[67]

There are numerous incidents of local activists around the country being threatened and injured by antienvironmentalist organizations. Lois Gibbs estimates that "40 percent of people protesting toxic waste sites and incinerators around the country have been intimidated." Andy Kerr, a member of the Oregon Natural Resources Council, claims, "Death threats come with the territory these days." He was hung in effigy. The home of Pat Costner, research director of Greenpeace's campaign against toxics, was destroyed in an arson attack, and thirty years of research went up in the flames.[68]

The private, antigovernment militias that have recently received much publicity are usually antienvironmentalist as well. Some ranchers, miners, loggers, and farmers claim that public lands should be free of all regulation and that private citizens should be able to do as they please to the nation's natural resources. In southern New Mexico, for instance, local newspapers are urging drastic action against environmentalists; one paper even suggesting they be drowned in a nearby river. Environmental organizations have asked that Congress and the Justice Department investigate the harassing of federal environmental officials by paramilitary organizations and antienvironmentalist organizations such as Wise Use.[69]

During the Reagan administration, the EPA's staff was cut by 25 percent; its budget was slashed by one-third. Cost-benefit analyses were used to determine whether safety standards were economically justifiable. These are again being proposed. A number of rules were suspended, canceled, or just ignored. The present Republican-dominated Congress is continuing the assault on environmental protections, rewriting legislation to undo long-standing environmental regulations. The oddly named Clean Water Act, for example, would allow regulations to be waived that have been in effect since 1972.

Unable to rely on companies to behave responsibly, or on the government to protect the general welfare, people in threatened areas have formed their own groups to deal with environmental threats. Such groups have gathered information about items such as the incidence of cancer and birth defects. Community health surveys have been undertaken as activists develop the skills and knowledge to respond collectively to the power of the corporations and their political allies. Demonstrations and other forms of protest have been organized to pressure for the protection of neighborhoods from incinerators and toxic waste dumps. Organizations such as the Citizens' Clearinghouse for Hazardous Wastes, the National Toxics Campaign, and the Environmental Research Foundation give technical assistance and conduct workshops for local activists.

In spite of formidable obstacles, many local communities are joining together to protect themselves, and there is now a national movement to fight environmental racism. In 1991, the first National People of Color Environmental Leadership Summit was held in Washington, D.C. The more than six hundred fifty participants came from many local and national groups, and there were even representatives from Puerto Rico, Mexico, and the Marshall Islands. The conference developed a set of principles calling for environmental protection throughout the world as the same companies that threaten the health of Americans menace communities in the Third World. Those seeking an end to environmental racism want no one, here or abroad, to be victims of the irresponsible practices of multinational corporations and their government allies.

Notes

1. Quoted in "Infant Deaths Tied to Poverty, Study Confirms," *New York Times*, 15 December 1995, p. A38; William S. Nersesian, "Infant Mortality in Socially Vulnerable Populations," *Annual Review of Public Health* 9 (1988): pp. 361, 364.
2. Matthew L. Wald, "Boston Child Study Finds Death Rate Higher among the Poor and the Black," *New York Times*, 8 August 1985; "Study of Poor Children Shows a Painful Choice: Heat over Food," *New York Times*, 9 September 1992; Esther B. Fein, "A Private Study Finds Many Children in Shelters Have Signs of Malnutrition," *New York Times*, 14 December 1994, p. B3.
3. Bert Burrason, "Infant Mortality in the United States: Racial Differences and Social Stratification," Paper presented at the 1994 meetings of the Pacific Sociological Association, pp. 9–10; "Study Finds Racial Disparity in Warnings to the Pregnant," *New York Times*, 20 January 1994, p. A16.
4. Sandra Blakeslee, "Concentrations of Lead in Blood Drop Steeply," *New York Times*, 27 July 1994, p. A18; "the short run," *Dollars and Sense* (July/August 1996), p. 5; Bureau of the Census, *Statistical Abstract of the United States, 1995*, Table 210, p. 139.
5. "Millions Cannot Afford Dental Help, Study Says," *New York Times*, 30 November 1994, p. C14; Susan T. Reisine, "The Impact of Dental Conditions on Social Functioning and the Quality of Life," *Annual Review of Public Health* 9 (1988): p. 5.
6. Elisabeth Rosenthal, "Shortage of Doctors in Poor Areas Is Seen as Barrier to Health Plans," *New York Times*, 18 October 1993, pp. A1, B4.
7. Michael Wines, and Robert Pear, "President Finds Benefits in Defeat on Health Care," *New York Times*, 30 July 1996, p. A1; Kaiser Health Reform Project, *Uninsured in America* (Henry J. Kaiser Family Foundation, 1994), pp. 2–3; Weitz, 133.
8. Bureau of the Census, *Statistical Abstract of the United States, 1994*, Tables 169, 171, pp. 118, 119.
9. Warren E. Leary, "Health Care Lagging among Blacks and Poor," *New York Times*, 12 September 1996, p. A18. The Health Care Financing Administration also found that lower-income whites were receiving less adequate care than whites with more money. Sandra Blakeslee, "Poor and Black Patients Slighted, Study Says," *New York Times*, 20 April 1994, p. B9.
10. Colin McCord, and Harold P. Freeman, "Excess Mortality in Harlem," in *Crisis in American Institutions*, 9th ed., eds. Jerome Skolnick and Elliot Currie (New York: HarperCollins, 1991), pp. 426–32.
11. Laurie Kaye Abraham, *Mamma Might Be Better Off Dead: The Failure of Health Care in Urban America* (Chicago: University of Chicago Press, 1993), p. 70.
12. "Blacks Far More Likely Than Whites to Have AIDS, Agency Says," *New York Times*, 9 September 1994, p. A16.
13. Deborah Wallace, "Roots of Increased Health Care Inequality in New York," *Social Science and Medicine* 31 (1990): pp. 1219–27; Rodrick Wallace, "Urban

13. Desertification, Public Health and Public Order: 'Planned Shrinkage,' Violent Death, Substance Abuse and AIDS in The Bronx," *Social Science and Medicine* 31 (1990): pp. 801–13.
14. Peter E. S. Freund, and Meredith B. McGuire, *Health, Illness and the Social Body: A Critical Sociology* (Englewood Cliffs, N.J.: Prentice-Hall, 1991), pp. 29–30; "Deadliest Heart Ailment in Blacks Is Enlargement," *New York Times*, 24 May 1995, p. C13.
15. Quoted in *Time*, 20 August 1965, p. 17.
16. Peter T. Kilborn, "A Family Spirals Downward in Waiting for Agency to Act," *New York Times*, 11 February 1995, pp. 1, 10.
17. Daniel Goleman, "Anger over Racism Is Seen as a Cause of Blacks' High Blood Pressure," *New York Times*, 24 April 1990, p. A16.
18. Melvin Konner, *Dear America: A Concerned Doctor Wants You to Know the Truth about Health Reform* (Reading, Mass.: Addison-Wesley, 1993), p. 35; Abraham, pp. 28–29; James E. Blackwell, *The Black Community: Diversity and Unity* (New York: HarperCollins, 1991), pp. 405–6.
19. Margaret S. Boone, *Capital Crime: Black Infant Mortality in America* (Newbury Park, Calif.: Sage, 1989), p. 131.
20. Peter T. Kilborn, "Sad Distinction for the Sioux: Homeland Is No. 1 in Poverty," *New York Times*, 20 September 1992, pp. 1, 32.
21. U.S. Congress, Office of Technology Assessment, *Indian Health Care* (Washington, D.C.: U.S. Government Printing Office, 1986), p. 89.
22. "The Pima Plague," segment of CNN, Special Assignment, broadcast, 19 March 1995.
23. U.S. Congress, *Indian Health Care*, p. 92.
24. Richard T. Schaefer, *Racial and Ethnic Groups*, 5th ed. (New York: HarperCollins, 1993), p. 172.
25. Dr. Joshua Lipsman, "White Man's Medicine," *Nation*, 26 March 1988, p. 401.
26. "Clinton to Hear Indians Upset over Health Cuts," *New York Times*, 23 March 1994, p. A22.
27. Jennifer Steinhauer, "Men Avoid Birth Control Responsibility, Poll Finds," *New York Times*, 23 May 1995, p. B10.
28. Susan Perry, and Jim Dawson, "Nightmare: Women and the Dalkon Shield," in *Corporate and Governmental Deviance: Problems of Organizational Behavior in Contemporary Society*, 3d ed., eds. M. David Ermann and Richard J. Lundman (New York: Oxford University Press, 1987), p. 154.
29. Quoted in Russell Mokhiber, *Corporate Crime and Violence: Big Business and the Abuse of Public Trust* (San Francisco: Sierra Club Books, 1988), p. 149.
30. Survival rate figures from Bureau of the Census, *Statistical Abstract of the United States, 1994*, Table 213, p. 143; "Breast Cancer Twice as Deadly in Blacks," *New York Times*, 28 September 1994, p. C10; Gina Kollata, "Deadliness of Breast Cancer in Blacks Defies Easy Answers," *New York Times*, 3 August 1994, p. C10; Rita Arditti, and Tatiana Schreiber, "Breast Cancer: The Environmental Connection," *Resist Newsletter* (May/June 1992), pp. 1–8.
31. "AIDS Cases Rising Sharply among Women," *New York Times*, 10 February 1995, p. A11.
32. Elizabeth Fee, and Nancy Krieger, "Health, Politics, and Power," *Women's Review of Books* 11 (July 1994), p. 4.
33. Gena Corea, *The Invisible Epidemic: The Story of Women and AIDS* (New York: HarperCollins, 1992), p. 4.

34. Bonnie Liebman, "For Women Only," *Nutrition Action Health Letter* 22 (March 1995), p. 4; Leonard K. Altman, "Study Finds Sexual Biases in Doctors' Choice of Pacemakers," *New York Times*, 15 February 1995, p. A16.
35. Mokhiber, 1988, pp. 28–29.
36. "SmithKline Is Fined for Failing to Report Side Effects of Drug," *New York Times*, 26 February 1985, p. A24.
37. Philip J. Hilts, "Manufacturer Admits Selling Untested Devices for Heart," *New York Times*, 16 October 1993, p. 1; Gina Kolata, "Manufacturer of Faulty Heart Valve Barred Data on Dangers, F.D.A. Says," *New York Times*, 21 March 1992, p. 50; "F.D.A. Faulted on Inspection of Medical Devices," *New York Times*, 26 March 1992, p. A17.
38. Joan Claybrook, *Retreat from Safety: Reagan's Attack on America's Health* (New York: Pantheon, 1984), pp. 1–8.
39. Russell Mokhiber, "The Ten Worst Corporations of 1993," *Multinational Monitor* 14, no. 12 (December 1993), p. 12; Cattle-King example from Claybrook, p. 22.
40. Todd S. Purdum, "Meat Inspections Facing Overhaul, First in 90 Years," *New York Times*, 7 July 1996, pp. 1, 11.
41. Quoted in David R. Simon, and D. Stanley Eitzen, *Elite Deviance*, 4th ed. (Boston: Allyn and Bacon, 1993), p. 122.
42. Claybrook, pp. 168–69.
43. Mark Dowie, "Pinto Madness," *The Best of Mother Jones* (Foundation for National Progress, 1985), pp. 59–69, quote p. 63.
44. From WBAI, 99.5 FM, New York City, evening news, 6 December 1994. Tape of broadcast available from Pacifica Radio Archive, 3729 Cahuenga Blvd. West, N. Hollywood, CA 91604.
45. Author's calculation from *Fortune*, 18 April 1993, p. 296.
46. Peter Freund, and George Martin, *The Ecology of the Automobile* (Montreal: Black Rose Books, 1993), p. 36.
47. Philip J. Hilts, "23 Million People Found Living Where Air Particles Exceed Code," *New York Times*, 30 April 1994, p. 9; "Study Ties Fouled Air to High Urban Death Rates," *New York Times*, 9 February 1993.
48. Examples of estimates can be found in Ann Misch, "Assessing Environmental Health Risks," in *State of the World: 1994*, ed. Linda Starke (New York: W. W. Norton & Co., 1994), p. 123; Samuel S. Epstein, *The Politics of Cancer* (San Francisco: Sierra Club Books), p. 23.
49. Edward A. Gargon, "Cancer Deaths Tied to Wastes in Jersey Study," *New York Times*, 8 July 1982; quoted in Tom Johnson, "Environmental Prosecutor Gets the Axe as Post Created by Florio Is Erased," *Star-Ledger*, 16 March 1994, p. 25.
50. Claybrook, p. 118.
51. Quoted in "Weedkillers Imperiling Tap Water," *Star-Ledger*, 19 October 1994, p. 14.
52. Barry Commoner, *The Closing Circle: Man, Nature & Technology* (New York: Bantam Books, 1971), has a useful discussion of the relationship between capitalism and pollution.
53. Quoted in William Greider, *Who Will Tell The People: The Betrayal of American Democracy* (New York: Simon and Schuster, 1992), p. 113.
54. Eula Bingham, and William V. Meader, "Governmental Regulation of Environmental Hazards in the 1990's," *Annual Review of Public Health* 11 (1990): p. 421; quoted in Hawley Truax, "Minorities at Risk," *Environmental Action* (January/February 1990), p. 21.

55. David Burnham, "1965 Memos Show Dow's Anxiety on Dioxin," *New York Times*, 19 April 1983, pp. A1, A18.
56. Quoted in Greider, p. 56.
57. Bruce Van Voorst, "Toxic Dumps: The Lawyers' Money Pit," *Time*, 13 September 1993, pp. 63–64.
58. Quoted in Marc Cooper, "Sickness on Evelina Street," *Village Voice*, 7 September 1993, pp. 33–37.
59. Allen R. Myerson, "This Is the House That Greed Built," *New York Times*, 2 April 1995, Section 3, pp. 1, 14; Solomon P. Ortiz, "America's Third World: Colonias," in *Annual Editions: Race and Ethnic Relations 91/92*, ed. John A. Kromkowski (Guilford, Conn.: Dushkin Publishing Group, 1991), pp. 80–82.
60. Ken Geiser, and Gerry Waneck, "PCBs and Warren County," in *Unequal Protection: Environmental Justice and Communities of Color*, ed. Robert D. Bullard (San Francisco: Sierra Club Books, 1994), pp. 43–52; Benjamin F. Chavis Jr., "Foreword" to *Confronting Environmental Racism: Voices from the Grassroots*, ed. Robert D. Bullard (Boston: South End Press, 1993), p. 3.
61. Robert Bullard, "Environmental Justice for All," in Bullard, ed., 1994, p. 17; Peter Marks, "Issues of Race and Pollution Trouble L.I. Town," *New York Times*, 12 November 1994, pp. 23, 27.
62. Bullard, ed., 1994, p. 9.
63. Bullard, ed., 1994, p. 9; Regina Austin, and Michael Schill, "Black, Brown, Red and Poisoned," in Bullard, ed., 1994, p. 55; Richard Moore, and Louis Head, "Building a Net That Works: SWOP," in Bullard, ed., 1994, p. 198.
64. Quoted in Bullard, ed., 1994, p. 5.
65. Jane Kay, "California's Endangered Communities of Color," in Bullard, ed., 1994, pp. 157–59.
66. Eric Mann, *L.A.'s Lethal Air: New Strategies for Policy, Organizing, and Action* (Los Angeles: Labor/Community Strategy Center, 1991), p. 5; Robert Reinhold, "Hard Times Dilute Enthusiasm for Clean-Air Law," *New York Times*, 26 November 1993, pp. A1, A30.
67. Alecia Swasy, *Soap Opera: The Inside Story of Procter & Gamble* (New York: Times Books, 1993), pp. 206–34. Many dangerous activities of this company are discussed throughout.
68. David Helvarg, "The War on Greens," *Nation*, 28 November 1994, p. 651; Liane Clorfene Casten, "Toxic Burn: Agent Orange's Forgotten Victims," *Nation*, 4 November 1991, p. 551.
69. James Ridgeway, "The Posse Goes to Washington: How the Militias and Far Right Got a Foothold on Capitol Hill," *Village Voice*, 23 May 1995, p. 17; John H. Cushman Jr., "Inquiry Urged into Possible Link Between Anti-Government Groups," *New York Times*, 5 May 1995, p. A22; Helvarg, p. 651.

7 / Militarism: The Circle of Violence, Interpersonal and Structural

Corporations and the government perpetuate the structural violence discussed previously. They also contribute to violence by supporting militarism. Even when wars are not being fought, structural violence results from the continuing effects of combat, accidents, and environmental contamination, as well as the economic impact of military spending. Interpersonal violence results from experimentation and the development of a "warrior" culture. Militarism also contributes to the erosion of democracy by making it harder to create a more egalitarian, less violent country.

Although the United States lags behind other developed capitalist countries in expenditures for social spending that can lessen violence, there is one area where this country has been and continues to be the biggest spender: the military. With about 6 percent of the world's population, in 1993, the United States accounted for 34 percent of the total military spending in the world. Our taxes pay the costs of war and preparation for war; the average family contributed over $3,000 annually to the military budget between 1975 and 1992.[1] The major victims of this spending are the people whose countries have been invaded and ravaged by U.S. military forces. Their enormous pain and suffering can only be alluded to here, but there have been many victims of U.S. militarism in this country as well.

The sums that have been spent on wars, invasions, weapons, and so on are hard to conceive, with the lowest estimate over $4 trillion since the end of World War II, about 75 percent of that amount spent during the Reagan–Bush years.[2] Between 1994 and 1999, the Pentagon will be spending another $1.2 trillion. In 1996, the military will have received at least $256.6 billion. This is the publicly acknowledged budget, but there is also a classified military budget, adding up to about $36 billion a year, most of which is accounted for by the CIA's classified appropriation of about $28 billion a year.[3] Military spending data do not include the military-related expenditures of NASA and the Department of Energy, which runs nuclear weapons installations and whose work on nuclear energy has many military implications.

One way to try to get a perspective on these vast sums is to suppose that you, the reader, have won a stupendous lottery. First, imagine you have won $1 million to be given to you in $1,000 checks, 50 weeks out of each year, until the money is all gone. If this were the case, you would receive your weekly check for the next 20 years. That would be nice, but what if you had won $1 billion? You and your heirs would get $1,000 a week for the next 20,000 years. And if you won $1 trillion, the checks would be in the mail, assuming there was one, for the next 20 million years.

From War to "Defense"

Military spending contributes to inequality by benefiting the already wealthy while diminishing the quality of life for the great majority of our population. The ways in which this happens will be detailed below. The public must believe this spending is in their interest. Because there is no obvious threat to the great majority from outside forces, fear must be created.

Creating the illusion that we are a nation under siege from hostile forces began very soon after World War II. The United States, unscathed among the warring nations, emerged as the world's economically strongest country. Yet the people of this country were soon led to believe they were in great danger and were told it was necessary to support an unprecedented peacetime military establishment.

The language manipulation discussed in chapter 2 was used to this end. For over one hundred and fifty years, the United States had a Department of War. Then, in 1947, in what euphemisms expert and Professor of English William Lutz describes as "the doublespeak coup of the century," the War Department was transformed into the Department of Defense.[4] Two years after the war officially ended, the general public may have felt financial resources could be used for peacetime purposes, but how can you argue against spending money to "defend" your country? The Soviet Union was depicted as a major threat to the United States.

The Soviet Union suffered immense destruction during World War II. Twenty million people were killed, 15 cities, 1,710 towns, 70,000 villages, 32,000 industrial enterprises, and the infrastructure of railroads, highways, and bridges were in ruins. Yet only a year after the War was over, the Cold War had begun. The U.S. public was taught by government, schools, Hollywood, and the media to fear our former wartime ally, a main force in the defeat of German fascism, the Soviet Union. The public was told the Soviets were engaged in a fearsome military buildup. We had to close the gap or become Soviet slaves. The only genuine gap was between the propaganda and the actuality of the arms race. The United States had a head start in this contest that it maintained until the collapse of the Soviet Union.

For its part, the Soviet Union had good reason to fear U.S. intentions. The United States stationed troops in over seventy countries, including Guam, Panama, Germany, Greece, the United Kingdom, Turkey, the Philippines, South Korea, and Cuba. Many of these bases, of course, are still in existence. The U.S. military can truthfully say, "the sun never sets on the United States flag." In contrast, as of 1980, Soviet troops were stationed in about six foreign countries, none of which bordered the United States.[5] These circumstances are at least a partial explanation of the Soviets' own arms program, which was then used to justify further the U.S. buildup.

If one looks at the sequence of events, almost all major arms buildups in the Soviet Union were in response to U.S. initiatives. In 1949, NATO was created as a military alliance of the United States, Western European countries, and Turkey. Particularly disquieting to the Soviets was the inclusion of Germany, which had invaded Russia twice in the twentieth century. The Warsaw Pact, a Soviet-led military alliance of the Eastern European countries, was formed two years later. The Soviet Union developed an atomic bomb in 1949, four years after the United States, and a hydrogen bomb in 1955, three years after this country.

Robert C. Aldridge, an expert in the arms race, pointed out in 1983:

> During almost four decades of the nuclear age it has been the United States which has led virtually every escalation in weapons production while the Soviet Union has, for the most part, tried to catch up. At only two points in the arms race did the Soviets have leading breakthroughs—when they launched the first intercontinental ballistic missile (ICBM) and when they put the first satellite into orbit; both in 1957. But their early accomplishments in those fields were shallow. The USSR had neither the resources nor the momentum to press ahead and they were soon surpassed by the U.S.[6]

The argument that the U.S. military buildup was a response to a Soviet threat does not hold up. This threat was knowingly exaggerated by government agencies and spokespeople to justify new weapons systems or greater military appropriations. Thus, during the Kennedy administration, U.S. citizens were warned there was a dangerous "missile gap"; they were not told it was the Soviets on the minus side.

Robert McNamara, secretary of defense from 1961 to 1968, former president of Ford Motors, later head of the World Bank, acknowledged in 1982 that the alleged gap under his watch

> was a function of forces within the Defense Department that... were

trying to support their particular program—in that case, an expansion of U.S. missile production—by overstating the Soviet force.[7]

In 1995, McNamara also admitted that the administrations in which he served consistently misled the U.S. public about the war in Vietnam. It was hoped that these lies would increase popular support for an increasingly unpopular war.[8]

Exaggerations, distortions, and falsehoods continued up until the collapse of our supposed enemy. The Reagan administration warned that the Soviets would be capable of a nuclear first strike that could destroy this country's defense system. Later administration officials admitted there was no real threat. The Pentagon has continued to use terms that imply or state directly the idea that the U.S. military might is used for defending all of us. The war against Iraq was first termed "Operation Desert Shield"; the 1989 invasion of Panama was "Operation Just Cause."

A study of military spending in the 1980s by the congressional investigating agency, the General Accounting Office (GAO), found a pattern of lies by the Pentagon to justify building very expensive weapons systems. Although parts of the report are classified, an unclassified summary claimed there had been

> dubious support for claims of . . . high performance, insufficient and often unrealistic testing, understated cost, incomplete or unrepresentative reporting, lack of systematic comparisons against the weapons they were to replace and unconvincing rationales for their development in the first place.[9]

Furthermore, Soviet efforts to reduce tensions were rejected without a public discussion of whether these should not at least be seriously explored as an alternative to an arms buildup.[10]

U.S. Citizens: Victims of the U.S. Military

MILITARY CASUALTIES

The most direct victims of the U.S. war machine are the military personnel killed, maimed, or psychologically traumatized by what they have seen and done. The Vietnam War killed over 1,921,000 Vietnamese and 58,000 U.S. troops. Many of those not killed or wounded also suffered. A Massachusetts study of white male Vietnam veterans found that their death rates for stroke, motor vehicle deaths, cancer, and suicide were higher than for comparable groups of nonveterans.

Over a million Vietnam vets have experienced post-traumatic stress disorder, suffering from:

... various psychiatric illnesses; they are five times more likely than those without the disorder to be unemployed; 70% have been divorced; almost half have been arrested or in jail at least once; and they are two to six times as likely to abuse alcohol or drugs.

The children of traumatized veterans are also at risk for emotional problems.[11]

Even the very short Gulf War produced problems for those experiencing its horrors firsthand. "Gulf Syndrome" is the term describing the diverse health problems of those who returned from the Persian Gulf. Military personnel received untested drugs and vaccines and were exposed to radiation from uranium in artillery shells and possibly to vapors from Iraqi chemical and biological weapons that were bombed by the United States. Some of these weapons had been sold to Iraq by U.S. companies.[12] Like their Vietnam predecessors, Gulf veterans are experiencing marital difficulties, alcohol abuse, high rates of unemployment, and homelessness. Studies show 10 to 15 percent have post-traumatic stress disorder. Children conceived by Gulf War personnel have very high rates of birth defects.[13]

The effects of war linger on. Even World War II still takes a toll on former service personnel. Since the 1940s, the United States has prepared for nuclear war against the Soviets. From one quarter to one half million troops were exposed to 184 nuclear bomb tests occurring between 1946 and the end of atmospheric testing in 1963. These "atomic veterans" were guinea pigs used by government scientists who were seeking information about the effects of radiation on a soldier's stress levels and the answer to the question, How would ground forces perform following a nuclear bomb?

The scientists already knew enough about radiation to wear protective clothing as they approached "ground zero." But ordinary soldiers walked into contaminated areas shielded by little more than reassurances that "radiation from an atomic weapon when burst in the air, is all gone in a minute and a half." Years later, many are dying from cancer. Nancy Cooper, widowed by her husband's leukemia, mournfully criticized the government: "They were promised checkups. If they had looked they would have found that Paul had leukemia.... I feel it's just the same as if they'd shot him. They took his life."[14]

CIVILIAN RISKS: "THE BUCHENWALD TOUCH"

Civilians are also victims of militarism. Beginning in the 1940s, the government knowingly exposed unwarned civilian populations to nuclear testing and radioactive substances. "Downwinders" are the thousands of people who lived in the seven Western states that were exposed to the radioactive fallout from open-air testing which contaminated air, food, and water. The cancer rates for downwinders are higher than for the general population.

Thousands of nuclear experiments were conducted secretly between 1944 and 1974. The secrecy was partly to prevent lawsuits and public criticism. In 1993, the government released a 1950 memo warning that if knowledge of the experiments became public, the Atomic Energy Commission (AEC) would be subject to considerable criticism for having "a little of the Buchenwald touch." Buchenwald was one of the Nazi concentration camps where human experiments were conducted. The risks were known at the time; indeed, there were debates among officials over whether a less populated area should be chosen for testing. But as one scientist, Dr. Gioacchino Failla, working for the AEC wrote in a memo, "The time has come when we should take some risk and get some information."[15]

The AEC conducted over four hundred experiments, including some on newborns who were given radioactive iodine. Scientists from Harvard and the Massachusetts Institute of Technology administered radioactive laced cereals to retarded boys at a Massachusetts state school. The boys were told they were part of a science club and given periodic blood tests. At the University of Rochester Medical Center, at least thirty-one patients were injected with plutonium and uranium in an effort to find out the possible consequences of radiation exposure should there ever be a nuclear war.[16]

In 1990, following years of agitation, the Radiation Exposure Compensation trust fund of $200 million was created by the federal government for persons having any one or more of thirteen specific types of cancer connected to radiation exposure. The money is difficult to claim, and obviously it cannot make up for the loss of family and friends. Claudia Peterson of St. George, Utah, watched her six-year-old daughter and thirty-seven-year-old sister die of cancer. She says, grievously, "I can't close my eyes and think about my daughter without it physically tearing my heart out." Many in St. George share her experiences. Her town, she laments, is "living a nightmare, and we can't wake up."[17]

Biological weapons have also been tested on human subjects. Between 1979 and 1988, the Army sprayed bacteria at the Dugway Proving Ground in Utah. This was a repeat of 239 tests done from 1949–69 at Washington National Airport, in New York City subways, and at sites in San Francisco, Minneapolis, St. Louis, Key West, and elsewhere. Political scientist Leonard Cole, who wrote a major study of the germ warfare program, estimates that "millions of citizens" were exposed to "countless trillions of bacteria and particles."

Germ warfare was justified as a means of protecting U.S. citizens against a ruthless enemy. In 1981, William M. Creasey, a retired major general involved in the programs, testified that testing in cities, as opposed to an unpopulated place such as a salt mine, was crucial, because biological warfare is "designed to work against people, and you have to test . . . in the kind of place where people live and work." A scientist claimed with a verbal shrug that where national security is involved, "We have to do some things that are possibly not the nicest things."[18]

Class factors and racism influenced the testing. Wanting to ensure minimal interference with their experiments in St. Louis, researchers chose a "slum district" as their test site, believing that the residents in this neighborhood would have less curiosity and concern about unusual activities. Should the community object, extra police were on hand "to quell any disturbances resulting from the presence of the test crew."

In at least one test, African-Americans were the unknowing subjects of a spraying with the bacterial agent, *Aspergillus fumigatus*, which can cause potentially fatal respiratory, ear, sinus, bone, and spinal infections. Believing that African-Americans might have different physiologies than whites and with a large number of blacks working as laborers, the army feared these workers might be especially vulnerable to the bacteria. The military argued they needed to see how a dispersal of this agent would spread among the blacks, because if they were incapacitated, this "would seriously affect the operation of the supply system." To this end they contaminated the crates these workers were handling at the Norfolk, Virginia Supply Depot.[19]

The military claims that the life-forms used in all tests were harmless, ignoring the dangers to infants, old people, and those with health problems. The army did not monitor those sprayed to see if any harm had occurred; civilian medical personnel at some test sites did, however, find unusual deaths and illnesses following the sprayings. It was one of these deaths, Edward Nevin in San Francisco, that led to a 1977 lawsuit that finally brought the biological warfare experiments to light. Leonard Cole concludes that "a fixation with national security" doesn't protect the public, rather "it encourages an ethos that permits suspension of safety and ethical considerations."[20]

DANGERS TO COMMUNITIES AND WORKERS

A current public health danger comes from nerve gas, which is stored before it is destroyed as a result of arms control agreements. A $450 million nerve-gas incinerator was constructed near Salt Lake City, Utah. The facility is flawed and some nerve gas has escaped. A safety manager employed by the builder, EG&G, was fired after he listed 119 problems with the plant. At least eight more similar incinerators, costing about $10 billion, are planned in eight more states if the army can override community opposition.

Unknown quantities of plutonium from the production of nuclear weapons are stored in thousands of plastic bags, metal cans, pipes, air ducts, and tanks in thirteen states, including Colorado, New Mexico, Tennessee, Texas, and California. Dr. Tara J. O'Toole, assistant secretary of energy, described the containment as "widely deficient" and noted that these "containers were really only intended to hold the stuff until we got around to recycling it in the next weapons campaign." The plutonium's radiation causes leaks in the drums. The Department of Energy released a report listing 299 problems with the plutonium storage and warned that there are "significant hazards to workers, the public and environment and little progress has been made to aggressively address the problem."[21]

Nuclear facilities are run by private corporations who bear a responsibility for what has happened to atomic workers. Rockwell International operated the DOE's plant at Rocky Flats, Colorado, where the company knowingly violated environmental laws. Toxic chemicals leaked into creeks running into the Denver water supply. Both Rockwell and the DOE lied about what was happening. In 1987, Rockwell received an $8.6 million bonus from the DOE for having "excellent management." The plant has a history of accidents and is considered the most hazardous of all the nuclear weapons manufacturing sites by the DOE itself.[22]

General Electric's nuclear weapons contracts led to pollution of a huge area of Washington State, helped make the Columbia River the most radioactive in the world, and exposed local populations to high levels of radiation. GE's Hanford, Washington, facility was used for producing nuclear weapons components and for testing the effects of radiation on health. The federal government used Hanford to test its fallout monitoring technology. Hanford families now suffer the consequences. In one area known locally as "Death Mile," twenty-seven out of twenty-eight families have severe health problems, including cancers and deformed births. The federal government and GE continue to fight the release of information about the Hanford experiments.

GE also operates a facility at the Knolls Atomic Laboratories outside Schenectady, New York. A Knolls engineer, Robert F. Coles, died of a cancer that had invaded his entire body after nine exposures to radiation. In a farewell letter to his brother, he wrote:

> I have been in pain for nearly a year and the thought of not being with them [his children] tears at my heart. . . . I do think it is through GE's negligent policies I was exposed to internal and external radiation of unknown quantities, and this is why I am now dying of cancer.[23]

The DOE has withheld data on the health impact of nuclear weapons, and the plants involved are exempt from OSHA inspections.

A *New York Times* investigation of the approximately sixty-seven thousand people working in weapons plants revealed that although the workers are highly patriotic, they are also afraid that they are being lied to and that they are in danger. At many plants, workers remember colleagues who died of brain tumors or some other form of cancer. In Fernold, Ohio, one worker told a reporter, "I figure we all got the same thing. I think we all got it in our system and some day it's going to kill us." Another said,

> All I can do is hope for the best, take out lots of insurance. You just keep thinking about payday. You just go home and play with the kids ... and you don't think about the plant.

DOE epidemiologist Dr. Shirley A. Fry had a more complacent view: "It's understandable that people are concerned.... But there are many other things that affect our health other than our jobs."[24]

SPENDING FOR THE MILITARY IS SPENDING FOR UNEMPLOYMENT

Throughout this book we have been emphasizing that prolonged unemployment affects people's health and their social relations in ways that fit our definition of violence. Very high levels of military spending contribute in several ways to increased joblessness, which, in turn, is associated with a rise in violence, as discussed in chapter 3.

Military production paradoxically creates jobs and unemployment. This is because money spent manufacturing military equipment creates fewer jobs per dollar than does civilian production. The Council on Economic Priorities estimated in the 1980s that for each billion dollars of military supply spending twenty-eight thousand jobs are generated. The same amount spent for mass transit would create thirty-two thousand jobs and for education, seventy-one thousand. A 1992 study by the Congressional Research Service claimed that each billion dollars transferred from the military to the civilian sector for things like repair or new construction of highways and streets, or health care, would produce a net gain of 4,054 jobs. Money transferred from the military to the civilian sector would also produce usable goods and services contributing to an improvement in the quality of life.[25]

Minority groups with the highest unemployment rates benefit the least from military spending. The engineers, computer specialists, and mathematicians who work in the weapons industry are likely to be white and male. Furthermore, military production is spread unevenly around the country. The "gunbelt" centers of military production are the ones least likely to be suffering from the problems of industrial decline. The traditional manufacturing centers discussed earlier, primarily in the Northeast and Midwest, have declined because of the declining competitiveness of U.S. products.

In addition, military production has made the United States less competitive internationally. Civilian products made in the United States do not do as well as those made in Japan and Germany, which means there will be less need for workers in the consumer manufacturing sector. The United States is a premier exporter of military technology, but the same is not true for other American products.

Money is spent on improving weapons, but not as much is spent for developing better consumer goods. About 70 percent of federal dollars for research and development goes for military purposes here; for Germany and Japan, the figures are 10 to 15 percent and 5 percent, respectively.[26] The siphoning of engineering talent to the aerospace industries has taken a toll on the steel, auto, consumer electronics, and machine tool industries. Markusen and Yudken summarize some of the consequences:

> While American firms labor to produce a Stealth bomber, a laser gun, or a software system to demanding military specifications, their counterparts abroad are free to lavish their best brains and resources on commercial developments with far greater payoffs to the economy.[27]

In 1989, the Federal Office of Technology Assessment compared the United States to Western Europe and Japan—countries that "construct their technology efforts with a greater emphasis on economic development over military development than does the United States."[28] Military intervention also affects employment. Repressive regimes, which are advantageous to corporate profits as discussed below, mean a loss of jobs in the United States.

The dissolution of the Soviet Union and the end of the Cold War heralded a chance for a "peace dividend," the reallocation of monies used for the military to more useful purposes. Although the international political situation has changed dramatically, reductions in U.S. military spending are relatively minor in comparison.

"WE DON'T HAVE ANY MONEY": WEAPONS OR SOCIAL SPENDING

True defense spending should increase a people's security, but in the United States, we are more insecure as a result of monies expended on the military. A better educated, healthier population is a goal few would argue against. Every dollar spent on war preparations is a dollar less for repairing our dangerously decaying infrastructure, feeding the hungry, sheltering the homeless, educating our entire population, providing recreation facilities, cleaning our contaminated environment, maintaining public libraries, and caring for the physically and mentally ill. Explaining why the federal government will be cutting Medicare and Medicaid funding, then Senate Majority Leader Robert Dole said, "We don't have any money."[29] Yet the House voted to give the Pentagon $7 billion more for 1996 and 1997 than had even been requested by the military.[30]

As Washington has increased military spending, it has decreased spending on other needed services. In 1996, Congress cut $12 billion from programs

Table 7.1 Federal Spending and Slashing for Selected Programs, 1980–95

Military	$1,116 billion
Corrections	$59 billion
Housing	Cut $390 billion
Aid to cities	Cut $117 billion
Job training	Cut $101 billion
Education	Cut $59 billion
Antipoverty programs	Cut $49 billion

Source: Common Agenda Coalition and the National Priorities Project, *Creating a Common Agenda*, p. 7.

Table 7.2 1995 Federal Budget

Military spending	$250 billion
Education	$33 billion
Housing	$27 billion
Environmental protection	$6 billion
Job training	$5 billion

Source: Common Agenda Coalition and the National Priorities Project, *Creating a Common Agenda*, p. 8.

sponsored by the Departments of Health and Human Services and the Department of Labor. In 1970, the federal government provided 17 percent of costs of higher education, making this more affordable; in 1992, it provided just 12 percent of the funding. Federal contributions to primary and secondary education have also declined.[31] The deficit is sometimes used as the justification for this, but a large part of the deficit itself can be traced to military spending.

At $1 billion a day, the minimal cost of the Gulf War was $49 billion. This six-and-a-half-week war cost more in dollars than the 1991 federal budget for education, job training, and employment services. Table 7.1 shows other recent priorities in federal spending.

The federal budget for 1995 is shown in Table 7.2. Does this make you feel more secure?

If social services were substituted for military spending, here are some trade-offs that could be made[32]:

One C-17 Cargo Plane = $340 million = Summer job training for 90,000 youths

One Centurion Submarine = $1.3 billion = Immunizations for every unimmunized child in the United States for next ten years

A 3 percent cut in military aid for South Korea = $3 billion = 424 new elementary schools

Critics of social spending like to say you can't solve a problem by throwing money at it, but they never claim this to be case with our military security. There is no guarantee that money not spent on the military would go for social spending; campaigns would still be needed for this. However, one major argument against this spending, "we just can't afford it," could be more easily countered.

"A WARRIOR NATION": TRAINED FOR VIOLENCE

On 4 April 1967, exactly one year before his assassination, Martin Luther King Jr. eloquently expressed his opposition to the Vietnam War. Speaking at the Riverside Church in New York City, he outlined how the war took away "skills and money like some demonic, destructive suction tube" and related how he had come "to see the war as an enemy of the poor."

King believed that the war had more than a material effect on the United States. It taught lessons of malice and violence to the troops, "injecting poisonous drugs of hate into the veins of people normally humane." King asked how he could preach against violence at home when young men would ask him, "What about Vietnam?" Isn't the United States

> using massive doses of violence to solve its problems, to bring about the changes it wanted? Their questions hit home, and I knew that I could never again raise my voice against the violence of the oppressed in the ghettos without having first spoken clearly to the greatest purveyor of violence in the world today—my own government.[33]

Since King's speech, U.S. military interventions have occurred in Laos and Cambodia, Grenada, Panama, Nicaragua, El Salvador, the Persian Gulf, and Somalia. People are still being taught that force is the way to achieve goals. As Senator Daniel Moynihan explained to Arab leaders in September 1990, "You must understand that Americans are a warrior nation."[34]

Recent presidents provide warrior-role models for dealing with crises. They have done this by attacking other countries with little provocation but with increases in their poll approval ratings. Pollsters refer to such matters as "rally events." Reagan's popularity increased after the 1983 invasion of Grenada, which, in turn, followed the bombing of a U.S. Marine installation in Lebanon. That humiliation was forgotten because of the success in Grenada. After the 1989 invasion of Panama, George Bush proudly described himself as a "macho man," and Lee Atwater, then chair of the Republican National Committee, declared that now Bush had "knocked the question about being timid and a wimp out of the stadium."[35]

On 26 June 1993, President Clinton ordered a U.S. missile attack on intelligence headquarters in the Iraqi capital of Baghdad. The president claimed that there was "compelling evidence that there was in fact a plot to assassinate former President Bush" as retaliation for the Gulf War in 1991. Twenty-three cruise missiles were launched, seven struck a civilian neighborhood, killing eight people and wounding many more. It is highly doubtful that such a plot existed. Clinton's action is not so different from Colin Ferguson who believed he had a right to kill LIRR passengers because whites and "Uncle Toms had mistreated him." Clinton's attack on Iraqi civilians won him a boost in the polls. In September 1996, with the election campaign in full swing, Clinton ordered Cruise missile strikes at Iraq again.[36]

WARRIOR MEN = PROBABLE SEX OFFENDERS

The military's influence is pervasive, as seen in popular movies, video games, toys, and in the rise of paramilitary organizations. The military has helped shape U.S. conceptions of masculinity, for years promising to make men out of boys. A real man is aggressive, a protector, and assertively heterosexual. This is one reason homosexuality was so anathema to the military, and why women have had a difficult time gaining equality in the armed forces. During training, recruits were called "faggots," "ladies," "girls" to show their trainers' contempt for their alleged weaknesses.

We noted earlier that sexual assaults can provide an affirmation of masculinity for some men. The view of masculinity encouraged by the military has been associated with sexual violence and a predatory attitude toward women. In basic training men used to chant

> This is my rifle.
> This is my gun. [Pointing to their crotch]
> One is for fighting.
> The other's for fun.

The military even helps to arrange the "fun." Prostitution is tolerated around U.S. bases, and rapes of foreign women are rarely punished. A thoroughly researched series of articles in the *Dayton Daily News* found a pattern of very lenient treatment given to hundreds of sex offenders by military courts.[37]

At least thirty-three Gulf servicewomen claimed they were raped by their own colleagues. One twenty-nine-year-old army mechanic, Jacqueline Ortiz, was among them. A year later she was suffering from insomnia, headaches, and nausea. She told Senate investigators: "It's very difficult to deal with. I was very proud to serve my country but not to be a sex slave to someone who had a problem with power." Specialist Ortiz and other women testified that their superiors were unresponsive to their complaints. A 1996 Pentagon study found that more than 55 percent of military women questioned had experienced some form of sexual harassment. Nearly 20 percent of the women did not report the incidents because they feared they would damage their careers.[38]

The tough-guy attitude toward women is also illustrated by the Tailhook scandal. At the annual naval aviators' convention in Las Vegas in 1991, ninety women were sexually assaulted by at least 117 young officers. Some of the men wore tee shirts emblazoned with the words "Women Are Property." The officers protected one another, and because the women could not identify individual attackers, none of the pilots were punished. Naval Inspector General Rear Admiral George W. Davis's report on the incident noted the nonchalance of the men involved:

> A common thread running through the overwhelming majority of interviews was "what's the big deal?" There is still little understanding of the nature, severity and number of assaults which occurred.[39]

WARRIOR MEN = PARAMILITARY ACTIVITIES

Right-wing militia members see the federal government as threatening their freedom. They have accepted the idea that the way to correct a problem is to identify those responsible for it and kill them—the military response to a troublesome situation.

Keystones in the paramilitary subculture are *Soldier of Fortune* (*SOF*) magazine and the National Rifle Association (NRA). Since 1981, *SOF* has hosted an annual four-day convention in Las Vegas, described by participant sociologist James William Gibson as "a celebration of violence." Conventioneers can attend seminars, some of which feature foreign military officers, and lectures such as the one with an *SOF* editor on "Submachine Guns: Their History and Use." They can buy tee shirts trivializing killing, such as one showing snipers with sophisticated weapons and the words, "Reach Out and Touch Someone." Given the association between militarism and male sexuality, it is not surprising that posters of scantily clad women decorate the convention site. Similarly undressed women are part of the exhibits and events.[40]

The federal government supports the *SOF* convention by sending agents from law enforcement agencies, such as the Drug Enforcement Agency, to give speeches. Local, state, and federal police also send personnel to gun schools run by those with close ties to paramilitary groups such as the NRA. One training camp in Arizona, the Gunsite Ranch, known more formally as the American Pistol Institute, is run by Jeff Cooper, formerly on the NRA board of directors. Cooper believes that patriotic Americans must defend themselves against the CLAMs, an acronym standing for "Congressional Left, Academics, and Media."[41] The Marine Corps, Department of Energy, and the Los Angeles Police Department are among those using the facilities at this ranch. Some police agents use their vacation time to teach at Cooper's Arizona school.

Little boys have long played war games, now adult males and a very few females play them, too, in the form of paintball. James William Gibson estimates that over 2 million men between 1988 and 1994 have put on camouflage uniforms and picked up their toy weapons at one of over a thousand sites all over the country. It is easy to buy a real gun at a store or through the pages of magazines. Since the end of the Vietnam War, in Vietnam, according to Gibson, "Millions of American men [have] purchased combat rifles, pistols and shotguns and begun training to fight their own personal wars."[42]

Some individuals have formed citizen militias who plan to fight the "enemy" on U.S. soil. As discussed earlier, the enemy can include African-Americans, gays, Jews, or federal employees. Radical or progressive groups may be targeted as well, labeled as Communists, the same justification the U.S. government has used for killing people around the world for two decades.

In Greensboro, North Carolina, in 1979, the paramilitary racist and anticommunist tendencies came together in a joint Neo-Nazi, Ku Klux Klan shooting of an anti-Klan march organized by a group called the Communist Workers Party. Five marchers were killed, and twelve of the neofascists were arrested. One of these was a former U.S. Army Special Forces sergeant who proudly declared that the shootings were "the only armed victory over communism in this country."[43] The April 1995 bombing in Oklahoma City also demonstrates the dangers posed by these groups.

Who Benefits?

THE MULTINATIONALS

The key to explaining the military buildup since 1945 is the threat to the profits of multinational corporations and the armaments industry.

Since the Second World War, and the rise of the multinational corporation, U.S. interests have extended to every part of the globe. Multinational corporations (MNCs) are now the dominant form of capitalist enterprises. Their headquarters are in one country, but their production and marketing operations are located in many others. MNCs are wealthy and powerful. The annual sales of the largest exceed the gross national products of some Third World countries with which they deal.

In 1945, the United States, the strongest capitalist country, replaced Great Britain as the dominant imperialist power. The figures below show the growth of U.S. corporate investment and assets abroad.[44]

1950	19 billion dollars
1970	119 billion
1980	396 billion
1993	716 billion

Overseas investments are an important source of corporate profits, with operations abroad accounting for about a quarter of these. To ensure profits, companies want the lowest possible labor costs, the largest possible markets, and the cheapest possible raw materials.

The multinationals use a "global assembly line," producing products or components where wages are low, and creating unemployment in the United States. For example, in 1970, 214,000 workers were making shoes in this country; by 1994, only 60,000 workers were still in this line of work. Nike's line of athletic shoes used to be produced in Maine by workers earning about $7 an hour. Now Nikes are all made in Asia. In Indonesia, a typical Nike worker is getting $1.03 a day, or 14 cents an hour, putting him/her below the Indonesian government's own poverty line, at no benefit to U.S. consumers. The price of the shoes does not go down along with labor costs.[45]

When the Star Spangled Banner is played at the beginning of a baseball game, most fans are unaware that the baseballs are manufactured in Haiti, by women earning about nine cents for each baseball they stitch, or about $3 a day. The balls sell for $3.50–$4 each in the United States.[46] The United States supported a series of dictators in Haiti and only reluctantly came to support Haiti's first democratically elected president, Jean Baptiste Aristide.

With friendly governments in power, U.S. corporations also have access to less regulated marketplaces. Goods that are banned here or that face declining demand can be sold profitably overseas. Tobacco products, pesticides, infant formula, and pharmaceutical products are among these dangerous exports.

At our local supermarkets, we increasingly can find flowers, fruits, vegetables, and seafood imported from Third World countries. There is no need to wait for spring and summer for asparagus, peas, strawberries, and so on. These products, imported by multinationals, are grown on land that used to be mainly used for subsistence agriculture. As agribusiness gains access to this land, poor peasants find themselves forced to leave, moving to the increasingly overcrowded cities in their own country or crossing the unfriendly borders of the United States where they are then blamed for unemployment that has been caused by the multinational corporations.

MAKING THE WORLD SAFE FOR CORPORATE INVESTMENT

A basic assumption of U.S. foreign policy has been that procapitalist governments are to be encouraged, supported, and, if necessary, put into power even against the resistance of their own populations. Intervention in support of business interests is not new; early in our history, this interest centered on the Caribbean and Latin America. Since the 1823 proclaiming of the Monroe Doctrine warning European powers to keep out of the Western hemisphere, the United States has intervened in this region of the world alone over sixty times. In 1935, Major General Smedley Butler, reflecting on his Marine career, made a still apt analysis of the role of the U.S. military:

> I spent thirty-three years and four months in active service.... And during that period I spent most of my time being a high-class muscle man for Big Business, for Wall Street and for the bankers.... I was a gangster for capitalism.... Thus I helped make Mexico ... safe for American oil interests in 1914. I helped make Haiti and Cuba a decent place for the National City Bank boys to collect revenues in ... I helped purify Nicaragua for the international banking house of Brown Brothers in 1909–12. I brought light to the Dominican Republic for American sugar interests in 1916.... In China in 1927 I helped see to it that Standard Oil went its way unmolested.[47]

Current problems in many countries, including Haiti and Guatemala, can be traced to these interventions.

Faced with intolerable conditions that result from national and international inequalities, people in the Third World form progressive movements. Socialist or strongly nationalist governments will want to use resources for the creation of services for the general population, not for increasing stockholder dividends in the developed capitalist countries.

The United States has opposed progressive change and revolutions since 1917 when, along with the other capitalist countries, there was armed intervention to prevent the Soviet revolution from succeeding. In the 1930s and 1940s, the United States supported the anti-Communist forces of Chiang Kai-shek against the Communist forces led by Mao Tse-tung in China. For over thirty years, the United States has been trying to overthrow the socialist government in Cuba.

Following the success of first the Soviet and then the Chinese revolutions, subsequent movements for progressive change were portrayed as examples of expanding communism. Starting in the 1950s in Southeast Asia, the United States tried to prevent a communist-led revolution from succeeding in Vietnam. As early as 1954, Secretary of State John Foster Dulles was declaring that in Southeast Asia, Communist Russia and its Chinese Communist ally were seeking to impose their totalitarian system, posing "a grave threat to the whole free community." He asserted that the United States must meet these threats resolutely and with "action."[48]

When the Soviet Union existed, it was held responsible for revolutionary movements around the world. El Salvador is a recent example of this. Documents "proving" the Soviets were behind nationally based efforts at social change have been fabricated. In this case, the State Department in early 1981 issued a "White Paper" that was supposed to show the rebels were agents of a Communist plot emanating from the USSR. According to the document, although there were real problems in El Salvador, the people were being exploited by "hostile outside forces," in particular, "Cuba, backed by the Soviet Union . . . operating through Nicaragua." These outsiders aim to transform any indigenous movement "into a totalitarian state, threatening the region and robbing the people of their hopes for liberty." Should they prove successful, this will be "a serious threat to the United States."[49] The principle author later admitted that portions of this document were exaggerated and "misleading."[50]

These arguments were fig leaves for violence and repression. In Latin America, as in Southeast Asia, U.S.-backed forces have engaged in some of the most horrible atrocities against populations recorded in recent years. Many of those directing terror operations against local civilian populations received their training at the U.S.-funded School of the Americas now located at Fort Benning, Georgia. Nicknamed the "School for Assassins" by critics, it has an annual budget of $4.2 million and has trained about sixty thousand military officers, many of whom have been accused of human rights violations. Training manuals used by the School advised beating and torturing prisoners, as well as threatening their families, and blackmail.[51]

Chile is a dramatic example of the nature of U.S. foreign policy. In 1970, a progressive candidate, Salvadore Allende, was elected president. His early reforms included nationalizing some industries and redistributing some land. Greater workplace democracy occurred when workers elected the managers of some factories. A full spectrum of political parties continued to exist.

The CIA, working with the Chilean military, was instrumental in the 1973 overthrow of Allende's government, aided by U.S. companies, especially International Telephone and Telegraph (ITT). The United States used its influence in international lending agencies such as the World Bank to ensure that economic assistance to the Allende government did not occur. A look at *New York Times* headlines regarding Chile illustrates what happened.

3/21/73	"C.I.A.-I.T.T. Plans on Chile Reported"
9/22/73	"Military Junta in Chile Prohibits Marxist Parties"
9/25/73	"Ousted Bosses Back at Chile's Plants"
9/26/73	"Chile's Military Chiefs Abolish Nation's Largest Labor Group"
10/20/73	"Chile to Return Seized Companies"
11/12/73	"Private U.S. Loans in Chile Up Sharply"
9/20/74	"C.I.A. Is Linked to Strikes in Chile That Beset Allende"
5/30/75	"Chile Accused of Killing Labor Leaders"
10/19/75	"Evidence Growing on Torture in Chile"

12/22/76	"World Bank Votes Loans to Chile of $60 Million with U.S. in Favor"
10/4/79	"Chile Attracts U.S. Business"

The torture and repression of tens of thousands of people did not deter investment. Referring to Goodyear's decision to invest in postcoup Chile, Jack Carter, the manager of the company's Chilean plant, commented, "I don't think we spent five minutes talking about human rights."[52]

In fact, there is a strong correlation between human rights abuses in a country, the receipt by that country of U.S. aid, and high levels of corporate investment. State Department approval is necessary for arms sales. A country's respect for human rights is not the criteria that decides if this approval will be made. The opposite seems true: repressive regimes accounted for nearly 75 percent of U.S. arms merchants customers in 1993, according to the State Department's own analysis.[53]

THE MILITARY-INDUSTRIAL COMPLEX

The *military-industrial complex* is a symbiotic alliance. Corporations get the contracts for military hardware, and after retirement high-ranking military personnel are offered lucrative positions in the corporate sector. While still in uniform, they obtain weapons to add to their status. These same military personnel will be advising on the purchases of weapons systems.

There are close connections between military officers, highly placed political figures, and the arms industry. Henry Kissinger, Nixon's secretary of state, for example, established a consulting firm in 1982 that had weapons manufacturers as major clients. Kissinger's service on President Reagan's Foreign Intelligence Advisory Board, described by the *New York Times* as "a hush-hush group with access to the nation's most sensitive intelligence," was a valuable resource for such clients.[54]

There were many other connections between the Reagan–Bush administrations and the military industry. Five Boeing executives were members of the Reagan administration, including Assistant Secretary of the Navy Melvyn R. Paisley, Deputy Assistant Secretary of the Navy Harold Kitson Jr., and Deputy Undersecretary of Defense Thomas K. Jones.

Reagan's joint chief of staff, General David Jones, joined General Electric's board of directors. Secretary of the Navy John F. Lehman had an economic interest in a military oriented consulting firm. Physicist Edward Teller, a long-time advocate of a strong military, encouraged Reagan's support for a laser-based defense system, the Strategic Defense Initiative or "Star Wars." He received stock in a laser company that would benefit from such a program as did other Reagan advisors and associates.[55]

John Tower, who as a Texas senator was chair of the Armed Services

Committee, became a consultant for Rockwell International, Textron, Martin Marietta, and LTV Aerospace and Defense. When his bid for secretary of defense under Bush failed, he was appointed to the Foreign Intelligence Advisory Board.[56]

In the Clinton administration, William Perry, secretary of defense, was an advisor on Strategic Defense Initiative programs while serving on the boards of directors of several military suppliers. Perry participated in other military budget discussions involving his interests. He is also a stockholder in United Technologies, which manufactures the Blackhawk helicopter, favored by Clinton even though the military itself wants to eliminate this particular aircraft.

These connections do not in themselves prove that particular weapons systems or strategies are not useful for defense. They do suggest the possibility, however, that self-interest rather than genuine national security needs are involved in military spending decisions.

The Pentagon does not encourage corporations to be patriotic by cutting their costs. Although politicians extol the magic of the marketplace and the wonders of competition, the Pentagon and the private sector have their own way of conducting business. There is little competitive bidding, and there are enormous opportunities to pad costs. Typically a cost-plus pricing system is used. The contractor gets back its stated costs of production plus a percentage, so the higher the costs the greater the profits.

The Pentagon pays ludicrously high prices for goods. Lockheed produced a toilet seat made of plastic and fiberglass for use in fighter planes. The seats cost $640.09 each. Pratt and Whitney charged much less for its bolt for the air force, only $17.59. Of course, if the air force purchasing officer had gone to a local hardware store, he or she could have bought this item for less than twenty-five cents. Boeing originally charged the air force $748 for pliers but reduced the price to only $90 when the higher price became a minor scandal. However, using creative bookkeeping, Boeing's total payment for the contract remained at its original figure.[57]

Given these figures, it is not surprising that corporations typically make heftier profits from their military contracts than their civilian ones, and military firms' profits exceed the average of civilian manufacturers. The General Accounting Office in 1987 reported that military contracts are 120 percent more profitable than nonmilitary ones.[58]

Subsidized by the taxpayers, profitable military industries take advantage of tax loopholes and sometimes do not even pay taxes. Between 1981 and 1983, this was the case with Grumann, Lockheed, General Electric, General Dynamics, and Boeing. Collectively these companies had $10.5 billion in profits. For these same years, the top twelve contractors who did pay taxes paid only an average rate of 1.5 percent on their reported profits.[59]

There are costly problems of mismanagement and outright fraud. The *New York Times* reported in 1990 that

> Twenty-five of the 100 largest Pentagon contractors have been found guilty of government fraud in the last seven years, some more than once. Yet not one has been barred from Government contracting.

The illegal acts included bribery, kickbacks, overcharging, and lying about weapons tests results.[60]

The Pentagon admits it has problems keeping track of its equipment; over a billion dollars worth of weapons a year are "lost." Additional costs occur when items are stockpiled as happened with a tool for the F-14 airplane. The navy bought 53,268 of these tools even though only four a year need to be replaced—this means they won't have to buy any more for over thirteen thousand years. As social critic Michael Parenti said describing this, "When it comes to defense, it's important to plan ahead."[61]

LOOKING FOR AN ENEMY

Although the socialist countries of eastern Europe, including the former Soviet Union, have become capitalist, we are apparently still not safe. The forces that benefit from intervention and military spending have found new "threats" to the well-being of the American people, new ways to justify keeping military spending at high levels. The Pentagon, with agreement from Commanders in Chief Bush and then Clinton, claims military strength must be sufficient to fight two wars in widely separated geographic areas. Yet in no other part of the world does any nation or even combination of nations come close to this country's spending.

There are several new "imperial alibis" for intervention and for keeping military spending high. The "drug war" mentioned earlier is one excuse. Another rationale is the "rogue-state" perspective that claims that such countries as North Korea, Iraq, Libya, and Syria are our enemies, armed with sophisticated weapons and led by moral renegades. Yet in 1994 the most allegedly dangerous nations spent about $9 billion together on their military budgets. This is less than 4 percent of the U.S. military budget of $258 billion.[62]

A brief look at the Gulf War shows the speciousness of recent arguments for intervention. Iraq was portrayed as an aggressor nation, armed with weapons of mass destruction. There was little mention of the fact that these weapons had been sold by Western companies with the approval of their governments. There was not much discussion either of the circumstances of Iraq's invasion of Kuwait, which was siphoning off Iraqi oil. It is possible that diplomacy and economic pressures could have achieved an Iraqi withdrawal without the carnage of the war. Neither strategy was given much chance.

Aggression itself is clearly not the reason why the war with Iraq occurred. Punishing another country for its aggression is a very selective process. If the United States based its foreign and military policy on deterring aggression, we would, for example, have intervened in Indonesia in 1975 to stop the invasion and occupation of East Timor, where two hundred thousand people, a third of the population, have been killed by Indonesian forces which (as of early 1997) were still occupying the country in defiance of international law.

Nonmilitary ways to achieve a more peaceful world are rarely publicly discussed. One way to protect the world against aggression by other powers would be to reduce sharply the international arms trade, in which U.S. companies play a leading role, now accounting for over 50 percent of the weapons sold in the world.[63] This could help prevent future wars but is an unlikely prospect.

WEAKENING OF DEMOCRATIC INSTITUTIONS

At different times, there are different rationales for the military spending that supposedly protects us and preserves our freedoms. We have discussed above how our physical well-being is actually lessened by the huge military budget and by military activities. Freedom and democracy have been jeopardized as well as part of the costs of protecting our way of life.

Transforming our society to a more egalitarian, less violent one is more difficult if we cannot exercise our democratic rights. The government has used the argument of protecting "national security" to weaken progressive dissent. Wars supposedly fought to protect our rights usually involve limiting these rights. During World War II, one hundred ten thousand Japanese, two-thirds of them U.S. citizens, were thrown into internment camps without any genuine proof that they had committed crimes or were a danger. The Cold War saw the antiprogressive repression identified with but not caused by Senator Joseph McCarthy. The Vietnam era was accompanied by the FBI's COINTELPRO, established in 1967 for the purpose of disrupting and destroying progressive groups. U.S. intervention in Central America during the Reagan–Bush administrations was accompanied by giving the CIA the right to spy on domestic dissenters. The threat of foreign terrorism is also being used as an argument for more repressive laws.[64]

Military strategies and technologies have been applied to domestic rebellions. Between 1964 and 1971, the National Guard was called on to quell 196 racial disturbances and about twenty campus protests, during which time there were the infamous shootings at Kent and Jackson state universities. When the 1992 uprising in Los Angeles took place, General Marvin L. Covault was put in charge of twelve thousand troops to be brought to the scene if his superiors thought it necessary. Covault developed the Army's "light infantry," units that can be rapidly deployed but have a great deal of firepower.

In New York City in 1995, when the police moved in to eject squatters forcibly from the building they had spent ten years renovating, they arrived in tanks. Watching the tanks roll down city streets, an observer exclaimed, "It's like we're at war with ourselves."[65]

The fight against communism and now against "terrorism" and "terrorist nations" has wasted resources and chipped away at our hard-won rights. The alleged battle to protect democracy has made us less democratic. We still, however, have rights and freedoms that can be used to fight for a more egalitarian, hopefully less violent society.

Notes

1. Military percentage from Bureau of the Census, *Statistical Abstract of the United States, 1995*, Table 555, p. 359; tax figure from Anne Markuson and Joel Yudken, *Dismantling the Cold War Economy* (New York: Basic Books, 1992), p. 10.
2. Michael Parenti, *Democracy for the Few*, 6th ed. (New York: St. Martin's Press, 1995), pp. 86–87.
3. Todd S. Purdham, "Clinton Signs Bill for $256.6 Billion for Armed Forces," *New York Times*, 24 September 1996, pp. A1, A20; Tim Weiner, "The Pentagon's Post-Cold War Black Budget Is Alive and Prospering," in *Censored: The News That Didn't Make the News—And Why*, ed. Carl Jensen (Chapel Hill, N.C.: Shelburne Press, 1993), p. 52; Tim Weiner, "The Worst-Kept Secret in the Capital," *New York Times*, 21 July 1994, p. B10. Weiner won a Pulitzer Prize in 1988 for his reporting on the secret military budget.
4. William Lutz, *DoubleSpeak* (New York: HarperCollins, 1989), p. 170.
5. Common Agenda Coalition and the National Priorities Project, *Creating a Common Agenda* (Northhampton, Mass.: National Priorities Project, n.d.), p. 58; David R. Simon, and D. Stanley Eitzen, *Elite Deviance*, 4th ed. (Boston: Allyn and Bacon, 1993), p. 166; Albert Szymanski, *The Logic of Imperialism* (New York: Praeger, 1981), p. 195.
6. Robert C. Aldridge, *First Strike! The Pentagon's Strategy for Nuclear War* (Boston: South End Press, 1983), p. 256.
7. Quoted in Stephen Rosskamm Shalom, *Imperial Alibis: Rationalizing U.S. Intervention after the Cold War* (Boston: South End Press, 1993), p. 28; discussions of distortions of Soviet military power can be found also in David Gold and Stephen Rose, *A Primer on the Arms Race* (Baltimore, Md.: Social Graphics Co., 1983); Simon and Eitzen, pp. 180–82.
8. For an example of McNamara's revised thinking, see R. W. Apple Jr., "McNamara Recalls, and Regrets, Vietnam," *New York Times*, 9 April 1995, pp. 1, 12. His thoughts are elaborated in his memoirs, *In Retrospect: The Tragedy and Lessons of Vietnam* (New York: Times Books, 1995).
9. Quoted in Tim Weiner, "Military Accused of Lies over Arms," *New York Times*, 28 June 1993, p. A10.

10. Shalom, p. 26.
11. Robert Jay Lifton, *Home from the War: Learning from Vietnam Veterans* (Boston: Beacon Press, 1992), p. ix.
12. Eric Schmitt, "The Gulf War Veteran: Victorious in War, Not Yet at Peace," *New York Times*, 28 May 1995, Section 4, p. 4; Laura Flanders, "Mal de Guerre," *Nation*, 7 March 1994, pp. 292–93. There continues to be controversy about this issue. As of late 1996, the Pentagon was denying U.S. troops had been exposed to chemical weapons, veterans were insisting they were, and a presidential committee claimed the Defense Department's accounts were not credible. Philip Shenon, "Gulf War Veterans in Navy Unit Tell of an Iraqi Chemical Attack," *New York Times*, 20 September 1996, pp. A1, A24; Shenon, "Presidential Panel Says Pentagon Lacks Credibility," *New York Times*, 6 September 1996, p. A22.
13. Jimmie Briggs, Kenneth Miller, and Derek Hudson, "The Tiny Victims of Desert Storm," *Life* (November 1995), pp. 46–52, 54, 56, 58–60, 62.
14. Quotes from Howard L. Rosenberg, *Atomic Soldiers: American Victims of Nuclear Experiments* (Boston: Beacon Press, 1980), pp. 17, 165.
15. Memo quoted in Keith Schneider, "1950 Note Warns about Radiation Tests," *New York Times*, 28 December 1993, p. A8; Failla quoted in Philip J. Hilts, "Fallout Risk Near Atom Tests Was Known, Documents Show," *New York Times*, 15 March 1995, p. A13.
16. Philip J. Hilts, "Radiation Test Secrecy Linked to Lawsuit Fears," *New York Times*, 15 November 1994; Philip J. Hilts, "'Thousands' of Human Experiments," *New York Times*, 22 October 1994; Philip J. Hilts, "Radiation Tests Used Some Healthy People," *New York Times*, 19 January 1995, p. B10; "44 Years Later, the Truth about the 'Science Club,'" *New York Times*, 31 December 1993, p. A18. Details of experiments in which plutonium was injected into eighteen people were reported in *The Albuquerque Tribune*, 15–17 November 1993.
17. Michael Janofsky, "Cold War Chill Lingers Downwind from a Nuclear Bomb-Testing Site," *New York Times*, 11 January 1994, p. A12.
18. Leonard A. Cole, *Clouds of Secrecy: The Army's Germ Warfare Tests over Populated Areas* (Totowa, N.J.: Rowman & Littlefield, 1988), p. 59; quotes from pp. 156, 140. The CIA also conducted experiments on unsuspecting subjects, including administering LSD to mental patients and to bar customers.
19. Quotes from Cole, pp. 64, 45–46. This use of African-Americans is reminiscent of the notorious Tuskegee syphilis experiment of 1932–72 described in James H. Jones, *Bad Blood: The Tuskegee Syphilis Experiment: A Tragedy of Race and Medicine* (New York: The Free Press, 1981).
20. Cole, p. 155.
21. Matthew L. Wald, "Stored Plutonium Is Liable to Leak, Government Says," *New York Times*, 7 December 1994, pp. A1, D20.
22. Quoted in David Johnston, "Weapons Plant Dumped Chemicals into Drinking Water, F.B.I. Says," *New York Times*, 10 June 1989, pp. 1, 10.
23. H. Jack Geiger, "Generations of Poison and Lies," *New York Times*, Op-Ed article, 5 August 1990; quote from the video *Deadly Deception*, produced by INFACT, which has organized a boycott of GE's consumer products in an effort to pressure the company to stop making weapons. The video was broadcast on PBS, Channel 13, New York City, 27 September 1992.
24. Quotes from William Glaberson, "Fear Corrodes Faith at Atomic Plants," *New York Times*, 11 December 1988, p. 36.

25. Elliot Currie, and Jerome Skolnick, *America's Problems: Social Issues and Public Policy*, 2d ed. (Glenview, Ill.: Scott, Foresman and Company, 1988), p. 394; Martin Tolchin, "Shift of Spending Seen as a Benefit," *New York Times*, 26 January 1993, p. A17; Markuson and Yudken, p. 134.
26. Currie and Skolnick, pp. 400–402.
27. Markusen and Yudken, p. 2. See also Seymour Melman, *The Permanent War Economy: American Capitalism in Decline* (New York: Simon and Schuster, 1985), pp. 74–104.
28. Markusen and Yudken, p. 64. They present figures stating that although the military was getting $23 billion for research and development from federal funds, the steel industy was given only $21 million.
29. This list is adapted from Seymour Melman, *The Demilitarized Society: Disarmament and Conversion* (Montreal: Harvest House, 1988), pp. 62–63; Dole quoted in Adam Clymer, "An Accidental Overhaul," *New York Times*, 26 June 1995, p. A1.
30. Eric Schmitt, "House Votes Big Increase in Military Budget for '96," *New York Times*, 16 June 1995, p. A20.
31. "Budget Scorecard," *New York Times*, 26 April 1996, p. A1. There were $23 billion cut altogether from federal programs. Education figures for 1970, Bureau of the Census, *Statistical Abstract of the United States, 1978*, Table 212, p. 136; for 1992, percentage calculated from *Statistical Abstract of the United States, 1995*, Table 284, p. 183.
32. Common Agenda Coalition and the National Priorities Project, *Creating a Common Agenda* (Washington, D.C., n.d), p. 14.
33. Quotes from "Declaration of Independence from the War in Vietnam," *Essay Series* (New York: A. J. Muste Memorial Institute, n.d.), pp. 37, 38. In November 1993, Clinton addressed a group of black ministers and imagined what King would say to violent ghetto youths were he still alive. The president fantasized that King would say he "did not fight for the right of black people to murder other black people." Clinton did not choose to quote what King actually said. See H. Bruce Franklin, "What King really would have said," *Philadelphia Inquirer*, 7 December 1993.
34. Quoted in Barbara Ehrenreich, "The Warrior Culture," in *Beyond the Storm: A Gulf Crisis Reader*, eds. Phyllis Bennis and Michel Moushabeck (New York: Olive Branch Press, 1991), p. 129.
35. Richard L. Berke, "Poll Shows Raid on Iraq Buoyed Clinton's Popularity," *New York Times*, 29 June 1993, p. A7; Bush quoted in Ehrenreich, p. 130; Atwater quoted in James William Gibson, *Warrior Dreams: Violence and Manhood in Post-Vietnam America* (New York: Hill and Wang, 1994), p. 291.
36. *Action Update*, International Action Center, vol. 1, no. 1 (Summer 1993). The FBI had reported that there was a plan to kill George Bush during his visit to Kuwait (April 1993) with a car bomb. A car bomb was discovered in Kuwait, but there was no evidence that it had been manufactured in Iraq or was in any way connected with Iraqi intelligence; Tim Weiner, "Plot by Baghdad to Assassinate Bush Is Questioned," *New York Times*, 25 October 1993; "Clinton Cites L.I.R.R. Shootings," *New York Times*, 12 December 1993, p. 57. For a critique of the 1996 attack, see editorial, "The Iraq Lesson," *Nation*, 23 September 1996, p. 3.
37. Russell Carollo, "Military Secrets," published 1–5 October. For an account of prostitution, see Sandra Pollock Sturdevant, and Brenda Stoltzfus, *Let the Good Times Roll: Prostitution and the U.S. Military in Asia* (New York: New Press, 1992).

38. Quoted in Anne Marie Connell, "Boys Will be Boys: The Tailhook Scandal," *On Guard* 13 (1992), p. 12; Tim Weiner, "Sexual Harassment Declining, Women in the Military Report," *New York Times*, 3 July 1996, p. A16. In a smaller 1988 survey, 64 percent of women respondents reported some form of sexual harassment.
39. Tee shirts described by Michael R. Gordon, "Pentagon Report Tells of Aviators Debauchery," *New York Times*, 24 April 1993; "Excerpts from the Pentagon Report," *New York Times*, 24 April 1993, p. 9; quote in Eric Schmitt, "Navy Says Dozens of Women Were Harassed at Pilots Convention," *New York Times*, 1 May 1992.
40. Gibson, 148–69.
41. Ibid., p. 172.
42. Ibid., p. 8.
43. Quoted in ibid., p. 215.
44. The 1950–70 figures are from the Bureau of the Census, *Statistical Abstract of the United States, 1980*, Table 1525, p. 863; 1980, 1993 *Statistical Abstract of the United States, 1995*, Table 1322, p. 805. I have used data that are directly comparable for these years; this may underestimate the most recent figure.
45. Number of workers, 1970, from U.S. Bureau of the Census, *Statistical Abstract of the United States, 1978*, Table 676, p. 416; for 1994, *Statistical Abstract of the United States, 1995*, Table 668, p. 427; Nike material from Jeffrey Ballinger, "The New Free-trade Heel," in *Annual Editions: Global Issues 93/94*, ed. Robert M. Jackson (Guilford, Conn.: Dushkin Publishing Group, 1993), pp. 130–31.
46. Allan Ebert, "Un-sporting Multinationals: Baseball Manufacturers Taking a Walk on Workers Rights," *Multinational Monitor* 6, no. 18 (December 1985), pp. 11–12.
47. A full list of U.S. military actions from 1798–1945 can be found in Appendix II, William Blum, *Killing Hope: U.S. Military and CIA Interventions since World War II* (Monroe, Maine: Common Courage Press, 1995), pp. 444–52; Butler quoted in Holly Sklar, *Chaos or Community: Seeking Solutions, Not Scapegoats for Bad Economics* (Boston: South End Press, 1995), p. 36.
48. Quoted in *Vietnam and America: A Documented History*, eds. Marvin E. Gettleman, Jane Franklin, Marilyn Young, and Bruce Franklin (New York: Grove Press Inc., 1985), p. 53.
49. *The Report of the President's National Bipartisan Commission on Central America* (New York: Macmillan Publishing Co., 1983), p. 5.
50. Shalom, 1993, p. 31. Anticommunism was also successfully used in the United States to weaken progressive movements, especially following the Second World War. Progressives of all political persuasions were labeled "Communists" and purged from the media, schools, the labor movement, and government positions. A good discussion of this can be found in Marty Jezer, *The Dark Ages: Life in the United States 1945–1960* (Boston: South End Press, 1982).
51. Steven Lee Myers, "Old U.S. Army Manuals for Latin Officers Urged Rights Abuses," *New York Times*, 22 September 1996, p. 13; Eric Schmitt, "School for Assassins, or Aid to Latin Democracy," *New York Times*, 3 April 1995; Roy Bourgeois, "Human Rights Watch: School of Assassins," *Z Magazine* (September 1993), pp. 14–16. Bourgeois is a Catholic priest affiliated with the Maryknoll Missionary Order, which has produced a seventeen-minute video titled *School of Assassins*.
52. Quoted in Juan de Onis, "Chile Attracts U.S. Business," *New York Times*, 4 October 1979.
53. Noam Chomsky, and Edward S. Herman, *The Washington Connection and Third*

World Fascism: The Political Economy of Human Rights, Volume I (Boston: South End Press, 1979), pp. 42–46; see also Edward S. Herman, *The Real Terror Network* (Boston: South End Press, 1982), pp. 128–30.
54. "Chronicle," *New York Times,* 16 February 1990.
55. Linda Greenhouse, "Boeing Wins Plea on Severance Pay," *New York Times,* 28 February 1990; Judith Miller, "Navy Secretary Said to Keep Ties to Company Aiding Arms Makers," *New York Times,* 27 December 1982, pp. A1, B11; Jeff Gerth, "Reagan Advisors Received Stock in Laser Concern," *New York Times,* 28 April 1983, p. A1.
56. Andrew Rosenthal, "Tower's Links to Contractors Factor in Choice for Pentagon," *New York Times,* 4 December 1988, pp. 1, 42.
57. Christopher Cerf, and Henry Beard, *The Pentagon Catalog* (New York: Workman Publishing Co., 1986), pp. 14, 16, 17; Bill Keller, "Navy Pays $660.00 Apiece for Two Ashtrays," *New York Times,* 29 May 1985; "Boeing Cuts Price of $748 Pliers but Contract Total Remains Same," *New York Times,* 23 March 1985.
58. Markusen and Yudken, p. 96; John S. Long, "Defense Department Is 'Big Daddy' to Many Major U.S. Corporations," *Star-Ledger,* 17 August 1987.
59. Wayne Biddle, "5 Big Military Builders Paid No Taxes for 3 Years," *New York Times,* 16 October 1984.
60. Richard W. Stevenson, "Many Caught but Few Are Hurt for Arms Contract Fraud in U.S.," *New York Times,* 12 November 1990, pp. A1, B8.
61. *Democracy for the Few,* p. 88.
62. The term "imperial alibis" is from Stephen R. Shalom's *Imperial Alibis;* the term "rogue state" comes from Michael Klare, *Rogue States and Nuclear Outlaws* (New York: Hill and Wang, 1995), a short version can be found in his "The New 'Rogue State' Doctrine," *Nation,* 8 May 1995, pp. 625–28. Figures from Chart 5.1, Common Agenda Coalition, p. 58. This same source also shows that Japan spent only $39 billion and Russia $27 billion.
63. "U.S. Accounts for Half of Global Arms Exports," *New York Times,* 4 June 1996.
64. Ironically, the U.S. government's past support for anticommunist fundamentalist forces is itself leading to American deaths. In November 1995, a military training complex was bombed in Riyadh, Saudi Arabia. The bombers were part of the rebellious forces that overthrew the pro-Soviet regime in Afghanistan. In June 1996, another explosion in Saudi Arabia killed nineteen American soldiers, and the bombing also was likely to have been done by Afghani war veterans. Philip Shenon, "Holy War Is Home to Haunt the Saudis," *New York Times,* 14 July 1996, Section 4, p. 3.
65. Jason DeParle, "General and Troops Have Domestic Mission," *New York Times,* 3 April 1992, p. 23; Vivian S. Toy, "Differing Viewpoints on Squatters Next Door," *New York Times,* 31 May 1995, p. B2.

8 / Reducing the Casualties

In the first chapter of this book, we stated that creating a more humane, less violent society requires expanding our concept of violence to include its structural as well as its interpersonal forms. Even if interpersonal violence, the focus of most media and political discussion, were drastically reduced, structural violence could still continue at high levels. However, the two types are linked, both rooted in the unequal distribution of power and wealth in our society. As we have tried to show, the economic and political inequalities that produce high unemployment, and the lack of opportunities leading to much interpersonal violence, also produce unhealthy working conditions, environmental degradation, unsafe products, and militarism.

Debates as to how best to deal with violent behavior should be trying to bring us to a better understanding of how to create social environments where violence is rare and where the violent consequences of elite decision making are minimized. Without large-scale changes, efforts to reduce violence drastically will have a limited impact at best.

Too much of the public discussion on violence focuses on lamenting the decline of values and fostering personal morality. Proposals to lessen youth violence frequently focus on making families more responsible for the behavior of their children. Of course, families should try to affect their children positively, and people should not deal dangerous illegal drugs nor use violence to solve their emotional or financial problems. By the same standards, capitalists should put the health and safety of workers and consumers before profits and take care not to degrade the environment. Politicians should put the public welfare before their own narrow career goals.

Republican presidential candidate Robert Dole, speaking in Ohio in May 1996, said we live in an "age of violence," but, he added, "The debate [is] not about root causes.... It [is] about right and wrong."[1] Dole is mistaken, violence can only be lessened if its roots are destroyed. Much of the violence in the United States, we have argued, stems from decisions made by a very small group of wealthy and powerful people protecting their class interests. Their decisions ripple into the lives of the rest of us, sometimes with devastating results.

Violence will lessen when we bring about progressive social change. This means working with others to build movements that can successfully challenge corporate power and government priorities. As Michael Parenti, in his discussion of the need for popular action, says,

> It is often frustrating and sometimes dangerous to challenge those who own and control the land, capital and technology of society. But in the long run it is even more dangerous not to do so.[2]

Capitalism has created many victims. Although some suffer more than others, an awareness of our common problems is a first step toward seeking common solutions. As social scientist William Ryan wrote in *Blaming the Victim*:

> Everyone who depends for the sustenance of [themselves] and their family on salary and wages, and who does not have a separate source of income through some substantial ownership of wealth is a potential victim in America. [They] are vulnerable to the disaster of catastrophic illness in a private-enterprise medical-care system; ... vulnerable to the deliberate manipulation of inflation and unemployment; ... vulnerable to the burden of grossly unfair taxes; ... vulnerable to the endemic pollution of air and food and to the unattended hazards of the factory and the highway that will likely kill [them] before [their] time; ... vulnerable to the greed of the great oil companies and food corporations.[3]

All the threats to well-being listed by Ryan are the result of an inequitable distribution of power that must be challenged. Thoughtful critics of American society—some cited in this book—have produced useful suggestions of what needs changing, how street and corporate crime can be reduced, how corporations can be made more accountable to workers and communities, and how government can be made more responsive to the will of the people.[4]

Capitalism, however, by its very nature, is irresponsible to the majority. As long as capitalism exists, we will have to find ways to lessen its harmful impact. Violence will not appreciably lessen in this country until we, the public, have more power over the economic and political institutions that most affect our lives. Communities and workers therefore need to find ways to exercise some control over capitalist enterprises. One often made suggestion is that corporate boards of directors should include voting representatives from the public and from the workers.

The Preamble to our Constitution says that government is intended to "promote the general welfare" and "domestic tranquility," not corporate welfare and general anxiety. The links that bind politicians to corporations need to be broken. This means changes in campaign financing and meaningful restrictions on corporate lobbying. In addition, the "general welfare" cannot be achieved without a truly progressive tax system that redistributes from the wealthy to the rest of the society in the form of social services. This will lessen structural violence. As we discussed in chapter 7, we still have a war economy even though we have no powerful enemies. Our money should be meeting human needs and not those of the military industries and their allies.

Government commitment to full employment will address some of the problems we have discussed, if the employment is reasonably paid and healthy. In addition, public ownership and control of vital services is necessary. If present trends continue, environmental rehabilitation and protection are not going to be high priorities. Affordable quality health care, child care, and housing are not going to be provided unless they make money. We need far less privatization of necessary services, not more.

Analysts of interpersonal violence have useful suggestions, especially for lessening street crime.[5] Instead of more punishment, more repression, and more revenge, they emphasize the need for more prevention and more rehabilitation. There may be people whose rehabilitation is so difficult that long-term incarceration of some kind is the only way to protect the public, but their numbers are going to be small. For many current inmates, prisons could provide socially valuable skills instead of honing their abilities to commit crimes while increasing their anger and bitterness.

No Struggle, No Progress

No strategies for change will be effective unless we organize and fight for their implementation. Frederick Douglass's 1853 admonition remains true. "If there is no struggle there is no progress.... Power concedes nothing without a demand, it never did and it never will."[6] We have democratic rights to speak, protest, organize, and vote. These rights are the result of struggles by past generations, and we can use them today and in the future to reduce the casualties of the present system. Injustices and suffering that seemed entrenched were overcome by the determined efforts of ordinary people, motivated by anger at injustice and by visions of a more just society. Learning about these past efforts teaches us how progressive changes are brought about, gives us respect for ordinary people, and provides inspiration and models for dealing with present problems. We can learn from our own history and the history of other countries as well.[7]

Making major social changes is always likely to seem an unrealistic goal. Looking only at the last hundred years, it must have seemed that legal segregation would never be abolished; women would never have reproductive choices, be able to vote, or have independent lives; gays and lesbians would always be treated as pariahs; child labor would not be abolished; or the working day would never shorten, work never become safer, or unions be recognized. In addition to making specific gains, movements past and present have deepened our knowledge of how our system works, knowledge that is vital to future struggles.

In the midst of the Depression, organized movements, many led by the Communist Party, built industrial unions, organized the unemployed, and helped bring about social programs that attacked poverty and unemployment. These programs are under siege today. The activism of the Depression was cut short by World War II and following that war by a corporate- and government-sponsored purge of activists in the 1950s, often called McCarthyism.

A new generation of activists emerged—first in the South, then in northern ghettos, fighting racism. Then came struggles against the war in Vietnam, poverty, sexism, and homophobia. There were victories, some of which we have discussed in earlier chapters. But government repression, internal conflicts, and political disagreements were among the factors that seriously weakened these movements.

Activism has continued. In the recent past, anti-intervention movements, critical of U.S. policy toward Central America, likely forestalled U.S. military invasions in that region, and solidarity movements have provided useful support to progressive forces abroad. New groups have emerged, for example, those fighting to protect affirmative action, immigrant rights, and public services such as education and health care.

Once change does occur, however, a collective amnesia is encouraged; we easily forget how our gains were won. When social reforms are described, they are "explained" as the result of alleged individual achievements and not as collective efforts. In describing the past, U.S. popular culture and most education emphasizes the role of individuals rather than showing the importance of collective action. Given this emphasis, it is easy to believe that a benevolent leadership or extraordinary individuals almost single-handedly created new social programs and policies. In addition, neglect by the media of current protests and grassroots actions encourages pessimism. For example, there is little news coverage of progressive political activities, and even nationally organized large demonstrations are usually covered in misleading ways. The numbers of people attending are frequently underestimated, and equal media attention is given to small numbers of dissenters, diluting the impact of the protesters' message.

Few Illusions

Even if most people are not protesting the system, there is an awareness that it is not working very well. We can be told over and over this is the greatest country in the world and that you can be anything you want, but personal experiences and knowledge of at least some of the injustices, corruption, and so forth have raised public awareness. Even with the collapse of the socialist bloc in Eastern Europe, faith in capitalism does not seem to have been heightened in this country.

The public does not have much confidence in business or in government, nor hope for the future. Commenting on trends shown by polling data, Richard T. Curtin, who heads the University of Michigan's Consumer Surveys, notes a growing pessimism among Americans. In his words, "We are recording a decline in people's expectations. And their uncertainty and anxiety grow the farther you ask them to look into the future."[8]

A 1996 Louis Harris Poll questioned a sampling of Americans about their opinion of the future, the importance of profits, and the influence of corporations on life in this country. When asked if the "American dream of equal opportunity, personal freedom and social mobility has become easier or harder to achieve in the past 10 years," 67 percent thought it had become harder. Only 5 percent agreed that corporate pursuit of profits is what "is best for America in the long term," with 95 percent agreeing that corporations "owe something to their workers and communities . . . and they should sometimes sacrifice profit for the sake of making things better." As this book has pointed out, this is not how corporations see things. And nearly three-fourths of the respondents also felt that business had too much power.[9]

However, if there is an awareness of the problems, there is less certainty about how to change things. Without a sense of an alternative social agenda to that set by corporate America, scapegoating, apathy, and cynicism will remain widespread. Even one of the easiest of political acts, voting, does not interest the majority of those eligible to cast ballots. In the 1994 congressional elections, a *New York Times*/CBS poll found widespread pessimism and alienation regarding the candidates. Sixty-eight percent of the respondents answered "not much" to the question, "How much say do you think people like yourself have about what the government does?" Nearly the same percentage could not find one elected official they admired, and 72 percent did not even know the name of their congressional representative.[10]

The United States has the lowest voter turnout of any advanced capitalist country. With neither major party in the United States committed to their interests, lower-income people are especially unlikely to vote, even though they could drastically affect the outcome of many elections. In 1992, only about 55 percent of those eligible to vote did so. Turnout is even lower in nonpresidential election years; thus the 1994 elections brought out only 45 percent of the eligible voters.

Registering and voting are more difficult in the United States than in other countries, a factor that affects turnout, but also significant is the fact that there is no party that represents working people, another unique feature of political life in this country. A 1996 poll sponsored by the League of Women Voters asked respondents whether government represented the people or big interests. About 70 percent of respondents answered, not surprisingly, "a few big interests."[11]

When there is a real choice, participation rises such as what happened in Burlington, Vermont, when socialist Bernard Sanders successfully ran for mayor and was able to improve the city's infrastructure and support youth employment programs. Although there are valid reasons for the belief that voting does not make much difference, not exercising the right to vote makes it easier for the powerful to feel free to act as they wish. And, after all, even the lesser of two evils means less harm will be done in the short run.

Voting alone will have limited effects but organized struggles are likely to have more far-reaching impacts. Two recent demonstrations are evidence that people want to protest the status quo, take a collective stand, and build a better society. The Million Man March brought virtually a million mostly African-American men to Washington, D.C., in October 1995; and in June 1996, about a quarter of a million people rallied at the nation's capital. One participant, Kathy Simons, a day care worker from Massachusetts, described why she had made the long trip:

> We're excited to come down here and have the opportunity to scream a little. There is such an overwhelming frustration in the compromises you have to make every day in quality and availability of child care.[12]

Fighting Back: Some Examples

With the political system unresponsive to people's needs without pressure from below, community organizations throughout the country are fighting against some of the problems discussed in this book. A few examples will illustrate the ways in which concerned groups are trying to make their communities safer, healthier, and more humane, some fighting around single issues and some with broader concerns.

In San Francisco, ¡PODER!, Spanish for power, organizes for alternatives to crime and gangs, demanding jobs and recreation instead of repression. In the city's 1995 election, the group helped create a coalition to fight a ballot referendum establishing a curfew for those aged under eighteen. ¡PODER! member fifteen-year-old Raquel Moreno saw the curfew as a form of scapegoating and as "part of a war going on between the police department and the community." ¡PODER! won the referendum.[13]

In Boston's Roxbury section, in 1995, an organization called the Dudley Street Neighborhood Initiative (DSNI) grew out of the despair of local residents who were trying to find a way to rebuild their blighted community. The conditions in Dudley were a result of the processes described in chapter 2, that is, decisions of government agencies, banks, and realtors had led to a downward spiral where Dudley ended up looking "like Beirut," according to Nelson Merced, a community activist.[14]

The ethnic makeup of Dudley includes African-Americans, Latinos from a number of areas, whites, and Portuguese-speaking immigrants from the Cape Verde Islands. A formal but democratic governing structure was created with representatives of all the community's ethnic groups, businesses, social service agencies, and religious organizations. It was at first difficult to convince people that they could make a difference. Knocking on doors, organizer Andrea Nagel found that "at times the negativity was really alarming."[15]

The group came up with the slogan "Don't Dump on Us" to emphasize residents' disgust with their neighborhood literally being used as a garbage dump. The often illegally dumped trash was not only an eyesore but a breeding ground for insects, rats, and disease. The slogan had another meaning as well: "Stop trashing the community" in other ways.

DSNI did more, however, than deal with specific problems such as sanitation. They created a vision of a multiuse urban village. One of the key elements in this was a concern for safety. The people of Dudley wanted stores, housing, and public spaces designed to encourage "eyes on the street." The development plan DSNI drew up provided not only for this but for improving employment opportunities, child care, recreation, and for protecting cultural diversity. This was an ambitious agenda for a neighborhood group, and outside support and advice were required. Nonetheless, the initiative and energy all came from a community, many of whose residents were stereotyped as criminals, lazy, and so forth. Eventually the DSNI got a $2 million loan from the Ford Foundation, and the power of eminent domain gave it some authority over land use.

With their resources, DSNI has been able to support a number of services, some especially relevant to the issues raised in this book, including community centers providing drug treatment, counseling to reduce substance abuse and child abuse, prenatal and postnatal advice, employment counseling, a rape crisis center, and the establishment of a local health care center. DSNI has also targeted environmental racism and lead poisoning. The neighborhood association has even engaged in a home building project.

The DSNI has intervened in cases of racist police actions, has challenged racist stereotypes in the media, involved young people in the organization's activities, and created an inspiring document, a declaration of community rights. If this declaration could be put into practice throughout communities in the United States, much of the violence we have discussed could very likely be reduced. In this neighborhood, demoralization, indifference, and despair have been replaced with optimism and a sense of community growth from the experiences of people working together to realize a common vision.

Another inspiring example comes from Los Angeles. Concerned with that city's severe air pollution, mentioned in chapter 6, veteran activist Eric Mann joined with others to create the Labor/Community WATCHDOG Organizing Committee in 1989. The Committee describes itself as "multiracial and anticorporate" with an emphasis on "rebuilding the labor movement, fighting for environmental justice, . . . mass transit and immigrant rights" while "actively opposing the growing criminalization, racialization and feminization of poverty."[16] It has established a center for research, publications, and outreach.

As with the DSNI, support from other groups, including unions, has helped build the Labor/Community WATCHDOG Organizing Committee, which takes the position that corporations, "along with the finest politicians their money can buy, are largely responsible for . . . toxic air." The organization also believes that because the corporate decision-making process excludes the affected public, creating a healthy environment means creating a more democratic one as well.[17]

The WATCHDOG group has organized a number of campaigns around issues of environmental degradation, transportation, and jobs. They also provide assistance to neighborhood activists such as Carlos Molina, organizer of Parents Against Pollution. He was concerned about the health of his daughter who was attending a school made unhealthy by a nearby oil refinery, a fertilizer factory, and a sewage plant. Molina met the WATCHDOG group and decided his organization would be more effective working with them. "They are looking for a permanent solution. We can find temporary solutions. We're the Band-Aids and they are curing the illness."[18]

The WATCHDOG Group maintains that affordable local transportation is an important issue. Working people need to be able to get to their jobs, those without jobs need transportation to look for employment. In 1995, as part of a coalition that included the NAACP, the Korean Immigrant Workers' Advocates, and the Southern Christian Leadership Conference in 1995, they were able to mount court challenges to the Los Angeles County Metropolitan Transit Authority. As a result, bus fares in Los Angeles were kept more affordable.[19]

WATCHDOG also organized a Boycott Texaco campaign with the slogan "Communities and Workers Demand Public Health Before Corporate

Profits." Texaco is a leading producer of carcinogens and other toxic products. It spends millions to lobby against air pollution regulations and engages in numerous unsafe practices in the United States and abroad. WATCHDOG hopes to pressure Texaco into reducing emissions of pollutants, funding health care clinics, allowing a community chosen inspector into its Wilmington, Los Angeles, plant, and cleaning up the damage it has caused in Ecuador. Even if these demands are not all met, through leafleting and demonstrating this organization, in conjunction with the Sierra Club, Greenpeace, Acción Ecológica, and the Rainforest Action Network, is doing more than protesting a problem. It is suggesting democratic solutions and demanding corporate responsibility, as well as helping to create a vision of a more egalitarian community.

The Labor/Community WATCHDOG group has been confronting structural violence. Community groups can also work against interpersonal violence. An impressive example of fighting racist violence comes from Billings, Montana, a town with a population of eighty-four thousand, whose residents, in the words of a documentary filmmaker, decided "the only way to really be safe is to take a stand." Montana is one of the five northwestern states that white supremacists describe as their future "Aryan homeland." Racist groups threatened Billings's residents. Death threats were sent to an African-American resident. The groups also tried to frighten the congregation of an African-American church by going to their services and standing in intimidating poses. A cinder block was thrown through the window of a Jewish family's home, where six-year-old Isaac Schnitzer had placed a cardboard Menorah in celebration of Chanukah. In addition, a Jewish cemetery was desecrated, and racist slogans were painted on the home of a Native American, Dawn Fast-Horse.

One of the organizers of antiracist activity was Randy Siemenes, president of the local laborers' union. He went to the labor council, which passed a strong resolution against hate groups. Union members worked with police to provide security at antihate meetings, and after their day's work, thirty members of the painters' union, along with one hundred other people, painted over the graffiti on the home of Dawn Fast-Horse. Gary Modie, one of the painters, said

> So many of the times when there's a cause, you end up standing on the sidelines too much.... I never really did a lot to do anything about anything and I was really glad to help paint the home, more so to help convey a message to these guys that the community will not stand for that.[20]

Many are involved in Billings's continued antiracist efforts, including unions, local human rights activists, religious leaders, journalists, the editor of the *Billings Gazette*, and the Billings police chief, Wayne Inman. Inman had been a member of the Portland, Oregon, Police Department when Ethiopian student Mulugeta Seraw (mentioned in chapter 4) was killed, and he didn't want to see racist violence in his hometown.

Using the model of the Danes who, during the Nazi invasion, put on yellow stars in support of their Jewish countrymen, in response to the attack on the Schnitzers' home, ten thousand families and businesses placed paper Menorahs in their windows. One business put up a sign reading "Not in Our Town. No Hate, No Violence." In support of the African-American congregation, members of other churches attended service at the church, conveying, in the words of the Reverend Bob Freeman, a distinct message: "If you bite one of us you bite us all. And that was a very good feeling we had."[21] Instead of having to face threats in isolation, perhaps arming themselves in desperation, those threatened in Billings got support and solidarity, and community ties were strengthened.

Groups can overcome their past antagonisms and build alliances when they realize they are in the same badly leaking boat. An example of this comes from northern Wisconsin, where white sports fishermen had mounted an ugly campaign against Ojibwa Indians who had exclusive treaty rights to spearfish. Using slogans such as "Save A Walleye—Spear an Indian," some whites engaged in shootings, arson, and beatings. Now both Ojibwas and the sportsmen have formed an alliance against EXXON, whose proposed mining operations would include the creation of an enormous toxic waste site, the size of three hundred football fields, endangering the whole Northern Wisconsin watershed.[22]

Efforts such as the ones described above are occurring throughout the United States. Another example comes from Massachusetts. Project HIP-HOP was started there in 1993 by the state chapter of the American Civil Liberties Union. For the past three years, an ethnically diverse group of high school students has traveled to the South on a "civil rights tour" where they speak to activists and learn that there is "unfinished business" that they have a role in completing. They not only learn about the past, but they meet members of current grassroots movements and become inspired. One youngster, Marco Garrida, described the transformation of his feelings:

> I have felt the spirit that fueled the movement.... HIP-HOP has stirred me to social consciousness.... I have also seen and heard and felt the injustice the movement sought to end. This injustice, which before had overwhelmed me, now angers me. Stronger, I accept my responsibility to continue what the Movement began, to finish the unfinished business.

The students share their experiences at schools and community centers and so far have addressed ten thousand other students. In the words of another participant, others are encouraged "to learn not to give in to that sense of helplessness."[23]

"We Can Build a New World"[24]

As the examples show, activism in the interests of social betterment continues. But reducing violence, extending and protecting our rights, and creating a more egalitarian society will take national movements and a political party that truly represents the majority of the population in this country.

A revitalized labor movement is a crucial part of any strategy for progressive change. We need a labor movement that can effectively fight for the interests of working people, that will have the resources and the collective strength to fight corporate power, and that can effectively pressure elected officials to act in the interest of the majority. The immense wealth the working people of this country produce needs to be used for social programs that benefit all of us, not a small group of investors.

There are some hopeful signs. Within the labor movement, the "New Voice" campaign has criticized a past leadership that had not done much organizing, had allowed women and people of color to be underrepresented in the leadership of the labor movement, and uncritically supported the U.S. government's foreign policy. At its 1996 convention, the AFL-CIO elected a new president, supported by New Voices, John Sweeney. Sweeney's previous position was president of the Service Employees International Union, one of the fastest growing labor organizations. He is aware, in his words, that "working-class Americans and their families are hurting as never before and we as a labor movement have got to respond as never before."[25] Of course, those words will have to be followed by effective actions if the problems are to be diminished.

More labor activists are now in leadership positions than in the past. One of these, Bob Wages, president of the Oil, Chemical and Atomic Workers' Union (OCAW), expressed his ambivalence about the direction of the labor movement, saying,

> I think the AFL-CIO can be a very powerful voice for working people. I think the federation can be visionary . . . it can lead strategic initiatives against . . . employers, against industry, against global capital. . . . The question is, will it?[26]

Unions are not enough, however. As we mentioned earlier, we need a political party that truly represents the vast majority of people in this country. OCAW has been instrumental in creating an organization to do this, the Labor Party Advocates (LPA). The LPA convened a meeting of one thousand four hundred unionists and grassroots activists in Cleveland in

June 1996 to make this a reality. Tony Mazzocchi of the OCAW, active in this endeavor, points out, "There are thousands of good people out there who care about democratic concepts, who share in wanting to fight to improve things for their fellow workers." He notes that the workplace is one of the few areas in American life where people of color and whites are likely to realize their common class interests.[27]

It is too soon to know how much difference these changes will mean. There are promising signs, such as a new emphasis on organizing the unorganized and representing the unrepresented. The labor organization's leadership is now more diverse, with a greater representation of women and people of color, and there is discussion of how to be connected to grassroots movements. Links between workers and students are being forged, using the model of Freedom Summer. During the Civil Rights Movement, students from many campuses went to the South to help local activists register voters. In 1996, over one thousand five hundred students were recruited for labor organizing efforts. There are also plans to create a "Strategic Action Center" to train unionists in conducting campaigns against particular corporations and helping those engaged in such campaigns.

Successful movements require visions of a better future. Is it absurd to imagine a society where everyone can have health care, a decent home, quality education, satisfying work, leisure, and a healthy environment? Is it unreasonable to expect to live in a country where everyone can walk the streets without fear, and where racism, sexism, homophobia, and violence are subjects only for the history books? United the people have won important victories in the past. We can organize to win them in the present and create that healthier, happier future.

There is no guarantee that a particular battle will end in victory, but even if we fail to reach a specific goal, the knowledge we gain, the skills we learn, the friendships we develop, and the cultures of resistance that we create remain. Our lives are enriched, and we are better able to succeed in future struggles.

Notes

1. Quoted in Katherine Q. Seelye, "Revisiting the Issue of Crime, Dole Offers List of Remedies," *New York Times*, 29 May 1996, pp. A1, B7.
2. Michael Parenti, *Land of Idols: Political Mythology in America* (New York: St. Martin's Press, 1994), p. 5.
3. William Ryan, *Blaming the Victim* (New York: Vintage Publications, 1976), p. xiii. Where Ryan used "he," I have substituted a more general pronoun.
4. Useful ideas can be found in Brad Erickson, ed., *CALL TO ACTION: Handbook for Ecology, Peace and Justice* (San Francisco: Sierra Club Books, 1990);

David R. Simon, and D. Stanley Eitzen, *Elite Deviance*, 4th ed. (Boston: Allyn and Bacon, 1993), pp. 335–62; Holly Sklar, *Chaos or Community? Seeking Solutions, Not Scapegoats for Bad Economics* (Boston: South End Press, 1995), pp. 161–77; Seymour Melman, *The Demilitarized Society: Disarmament & Conversion* (Montreal: Harvest House, 1988). These are just a few of the sources that an interested reader can investigate.
5. These include Albert J. Reiss, and Jeffery A. Roth, eds., *Understanding and Preventing Violence* (Washington, D.C.: National Research Council, 1993); Felice J. Levine, and Katherine J. Rosich, *Social Causes of Violence: Crafting a Science Agenda* (Washington D.C.: American Sociological Association, 1996); American Psychological Association, *Violence & Youth: Psychology's Response*, Vol. I: *Summary Report of the American Psychological Association on Violence and Youth* (Washington, D.C.: American Psychological Association, 1993); Steven R. Donziger, ed., *The Real War on Crime: The Report of the National Criminal Justice Commission* (New York: Harper Perennial, 1996), pp. 195–253; Elliot Currie, *Reckoning: Drugs, the Cities and the American Future* (New York: Hill and Wang, 1993), pp. 280–332.
6. Quoted in Lerone Bennett Jr., *Before the Mayflower* (New York: Penguin Books, 1984), pp. 160–61.
7. This book concentrates on the United States, but we can learn from, for example, the antiapartheid struggle in South Africa, the achievements in Cuba and of the Sandinista regime in Nicaragua, Kerala State, India, and even from what was successfully achieved by Eastern European socialism. On Kerala, see Richard W. Franke and Barbara H. Chasin *Kerala: Radical Reform as Development in an Indian State*, 2d ed. (Oakland, Calif: Institute for Food and Development Policy, 1994).
8. Quoted in Louis Uchitelle, "The Rise of the Losing Class," *New York Times*, 20 November 1994, Section 4, p. 5.
9. "Business Week/Harris Poll: America, Land of the Shaken," *Business Week*, 11 March 1996, pp. 64–65.
10. Katherine Q. Seelye, "Voters Disgusted with Politicians as Election Nears," *New York Times*, 3 November 1994, pp. A1, A28.
11. Harold R. Kerbo, *Social Stratification and Inequality: Class Conflict in Historical and Comparative Perspective*, 3rd ed. (New York: McGraw-Hill Companies, Inc., 1996), pp. 237–38; Frances Fox Piven, and Richard A. Cloward, *Why Americans Don't Vote* (New York: Pantheon, 1989); Michael Parenti, *Democracy for the Few*, 6th ed. (New York: St. Martin's Press, 1995), p. 198. Sanders is currently Vermont's Congressional representative. Richard L. Berke, "Nonvoters are No More Alienated Than Voters, a Survey Shows," *New York Times*, 30 May 1996, p. A21.
12. Quoted in Tim Weiner, "A Capital Rally Attracts Groups from Across the Nation to Focus on Children's Needs," *New York Times*, 2 June 1996, p. 30.
13. Quoted in Lisa Pagan, "Being Young Is Not a Crime: Youth Organizing in San Francisco," *Resist Newsletter* (May 1996), p. 4.
14. Peter Medoff, and Holly Sklar, *Streets of Hope: The Fall and Rise of an Urban Neighborhood* (Boston: South End Press, 1994). Beirut quote, p. 42.
15. Quoted in Medoff and Sklar, p. 69.
16. From their Web site, http://www.igc.apc.org/lctr/, 31 May 1996.
17. Eric Mann, *L.A.'s Lethal Air: New Strategies for Policy, Organizing, and Action* (Los Angeles: Labor/Community Strategy Center, 1991), p. 6.

18. Quoted in Laureen Lazarovici, "Air Battles: The Watchdog Wades into the Pollution Wars on Behalf of the Other L.A.," *LA Weekly*, 6–12 December 1991.
19. Robin G. Kelley, "Freedom Riders (the Sequel)," *Nation*, 5 February 1996, p. 19.
20. Quoted in video *Not In Our Town*. This video was broadcast on PBS, Channel 13, New York City, 17 December 1995.
21. Quoted in video *Not In Our Town*.
22. The Institute for Natural Progress, "In Usual and Accustomed Places: Contemporary American Indian Fishing Rights Struggles," in *The State of Native America*, ed. M. Annette Jaimes (Boston: South End Press, 1992), pp. 231–35; News broadcast, WBAI-FM, New York, 15 April 1996.
23. Quoted in Nancy Murray, "Rolling Through History: Project HIP-HOP Teaches Lessons of Activism," *Resist Newsletter* (May 1996), pp. 2–3.
24. This is, of course, part of the line from the old union song, "Solidarity Forever." The whole line is "We can build a new world from the ashes of the old, for the union makes us strong."
25. Quoted in Steven Greenhouse, "Labor's Labors Not Lost," *New York Times*, 12 May 1996, Section 4, p. 4.
26. Jeremy Brecher, and Tim Costello, "A New Labor Movement in the Shell of the Old: New Voice in Labor Organizing," *Z Magazine* (April 1996), pp. 45–49; quote from Laura McClure, "Union Organizing: AFL-CIO Changes," *Z Magazine* (January 1996), p. 21.
27. Quoted in Laura McClure, "Labor Party Advocates," *Z Magazine* (April 1995), p. 16. There are other attempts at party building as well. See, for example, Howie Hawkins, "Progressive Politics: Independent Progressive Politics Network," *Z Magazine* (June 1996), pp. 17–21.

Bibliography

Abraham, Laurie Kaye. *Mama Might Be Better Off Dead: The Failure of Health Care in Urban America.* Chicago: University of Chicago Press, 1993.

Aldridge, Robert C. *First Strike! The Pentagon's Strategy for Nuclear War.* Boston: South End Press, 1983.

Allen, Laura. "Women Workers at Perdue: A Chicken in Every Pot, Health Hazards in Every Shop." *Resist Newsletter* (October 1988): 3–6.

American Psychological Association. *Violence & Youth: Psychology's Response,* Vol. I: *Summary Report of the American Psychological Association on Violence and Youth.* Washington, D.C.: American Psychological Association. 1993.

American Public Health Association. Position Paper, 9211, Domestic Violence. Washington: D.C., APHA, n.d.

Amnesty International. *United States of America: Police Brutality and Excessive Force in the New York City Police Department.* New York: Amnesty International, 1996.

Amott, Theresa. *Caught in the Crisis: Women and the U.S. Economy Today.* New York: Monthly Review Press, 1993.

Anderson, David C. "The Crime Funnel." *New York Times Magazine,* 12 June 1994, 56–58.

Aponte, Robert. "Urban Employment and the Mismatch Dilemma: Accounting for the Immigration Exception." *Social Problems* 43 (1996): 268–83.

Arditti, Rita, and Tatiana Schreiber. "Breast Cancer: The Environmental Connection." *Resist Newsletter* (May/June 1992): 1–8.

Austin, Regina, and Michael Schill. "Black, Brown, Red and Poisoned." In *Unequal Protection: Environmental Justice and Communities of Color.* Edited by Robert D. Bullard, 53–74. San Francisco: Sierra Club Books, 1994.

Balkan, Sheila, Ronald J. Berger, and Janet Schmidt. *Crime and Deviance in America: A Critical Approach.* Belmont, Calif.: Wadsworth Publishing Co., 1980.

Ballinger, Jeffrey. "The New Free-Trade Heel." In *Annual Editions: Global Issues 93/94.* Edited by Robert M. Jackson, 130–131. Guilford, Conn.: Dushkin Publishing Group, 1993.

Baron, Larry, and Murray A. Straus. *Four Theories of Rape in American Society: A State-Level Analysis.* New Haven, Conn.: Yale University Press, 1989.

Bellant, Russ. *The Coors Connection: How Coors Family Philanthropy Undermines Democratic Pluralism.* Boston: South End Press, 1991.

Berman, Daniel. *Death on the Job: Occupational Health and Safety Struggles in the United States*. New York: Monthly Review Press, 1978.
Bennett, Jr., Lerone. *Before the Mayflower*. New York: Penguin Books, 1984.
Berrill, Kevin T. "Anti-Gay Violence and Victimization in the United States: An Overview." In *Hate Crimes: Confronting Violence Against Lesbians and Gay Men*. Edited by Gregory M. Herek and Kevin T. Berrill, 19–45. Newbury Park, Calif.: Sage Publications, 1992.
Bingham, Eula, and William V. Meader. "Governmental Regulation of Environmental Hazards in the 1990's." *Annual Review of Public Health* 11 (1990): 419–34.
Bird, Kai. *The Chairman: John J. McCloy and the Making of the American Establishment*. New York: Simon and Schuster, 1992.
Birnbaum, Jeffrey R. *The Lobbyists: How Influence Peddlers Work Their Way in Washington*. New York: Times Books, 1993.
Blackburn, McKinley L., David E. Bloom, and Richard B. Freeman. "The Declining Economic Position of Less Skilled Men." In *A Future of Lousy Jobs: The Changing Structure of U.S. Wages*. Edited by Gary Burtless, 31–76. Washington, D.C.: The Brookings Institution, 1990.
Blackwell, James E. *The Black Community: Diversity and Unity*. New York: HarperCollins, 1991.
Blank, Rebecca M. "Are Part-Time Jobs Bad Jobs?" In *A Future of Lousy Jobs: The Changing Structure of U.S. Wages*. Edited by Gary Burtless, 123–64. Washington, D.C.: The Brookings Institution, 1990.
Bluestone, Barry, and Bennett Harrison. *The Deindustrialization of America: Plant Closings, Community Abandonment and the Dismantling of Basic Industry*. New York: Basic Books, 1982.
Blumberg, Paul. *The Predatory Society: Deception in the American Marketplace*. New York: Oxford University Press, 1989.
Blumstein, Alfred. "Violence by Young People: Why the Deadly Nexus?" *National Institute of Justice Journal* (August 1995): 2–9.
Boisjoly, Russell, Ellen Foster Curtis, and Eugene Mellican. "Ethical Dimensions of the Challenger Disaster." In *Corporate and Governmental Deviance*. 5th ed. Edited by M. David Ermann and Richard J. Lundman, 207–31. New York: Oxford University Press, 1996.
Bok, Derek. *The Cost of Talent: How Executives and Professionals Are Paid and How It Affects America*. New York: Free Press, 1993.
Bonaich, Edna, and David W. Waller. "Mapping a Global Industry: Apparel Production in the Pacific Rim Triangle." In *Global Production: The Apparel Industry in the Pacific Rim*. Edited by Edna Bonaich, Lucie Cheng, Norma Chinchilla, Nora Hamilton, and Paul Ong, 21–41. Philadelphia: Temple University Press, 1994.
Bourgeois, Roy. "Human Rights Watch: School of Assassins." *Z Magazine* (September 1994): 14–16.
Bourgois, Philippe. "Just Another Night on Crack Street." *New York Times Magazine*, 12 November 1989, 52+.
Braverman, Harry. *Labor and Monopoly Capital: The Degradation of Work in the Twentieth Century*. New York: Monthly Review Press, 1974.
Brecher, Jeremy, and Tim Costello. "A New Labor Movement in the Shell of the Old: New Voice in Labor Organizing." *Z Magazine* (April 1996): 45–49.
Brenner, Claudia. "Survivor's Story." In *Hate Crimes: Confronting Violence Against Lesbians and Gay Men*. Edited by Gregory M. Herek and Kevin T. Berrill, 11–15. Newbury Park, Calif.: Sage Publications, 1992.

Brenner, M. Harvey. *Economy, Society and Health*. Washington, D.C.: Economic Policy Institute, 1992.
Brown, Jonathan. "Opening the Book on Lending Discrimination." *Multinational Monitor* 13, no. 11 (November 1992): 8–14.
Bullard, Robert D. "Environmental Justice for All." In *Unequal Protection: Environmental Justice and Communities of Color*. Edited by Robert D. Bullard, 3–22. San Francisco: Sierra Club Books, 1994.
Burghardt, Tom. "Neo-Nazis Salute the Anti-Abortion Zealots." *CovertAction Quarterly* (Spring 1995): 26–33.
Burrason, Bert. "Infant Mortality in the United States: Racial Differences and Social Stratification." Paper presented at the annual meeting of the Pacific Sociological Association. San Diego, California, April 1994.
Burtless, Gary. "Introduction and Summary." In *A Future of Lousy Jobs: The Changing Structure of U.S. Wages*. Edited by Gary Burtless, 1–30. Washington, D.C.: The Brookings Institution, 1990.
Carey, James. "Benton Harlow: Distributor of Unsafe Drugs." In *Corporate Violence: Injury and Death for Profit*. Edited by Stuart Hill, 163–69. Totowa, N.J.: Rowman & Littlefield, 1987.
Casten, Liane Clorfene. "Toxic Burn: Agent Orange's Forgotten Victims." *Nation* (4 November 1991): 550–54.
Chambliss, William J. "Policing the Ghetto Underclass: The Politics of Law and Law Enforcement." *Social Problems* 41 (1994): 177–94.
Chavis Jr., Benjamin F. "Foreword." In *Confronting Environmental Racism: Voices from the Grassroots*. Edited by Robert D. Bullard, 3–5. Boston: South End Press, 1993.
Chomsky, Noam, and Edward S. Herman, *The Washington Connection and Third World Fascism: The Political Economy of Human Rights, Volume I*. Boston: South End Press, 1979.
Clawson, Dan Alan Neustadtl, and Denise Scott. *Money Talks: Corporate PACS and Political Influence*. New York: Basic Books, 1992.
Claybrook, Joan. *Retreat from Safety: Reagan's Attack on America's Health*. New York: Pantheon, 1984.
Clinard, Marshall. *Corporate Corruption: The Abuse of Power*. New York: Praeger, 1990.
Clinard, Marshall, and Peter Yeager. *Corporate Crime*. New York: The Free Press, 1980.
Cockburn, Alexander. "Beat the Devil." *Nation* (11 December 1995): 736–37.
Cole, Leonard A. *Clouds of Secrecy: The Army's Germ Warfare Tests over Populated Areas*. Totowa, N.J.: Rowman & Littlefield, 1988.
Coleman, James W. *The Criminal Elite: The Sociology of White-Collar Crime*. 3d ed. New York: St. Martin's Press, 1994.
Coleman, Wanda. "Remembering Latasha: Blacks, Immigrants and America." *Nation* (15 February 1993): 187–91.
Common Agenda Coalition and the National Priorities Project. *Creating a Common Agenda*. Northhampton, Mass.: National Priorities Project, n.d.
Commoner, Barry. *The Closing Circle: Man, Nature & Technology*. New York: Bantam Books, 1971.
Cooper, Marc. "Sickness on Evelina Street." *Village Voice*, 7 September 1993, 33–37.
Corea, Gena. *The Invisible Epidemic: The Story of Women and AIDS*. New York: HarperCollins, 1992.
Cottle, Thomas. "When You Stop, You Die: The Human Toll of Unemployment."

In *Crisis in American Institutions*. 9th ed. Edited by Jerome Skolnick and Elliot Currie, 75–81. New York: HarperCollins, 1994.
Currie, Elliot. *Confronting Crime*. New York: Pantheon Books, 1985.
———. *Reckoning: Drugs, the Cities and the American Future*. New York: Hill and Wang, 1993.
Currie, Elliot, and Jerome Skolnick. *America's Problems: Social Issues and Public Policy*. 2d ed. Glenview, Ill.: Scott, Foresman and Company, 1988.
Davis, Mike. *City of Quartz: Excavating the Future in Los Angeles*. New York: Vintage, 1990.
Davis, Robert. "Racial Differences in Mortality: Current Trends and Perspectives." In *Race and Ethnicity in America: Meeting the Challenge in the 21st Century*. Edited by Gail Thomas, 115–28. Washington, D.C.: Taylor & Francis, 1995.
Derber, Charles. *The Wilding of America: How Greed and Violence Are Eroding Our Nation's Character*. New York: St. Martin's Press, 1996.
Domhoff, G. William. *The Powers That Be: Processes of Ruling Class Domination in America*. New York: Vintage, 1979.
Donziger, Steve R., ed. *The Real War on Crime: The Report of the National Criminal Justice Commission*. New York: HarperPerennial, 1996.
Dowie, Mark. "Pinto Madness." In *The Best of Mother Jones*. Edited by Richard Reynolds, 59–69. Foundation for National Progress, 1985.
Dye, Thomas R. *Who's Running America: The Conservative Years*. 4th ed. Englewood Cliffs, N.J.: Prentice-Hall, 1986.
Ebert, Allan. "Un-sporting Multinationals: Baseball Manufacturers Taking a Walk on Workers Rights." *Multinational Monitor* 6, no. 18 (December 1985): 11–12.
Ehrenreich, Barbara. "The Warrior Culture." In *Beyond the Storm: A Gulf Crisis Reader*. Edited by Phyllis Bennis and Michel Moushabeck, 129–31. New York: Olive Branch Press, 1991.
Ehrlich, Howard J. "Reporting Ethnoviolence." *Z Magazine* (June 1994): 53–58.
Elliot, Delbert. "Serious Violent Offenders: Onset, Developmental Course, and Termination." *Criminology* 32 (1994): 5–14.
Epstein, Samuel S. *The Politics of Cancer*. San Francisco: Sierra Club Books, 1978.
Erickson, Brad, ed. *Call to Action: Handbook for Ecology, Peace and Justice*. San Francisco: Sierra Club Books, 1990.
Ermann, M. David, and Richard J. Lundmann. "Overview." In *Corporate and Governmental Deviance*. 4th ed. Edited by M. David Ermann and Richard J. Lundmann, 3–43. New York: Oxford University Press, 1987.
Fagan, Jeffrey. "Drug Selling and Licit Income in Distressed Neighborhoods: The Economic Lives of Street-Level Drug Users and Dealers." In *Drugs, Crime and Social Isolation: Barriers to Urban Opportunity*. Edited by Adele V. Harrell and George E. Peterson, 99–146. Washington, D.C.: Urban Institute Press, 1992.
———. "Interactions Among Drugs, Alcohol and Violence." *Health Affairs* 12 (1993): 65–79.
Fee, Elizabeth, and Nancy Krieger. "Health, Politics, and Power." *Women's Review of Books* 11 (1994): 4–5.
Ferraro, Kathleen J. "Cops, Courts, and Woman Battering." In *Violence Against Women: The Bloody Footprints*. Edited by Pauline B. Bart and Eileen Geil Morgan, 165–76. Newbury Park, Calif.: Sage Publications, 1993.
Flanders, Laura. "Mal de Guerre." *Nation* (7 March 1994): 292–93.
———. "Is It Real . . . Or Is It Astroturf: PR Firm Finds 'Grassroots' Support for Breast Implants." *EXTRA!* (July/August 1996): 6.

Fontanarosa, P. B. "The Unrelenting Epidemic of Violence in America." *JAMA* 273, no. 22 (14 June 1995): 1792–93.
Fox, Robin. *The Challenge of Anthropology: Old Encounters and New Excursions.* New Brunswick, N.J.: Transaction Publishers, 1994.
Franke, Richard W. and Barbara H. Chasin. *Kerala: Radical Reform as Development in an Indian State.* 2d ed. Oakland, Calif.: Institute for Food and Development Policy, 1994.
Freeman, Richard B. "Crime and the Employment of Disadvantaged Youths." In *Urban Labor Markets and Job Opportunity.* Edited by George Peterson and Wayne Vroman, 202–37. Washington, D.C.: Urban Institute Press, 1992.
———. "How Much Has De-Unionization Contributed to the Rise in Male Earnings Inequality?" In *Uneven Tides: Rising Inequality in America.* Edited by Sheldon Danziger and Peter Gottschalk, 133–63. New York: Russell Sage Foundation, 1993.
Freund, Peter, and George Martin. *The Ecology of the Automobile.* Montreal: Black Rose Books, 1993.
Freund, Peter E. S., and Meredith B. McGuire. *Health, Illness and the Social Body: A Critical Sociology.* Englewood Cliffs, N.J.: Prentice-Hall, 1991.
Fried, Albert. *The Rise and Fall of the Jewish Gangster in America.* New York: Holt Rinehart and Winston, 1980.
Fried, Marlene Gerber. "Reproductive Wrongs." *Women's Review of Books* (July 1994): 6–7.
Galtung, John. *The True Worlds.* New York: The Free Press, 1980.
Gans, Herbert. "Deconstructing the Underclass." In *Race, Class and Gender in the United States.* 3rd ed. Edited by Paula S. Rothenberg, 51–57. New York: St. Martin's Press, 1995.
Gelles, Richard, J., and Murray A. Straus. *Intimate Violence: The Causes and Consequences of Abuse in the American Family.* New York: Simon and Schuster, 1988.
Gettleman, Marvin E., Jane Franklin, Marilyn Young, and Bruce Franklin, eds. *Vietnam and America: A Documented History.* New York: Grove Press Inc., 1985.
Gibbs, Nancy. "Till Death Do Us Part." In *Crisis in American Institutions.* 9th ed. Edited by Jerome H. Skolnick and Elliott Currie, 231–42. New York: HarperCollins, 1994.
Gibson, James William. *Warrior Dreams: Violence and Manhood in Post-Vietnam America.* New York: Hill and Wang, 1994.
Gilbert, Dennis, and Joseph A. Kahl. *The American Class Structure: A New Synthesis.* 4th ed. Belmont, Calif.: Wadsworth, 1993.
Glazer, Myron Peretz, and Penina Migdal Glazer. *The Whistleblowers: Exposing Corruption in Government & Industry.* New York: Basic Books, 1989.
Glazer, Nathan, and Daniel Patrick Moynihan. *Beyond the Melting Pot: The Negroes, Puerto Ricans, Jews, Italians and Irish of New York City.* Cambridge, Mass.: M.I.T. Press, 1970.
Global Exchanges 27 (Summer 1996) "Globalization and the Downsizing of the American Dream," special insert, 2.
Gold, David, and Stephen Rose. *A Primer on the Arms Race.* Baltimore, Md.: Social Graphics Co., 1983.
Goldsmith, William W., and Edward J. Blakely. *Separate Societies: Poverty and Inequality in U.S. Cities.* Philadelphia: Temple University Press, 1992.
Goldstein, Richard. "The New Anti-Semitism: A *Geshrei.*" In *Blacks and Jews: Alliances and Arguments.* Edited by Paul Berman, 204–16. New York: Delta, 1994.

Goode, Judith. "Polishing the Rustbelt: Immigrants Enter a Restructuring Philadelphia." In *Newcomers in the Workplace*. Edited by Louise Lamphere, Alex Stepick, and Guillermo Grenier, 199–230. Philadelphia: Temple University Press, 1994.

Greider, William. *Who Will Tell the People: The Betrayal of American Democracy*. New York: Simon and Schuster, 1992.

Grofman, Bernard, and Chandler Davidson, eds. *Controversies in Minority Voting: The Voting Rights Act in Perspective*. Washington, D.C.: The Brookings Institution, 1992.

Hall, Bob. "Perdue Farms: Poultry and Profits." *Multinational Monitor* 10, no. 9 (September 1989): 18–20.

Hardert, Ronald A. "Environmental Whistle-blowers, Anger and the Power Elite." Working paper presented at the annual meeting of the Pacific Sociological Association. San Diego, Calif. April 1994.

Harrell, Adele V., and George E. Peterson, eds. *Drugs, Crime and Social Isolation: Barriers to Urban Opportunity*. Washington, D.C.: Urban Institute Press, 1992.

Harris, Marvin. *America Now: The Anthropology of a Changing Culture*. New York: Simon and Schuster, 1981.

Hawkins, Howie. "Progressive Politics: Independent Progressive Politics Network." *Z Magazine* (June 1996): 17–21.

Heiss, Jerold. "Effects of African American Family Structure on School Attitudes and Performance." *Social Problems* 43 (1996): 246–67.

Helvarg, David. "The War on Greens." *Nation* (28 November 1994): 646–51.

Herman, Edward S. *The Real Terror Network*. Boston: South End Press, 1982.

———. "The Natural Rate of Unemployment." *Z Magazine* (November 1994): 62–65.

Herman, Edward S., and Noam Chomsky. *Manufacturing Consent: The Political Economy of the Mass Media*. New York: Pantheon, 1988.

Higham, Jon. *Strangers in the Land: Patterns of American Nativism, 1860–1925*. New Brunswick, N.J.: Rutgers University Press, 1966.

Hill, Richard C., and Cynthia Negry. "Deindustrialization and Racial Minorities in the Great Lakes Region, USA." In *The Reshaping of America: Social Consequences of the Changing Economy*. Edited by D. Stanley Eitzen and Maxine Baca Zinn, 168–78. Englewood Cliffs, N.J.: Prentice-Hall, 1989.

Hills, Stuart L. "Epilogue." In *Corporate Violence: Injury and Death for Profit*. Edited by Stuart L. Hills, 187–206. Totowa, N.J.: Rowman & Littlefield, 1987.

Holmes, Ronald M., and Stephen T. Holmes. *Murder in America*. Thousand Oaks, Calif.: Sage Publications, 1994.

Horn, Patricia. "Beating Back the Revolution." *Dollars & Sense* (December 1992): 12–13, 21–22.

Institute for Natural Progress. "In Usual and Accustomed Places: Contemporary American Indian Fishing Rights Struggles." In *The State of Native America*. Edited by M. Annette Jaimes, 217–39. Boston: South End Press, 1992.

Isaac, Katherine. "Losing Jobs to 936." *Multinational Monitor* 14, no. 7 (July/August 1993): 6–7.

Jackall, Robert. *Moral Mazes: The World of Corporate Managers*. New York: Oxford University Press, 1989.

Jackson, Janine, and Jim Naureckas. "*U.S. News* Illustrates Flaws in Crime Coverage." *EXTRA!* (May/June 1994): 10–13.

Jaffe, Frederick S., Barbara L. Lindheim, and Philip R. Lee. "Legal Abortion Improves Public Health." In *Abortion: Opposing Viewpoints*. Edited by Bonnie Szumski, 147–51. St. Paul, Minn.: Greenhaven Press, 1986.

James, David, and Michael Soref. "Managerial Theory: Unmaking of the Corporation President." *American Sociological Review* 46 (1981): 1–18.

Janis, Irving. *Victims of GroupThink: A Psychological Study of Foreign Policy Decisions and Fiascoes.* Boston: Houghton Mifflin Company, 1972.

Jennings, James. *Understanding the Nature of Poverty in America.* Westport, Conn.: Praeger, 1994.

Jezer, Marty. *The Dark Ages: Life in the United States 1945–1960.* Boston: South End Press, 1982.

Jones, Jacqueline. *The Dispossessed: America's Underclasses from the Civil War to the Present.* New York: Basic Books, 1992.

Jones, James. *Bad Blood: The Tuskegee Syphilis Experiment: A Tragedy of Race and Medicine.* New York: The Free Press, 1981.

Kaiser Health Reform Project. *Uninsured in America.* Henry J. Kaiser Family Foundation, 1994.

Kaplan, Janice. "Are Talk Shows Out of Control?" *TV Guide*, 1 April 1995, 8–10.

Kasarda, John D. "The Severely Distressed in Economically Transforming Cities." In *Drugs, Crime and Social Isolation: Barriers to Urban Opportunity.* Edited by Adele V. Harrell and George E. Peterson, 45–98. Washington, D.C.: Urban Institute Press, 1992.

Katz, Michael B., ed. *The "Underclass" Debate: The View from History.* Princeton, N.J.: Princeton University Press, 1993.

Kay, Jane. "California's Endangered Communities of Color." In *Unequal Protection: Environmental Justice and Communities of Color.* Edited by Robert D. Bullard, 155–88. San Francisco: Sierra Club Books, 1994.

Kelley, Robin G. "Freedom Riders (the Sequel)." *Nation* (5 February 1996): 18–22.

Kerbo, Harold R. *Social Stratification and Inequality: Class Conflict in Historical and Comparative Perspective.* 3d ed. New York: McGraw-Hill Companies, Inc., 1996.

King Jr., Martin Luther. "Declaration of Independence from the War in Vietnam." *Essay Series.* New York: A. J. Muste Memorial Institute, n.d., 35–50.

Klare, Michael. *Rogue States and Nuclear Outlaws.* New York: Hill and Wang, 1995.

———. "Making Enemies for the '90's: The New 'Rogue State Doctrine.'" *Nation* (8 May 1995): 625–28.

Kloby, Jerry. "Increasing Class Polarization in the United States: The Growth of Wealth and Income Inequality." In *Critical Perspectives in Sociology.* Edited by Berch Berberoglu, 39–53. Dubuque, Iowa: Kendell/Hunt Publishing Co., 1991.

Konner, Melvin. *Dear America: A Concerned Doctor Wants You to Know the Truth about Health Reform.* Reading, Mass.: Addison-Wesley, 1993.

Kozol, Jonathan. *Savage Inequalities: Children in America's Schools.* New York: HarperCollins, 1991.

Kurz, Demie. "Battering and the Criminal Justice System: A Feminist View." In *Domestic Violence: The Changing Criminal Justice Response.* Edited by Eve S. Buzawa and Carl G. Buzawa, 21–38. Westport, Conn.: Auburn House, 1992.

Kwik, Phill. "Pittston Power." *Nation* (16 October 1989): 409.

Langer, Elinor. "The American Neo-Nazi Movement Today." *Nation* (16/23 July 1990): 82–107.

Larson, Erik. *Lethal Passage: How the Travels of a Single Handgun Expose the Roots of America's Gun Crisis.* New York: Crown Publishers, 1994.

Lawson, Bill E., ed. *The Underclass Question.* Philadelphia: Temple University Press, 1992.

Lazarovici, Laureen. "Air Battles: The Watchdog Wades into the Pollution Wars on Behalf of the Other L.A." *LA Weekly* (6–12 December 1991).
Lemann, Nicholas. *The Promised Land: The Great Black Migration and How It Changed America.* New York: Vintage Books, 1991.
Lerman, Lisa G. "Prosecution of Wife Beaters: Institutional Obstacles and Innovations." In *Violence in the Home: Interdisciplinary Perspectives.* Edited by Mary Lystad, 262–65. New York: Brunner/Mazel, 1986.
Levin, Jack, and Jack McDevitt. *Hate Crimes: The Rising Tide of Bigotry and Backlash.* New York: Plenum Press, 1993.
Levine, Felice J., and Katherine J. Rosich. *Social Causes of Violence: Crafting a Science Agenda.* Washington, D.C.: American Sociological Association, 1996.
Leviton, David, ed. *Horrendous Death: Health and Well-Being.* New York: Hemisphere Publishing, 1991.
Liam, Ramsey, and Paula Rayman. "Health and Social Costs of Unemployment." *American Psychologist* 37 (1982): 1116–23.
Liebman, Bonnie. "For Women Only." *Nutrition Action Health Letter* 22 (March 1995): 4–7.
Lifton, Robert Jay. *Home from the War: Learning from Vietnam Veterans.* Boston: Beacon Press, 1992.
Lipsman, Dr. Joshua. "White Man's Medicine." *Nation* (26 March 1988): 401.
Livingston, Jay. *Crime & Criminology.* Englewood Cliffs, N.J.: Prentice-Hall, 1992. 2d ed. 1994.
Lunneborg, Patricia. *Abortion: A Positive Decision.* New York: Bergin & Garvery, 1992.
Lusane, Clarence. *Pipe Dream Blues: Racism and the War on Drugs.* Boston: South End Press, 1991.
Lutz, William. *Doublespeak: From "Revenue Enhancement to Terminal Living": How Government, Business Advertisers and Others Use Language to Deceive You.* New York: Harper Perennial, 1989.
Malcolm X. *By Any Means Necessary.* New York: Pathfinder Press. Inc., 1970.
Mann, Eric. *L.A.'s Lethal Air: New Strategies for Policy, Organizing, and Action.* Los Angeles: Labor/Community Strategy Center, 1991.
Markuson, Anne, and Joel Yudken. *Dismantling the Cold War Economy.* New York: Basic Books, 1992.
Marx, Karl. *Capital.* Vol. 1. Moscow: Foreign Languages Publishing House, n.d. Originally published 1887.
Massey, Douglas, and Nancy A. Denton. *American Apartheid: Segregation and the Making of the Underclass.* Cambridge, Mass.: Harvard University Press, 1993.
Mauer, Marc. "A Generation Behind Bars: Black Males and the Criminal Justice System." In *The American Black Male: His Present Status and His Future.* Edited by Richard G. Majors and Jacob U. Gordon, 81–93. Chicago: Nelson-Hall, 1994.
McClure, Laura. "Union Organizing: AFL-CIO Changes." *Z Magazine* (January 1996): 18–21.
McCord, Colin, and Harold P. Freeman. "Excess Mortality in Harlem." In *Crisis in American Institutions.* 9th ed. Edited by Jerome Skolnick and Elliot Currie, 426–32. New York: HarperCollins, 1991.
McCoy, Alfred W. *The Politics of Heroin: CIA Complicity in the Global Drug Trade.* New York: Lawrence Hill Books, 1991.
McGehee, Ralph. *Deadly Deceits: My 25 Years in the CIA.* New York: Sheridan Square Press, 1983.

Medoff, Peter, and Holly Sklar. *Streets of Hope: The Fall and Rise of an Urban Neighborhood.* Boston: South End Press, 1994.
Melman, Seymour. *The Demilitarized Society: Disarmament and Conversion.* Montreal: Harvest House, 1988.
Milgram, Stanley. *Obedience to Authority.* New York: Harper and Row, 1969.
Merva, Mary, and Richard Fowles. *Effects of Diminished Economic Opportunities on Social Stress: Heart Attacks, Strokes and Crime.* Washington, D.C.: Economic Policy Institute, n.d.
Mills, C. Wright. "The Cultural Apparatus." In *Power, Politics and People: The Collected Essays of C. Wright Mills.* Edited by Irving L. Horowitz, 405–22. New York: Ballantine Books, 1963.
Misch, Ann. "Assessing Environmental Health Risks." In *State of the World: 1994.* Edited by Linda Starke, 117–36. New York: W. W. Norton & Co., 1994.
Mishel, Lawrence, and Jared Bernstein. *The State of Working America, 1992–1993.* Armonk, N.Y.: M. E. Sharpe, Inc., 1993.
Mokhiber, Russell. *Corporate Crime and Violence: Big Business Power and the Abuse of Public Trust.* San Francisco: Sierra Club Books, 1988.
———. "The 10 Worst Corporations of 1993." *Multinational Monitor* 14, no. 12 (December 1993): 9–16.
Mokhiber, Russell, Julie Gozan, and Holley Knaus. "The Corporate Rap Sheet: The 10 Worst Corporations of 1992." *Multinational Monitor* 13, no. 12 (December 1992): 7–16.
Moore, Joan. "Gangs, Drugs, and Violence." In *Gangs: The Origins and Impact of Contemporary Youth Gangs in the United States.* Edited by Scott Cummings and Daniel J. Monti, 27–46. Albany, N.Y.: State University of New York Press, 1993.
Moore, Richard, and Louis Head. "Building a Net That Works: SWOP." In *Unequal Protection: Environmental Justice and Communities of Color.* Edited by Robert D. Bullard, 191–206. San Francisco: Sierra Club Books, 1994.
Moses, Marion. "Farmworkers and Pesticides." In *Confronting Environmental Racism.* Edited by Robert D. Bullard, 161–78. Boston: South End Press, 1993.
Murray, Nancy. "Rolling Through History: Project HIP-HOP Teaches Lessons of Activism." *Resist Newsletter* (May 1996): 1–3.
Nader, Ralph, and William Taylor. *The Big Boys: Power and Position in American Business.* New York: Pantheon, 1986.
National Issues Forum. *Crime: What We Fear, What Can Be Done.* Dayton, Ohio: National Issues Forum, 1987.
Nersesian, William S. "Infant Mortality in Socially Vulnerable Populations." *Annual Review of Public Health* 9 (1988): 361–77.
New Jersey Council of Churches. *The Reshaping of New Jersey: The Growing Separation.* East Orange, N.J.: New Jersey Council of Churches, 1988.
Noble, Charles. *Liberalism at Work: The Rise and Fall of OSHA.* Philadelphia: Temple University Press, 1986.
Ortiz, Solomon P. "America's Third World: Colonias." In *Annual Editions: Race and Ethnic Relations 91/92.* Edited by John A. Kromkowski, 80–82. Guilford, Conn.: Dushkin Publishing Group, 1991.
Osborn, Barbara Bliss. "If It Bleeds It Leads—If It Votes It Don't: A Survey of L.A.'s Local News Shows," *EXTRA!* (September/October 1994): 15.
Pagan, Lisa. "Being Young Is Not a Crime: Youth Organizing in San Francisco." *Resist Newsletter* (May 1996): 4–5.

Parenti, Michael. *Inventing Reality: The Politics of News Media.* 2d ed. New York: St. Martin's Press, 1993.
———. *Land of Idols: Political Mythology in America.* New York: St. Martin's Press, 1994.
———. *Democracy for the Few.* 6th ed. New York: St. Martin's Press, 1995.
Perry, Susan, and Jim Dawson. "Nightmare: Women and the Dalkon Shield." In *Corporate and Governmental Deviance: Problems of Organizational Behavior in Contemporary Society.* 3d ed. Edited by M. David Ermann and Richard J. Lundman, 145–62. New York: Oxford University Press, 1987.
Phillips, Kevin. *The Politics of Rich and Poor: Wealth and the American Electorate in the Reagan Aftermath.* New York: HarperPerennial, 1990.
Pinderhughes, Howard. "The Anatomy of Racially Motivated Violence in New York City: A Case Study of Youth in Southern Brooklyn." *Social Problems* 40 (1993): 478–91.
———. "'Down with the Program': Racial Attitude and Group Violence among Youth in Bensonhurst and Gravesend." In *Gangs: The Origin and Impact of Contemporary Youth Gangs.* Edited by Scott Cummings and Daniel J. Monti, 75–94. Albany, N.Y.: SUNY Press, 1993.
Piven, Frances Fox, and Richard A. Cloward. "The Historical Sources of the Contemporary Welfare Debate." In *The Mean Season: The Attack on the Welfare State.* Edited by Fred Block, Richard A. Cloward, Barbara Ehrenreich, and Frances Fox Piven, 3–43. New York: Pantheon Books, 1987.
———. *Why Americans Don't Vote.* New York: Pantheon, 1989.
———. *Regulating the Poor: The Functions of Public Welfare.* Updated ed. New York: Vintage Books, 1993.
President's National Bipartisan Commission on Central America. *The Report of the President's National Bipartisan Commission on Central America.* New York: Macmillan Publishing Co., 1983.
Rabin, Yale. "Highways as a Barrier to Equal Access." In *Majority and Minority: The Dynamics of Racial and Ethnic Relations.* 2d ed. Edited by Norman R. Yetman and C. Hoy Steele, 463–75. Boston: Allyn and Bacon, Inc., 1975.
Reiman, Jeffrey. *The Rich Get Richer and the Poor Get Prison.* 3d ed. New York: Macmillan, 1990.
Reisine, Susan T. "The Impact of Dental Conditions on Social Functioning and the Quality of Life." *Annual Review of Public Health* 9 (1988): 1–19.
Reiss, Albert J., and Jeffrey A. Roth. *Understanding and Preventing Violence.* Washington, D.C.: National Academy Press, 1993.
Ridgeway, James. "The Posse Goes to Washington: How the Militias and Far Right Got a Foothold on Capitol Hill." *Village Voice*, 23 May 1995.
Rose, Stephen J. *Social Stratification in the United States: The American Profile Poster.* New York: New Books, 1992.
Rosenberg, Howard L. *Atomic Soldiers: American Victims of Nuclear Experiments.* Boston: Beacon Press, 1980.
Rosenberg, Mark L. "Violence Is a Public Health Problem." In *Unnatural Causes: The Three Leading Killer Diseases in America.* Edited by Russell C. Maulitz, 147–68. New Brunswick, N.J.: Rutgers University Press, 1988.
Rubenstein, Richard L. *The Age of Triage: Fear and Hope in an Overcrowded World.* Boston: Beacon Press, 1983.
Ruel, Susan. "Body Bag Journalism: Crime Coverage by the U.S. Media." Paper presented at International Conference on Violence in the Media, St. John's University, New York, 3 October 1994.

Russell, George. "Corporate Restructuring." In *The Reshaping of America: Social Consequences of the Changing Economy*. Edited by D. Stanley Eitzen and Maxine Baca Zinn, 33–36. Englewood Cliffs, N.J.: Prentice-Hall, 1989.

Ryan, William. *Blaming the Victim*. Revised edition. New York: Vintage Publications, 1976.

Salmi, Jamil. *Violence and Democratic Society: New Approaches to Human Rights*. Atlantic Highlands, N.J.: Zed Books, 1993.

Sampson, Robert J., and W. Byron Groves. "Community Structure and Crime: Testing Social-Disorganization Theory." *American Journal of Sociology* 94 (1989): 774–802.

Schaefer, Richard T. *Racial and Ethnic Groups*. 5th ed. New York: HarperCollins, 1993.

Scully, Diane. *Understanding Sexual Violence: A Study of Convicted Rapists*. Boston: Unwin-Hyman, 1992.

Serrin, William. "The Wages of Work." *Nation* (28 January 1994): 80–81.

Shalom, Stephen Rosskamm. "Drug Policy & Program." *Z Papers* (January 1992): 9–17.

———. *Imperial Alibis: Rationalizing U.S. Intervention After the Cold War*. Boston: South End Press, 1993.

Sheahen, Allen. "Poverty in America Is a Serious Problem." In *Poverty: Opposing Viewpoints*. Edited by William Dudley, 17–24. St. Paul, Minn.: Greenhaven Press, 1988.

Sherman, Lawrence W., and Richard A. Berk. "The Specific Deterrent Effects of Arrest for Domestic Assault." *American Sociological Review* 49 (1984): 261–72.

Shernoff, David. "Workers at Risk." *Multinational Monitor* 9, no. 10 (October 1988): 21–22.

Simon, David R. *Elite Deviance*. 5th ed. Boston: Allyn and Bacon, 1996.

Simon, David R., and D. Stanley Eitzen. *Elite Deviance*. 4th ed. Boston: Allyn and Bacon, 1993.

Sklar, Holly. *Chaos or Community: Seeking Solutions, Not Scapegoats for Bad Economics*. Boston: South End Press, 1995.

Skolnick, Jerome H., and James J. Fyfe. *Above the Law: Police and the Excessive Use of Force*. New York: The Free Press, 1993.

Solomon, Norman. "The Media's Favorite Think Tank: How the Heritage Foundation Turns Money into Media." *EXTRA!* (July/August 1996): 9–12.

Southern Poverty Law Center. *Intelligence Report* (March 1994).

Sponsel, Leslie E. "The Mutual Relevance of Anthropology and Peace Studies." In *The Anthropology of Peace and Nonviolence*. Edited by Leslie E. Sponsel and Thomas Gregor, 1–36. Boulder, Colo.: Lynne Rienner, 1994.

Squires, Gregory D. "Runaway Factories Are Also a Civil Rights Issue." In *The Reshaping of America: Social Consequences of the Changing Economy*. Edited by D. Stanley Eitzen and Maxine Baca Zinn, 179–81. Englewood Cliffs, N.J.: Prentice-Hall, 1989.

Stark, Evans, and Anne H. Flitcraft. "Women and Children at Risk: A Feminist Perspective on Child Abuse." *Women's Health, Politics and Power: Essays on Sex/Gender, Medicine, and Public Health*. Edited by Elizabeth Fee and Nancy Krieger, 307–31. Amityville, N.Y.: Baywood Publishing Co., Inc., 1994.

Steinberg, Stephen. *The Ethnic Myth: Race, Ethnicity, and Class in America*. Boston: Beacon Press, 1989.

Sturdevant, Sandra Pollock, and Brenda Stoltzfus. *Let the Good Times Roll: Prostitution and the U.S. Military in Asia*. New York: New Press, 1992.

Sutherland, Edwin H. "White Collar Criminality." In *Crime and Delinquency: A Reader*. Edited by Carl Bersani, 25–34. Toronto: Macmillan, 1970.
Swasy, Alecia. *Soap Opera: The Inside Story of Procter & Gamble*. New York: Times Books, 1993.
Sweezy, Paul. *The Theory of Capitalist Development*. New York: Monthly Review Press, 1942.
Szymanski, Albert. *The Logic of Imperialism*. New York: Praeger, 1981.
Tabor, Michael. "The Plague: Capitalism+Dope=Genocide." In *The Triple Revolution Emerging: Social Problems in Depth*. Edited by Robert Perrucci and Mark Pilisuk, 241–49. Boston: Little Brown and Company, 1971.
Thompson, E. P. *The Making of the English Working Class*. New York: Vintage, 1963.
Tiger, Lionel, and Robin Fox. *The Imperial Animal*. New York: Delta, 1971.
Tonry Michael. "Sentencing Guidelines, Disadvantaged Offenders, and Racial Disparities." *Report from the Institute for Philosophy and Public Policy* (Summer/Fall 1994): 7–13.
———. *Malign Neglect*. New York: Oxford University Press, 1995.
Truax, Hawley. "Minorities at Risk." *Environmental Action* (January/February 1990): 21.
United Nations Development Program. *Human Development Report, 1994*. New York: Oxford University Press, 1994.
U.S. Bureau of the Census. *Statistical Abstract of the United States, 1995* (also 1994, 1993, 1987, 1983, 1980). Washington, D.C.: Government Printing Office.
U.S. Commission on Civil Rights. *Civil Rights Issues Facing Asian Americans in the 1990's* (February 1992).
U.S. Congress. Committee on Education and Labor, House of Representatives. *Hearings on H.R. 1280, Comprehensive Occupational Safety and Health Reform Act*, 28 April, 29 July, 1993.
U.S. Congress. Office of Technology Assessment. *Indian Health Care*. Washington, D.C.: U.S. Government Printing Office, 1986.
U.S. Department of Justice. *SourceBook of Criminal Justice Statistics—1994*. 1995.
U.S. Department of Justice. *Comparing Federal and State Prison Inmates, 1991*.
U.S. Department of Justice. *Drugs and Crime Facts, 1993*.
U.S. Department of Justice. *Drugs and Crime Facts, 1994*.
U.S. Department of Justice. *Crime and Neighborhoods* (June 1994).
U.S. Department of Justice. *Criminal Victimization in the United States: 1973–1992 Trends* (July 1994).
U.S. Department of Justice. *Violence between Intimates* (November 1994).
U.S. Department of Justice. *Prisoners in 1994* (August 1995).
U.S. Government. *The Congressional Record*, Vol. 135, no. 62 (16 May 1989).
U.S. Riot Commission. *Report of the National Advisory Commission on Civil Disorders*. New York: Bantam Books, 1968.
Useem, Michael. *Executive Defense: Shareholder Power and Corporate Reorganization*. Cambridge, Mass.: Harvard University Press, 1993.
Voorst, Bruce Van. "Toxic Dumps: The Lawyers' Money Pit." *Time*, 13 September 1993, 63–64.
Wallace, Deborah. "Roots of Increased Health Care Inequality in New York." *Social Science and Medicine* 31 (1990): 1219–27.
Wallace, Rodrick. "Urban Desertification, Public Health and Public Order: 'Planned Shrinkage,' Violent Death, Substance Abuse and AIDS in the Bronx." *Social Science and Medicine* 31 (1990): 801–13.
Weiner, Tim. "The Pentagon's Post-Cold War Black Budget Is Alive and Prosper-

ing." In *Censored: The News That Didn't Make the News—And Why.* Edited by Carl Jensen. Chapel Hill, N.C.: Shelburne Press, 1993.

Weinstein, Deena. *Bureaucratic Opposition: Challenging Abuses of the Workplace.* New York: Pergamon Press, 1979.

Weitz, Rose. "Sex, Class, Race: Health and Illness in the United States." *Race, Sex and Class* 2 (1994): 127–43.

Whitman, Steve. "The Crime of Black Imprisonment." *Z Magazine* (May/June 1992): 69–72.

Widon, Cathy Spatz. *The Cycle of Violence.* Washington, D.C.: U.S. Department of Justice, 1992.

Wilson, Edward O. *Sociobiology: The New Synthesis.* Cambridge, Mass.: Harvard University Press, 1971.

Wilson, William J. *The Truly Disadvantaged: The Inner City, the Underclass and Public Policy.* Chicago: University of Chicago Press, 1987.

———, ed. "The Ghetto Underclass: Social Science Perspectives." *Annals of the American Academy of Political and Social Science* 501 (1989).

———. "Work." *New York Times Magazine,* 18 August 1996, 26–31, 40, 48, 52.

Wolf, Edward N. *Top Heavy: A Study of the Increasing Inequality of Wealth in America.* New York: The Twentieth Century Fund, 1995.

World Bank. *World Development Report, 1994.* New York: Oxford University Press, 1994.

Zawitz, Marianne W. *Guns Used in Crime.* U.S. Department of Justice, Bureau of Justice Statistics, 1995.

VIDEOS

Not In Our Town. 1995. California Working Group, P.O. Box 10326, Oakland, CA 94610, 510-547-8484. Running time, 25 minutes.

Pockets of Hate. 1988. Films for the Humanities, Inc., P.O. Box 2053, 743 Alexander Road, Princeton, NJ 08540. Running time, 26 minutes.

School of Assassins. Maryknoll World Productions, P.O. Box 308, Maryknoll, NY 10545-0308, 1-800-227-8523. Running time, 18 minutes.

The Wrath of Grapes. United Farm Workers of America, P.O. Box 62, Keene, CA 93531. Running time, 15 minutes.

Index

abortion, 77, 84–86; and clinic violence, 86; illegal, 85; limits on, 85
Abrams, Robert, 106
accidents, 3, 132; and guns, 38–39. See also fire deaths
Aetna Insurance, 36
Affirmative Action, 20, 91, 181
AFL-CIO, 108, 188
African-American family, 59–60
African-Americans, 6; and bias crimes, 99; and child abuse, 80; class and, 15; and crime, 48; crime fears, 45; and housing, 51–52; and income, 20; infant mortality rate, 125; and interpersonal violence, 89–90; migration north, 50; and prison, 55, 68; and racial violence, 93; stereotypes of, 47; and unemployment, 53. See also environmental racism; race; Tatum
agribusiness, 137, 166
agricultural labor, 112
Aid to Families with Dependent Children (AFDC), 67, 125
AIDS, 128–29; and gender, 134–35
air pollution, 140
Alabama, 144
Alaska, 83
alcohol use, 130
Aldridge, Robert C., 153
Allende, Salvatore, 168
Allied Signal Corporation, 116
American Clothing and Textile Workers' Union, 18

American Humane Association, 80
American Lung Association, 146
American Medical Association, 78
American Pistol Institute. See Gunsite Ranch
American Psychological Association, 2
American Sociological Association, 2
Amnesty International, 96, 97
anger: and domestic violence, 80
anti-Asian violence, 1. See also Asian Indians; Chin
anticommunism, 165, 167–68. See also Cold War
anthropology: theories of rape, 83; theories of violence, 10
Aristide, Jean Baptiste, 166
arms build-up. See Cold War; weapons gap
arrest rates, 48, 49; of Vietnam veterans, 155
Asian-Americans, 92. See also Asian Indians; Chin
Asian Indians: violence toward, 92
AT&T, 28, 33, 34
atomic bomb, 153
Atomic Energy Commission (AEC), 26, 156
atomic testing, 155
atomic veterans, 155
attitudes, 182
Atwater, Lee, 162
Aucher, Thorne, 110
authority: and class, 14. See also bureaucracy; command posts; Milgram

automobile safety, 108, 138.
　　See also cost-benefit analysis; Pinto

baby formula, 136
Baldwin, James, 97, 129
Baltimore, 58
banks: and narcotics, 65, 66
Bard, Inc., C. R., 136
Baron, Larry, 83
Bensonhurst, 90
Berg, Alan, 94
B. F. Goodrich, 27
bias crimes: increase in, 91–92.
　　See also anti-Asian; Asian Indian;
　　Chin; Griffith; Hawkins;
　　homophobic violence; racist
　　violence
Billings, Montana, 186–87
Billings, Robert J., 84
biological determinism, 8–9
biological warfare, 156–57.
　　See also Gulf syndrome.
birth control, 132–33. See also Dalkon
　　Shield
blacks. See African-Americans
Black Panther Party, 69
black power, 93
Blue Cross/Blue Shield, 36
Bluestone, Barry, 117
Blumstein, Alfred, 62
Bobbitt, Lorena, 77
Boeing, 170
Bok, Derek, 106
bootlegging. See Prohibition
Boston, 47, 86, 184
Bourgois, Philippe, 61, 63
Boxer, Barbara, 65
breast cancer, 133–34
Brenner, M. Harvey, 118
Brookings Institution, 36
Buchenwald, 156
Bureau of Indian Affairs (BIA), 131
bureaucracy, 21–30; and police
　　violence, 97. See also command
　　posts; doublespeak; Milgram
Burghardt, Tom, 86
Burns, David, 35
Bush, George, 34, 47, 98, 162.
　　See also Reagan–Bush administration
Business Council, 36, 105

Butler, Major General Smedley, 167
Byrd, Robert, 88

California, 141
Camden, N.J., 45
campaign costs, 32
campaign financing, 32
cancer, 114; and the environment,
　　140; and work, 110. See also atomic
　　testing; carcinogens; environmental
　　racism
"capital flight," 115. See also
　　suburbanization
capitalism: and racial inequality, 76;
　　and structural violence, 104; victims
　　of, 179
capitalists, 14, 178; and government,
　　30–36
Capone, Al, 105
carcinogens, 29. See also cancer
cardiovascular disease, 114, 118, 128,
　　135; and stress, 129. See also Bard;
　　Shiley
Carey, James, 27
carpal tunnel syndrome, 114
Carter administration, 142
Catholics, 85
Center for Indoor Air Research, 34
Centers for Disease Control, 2, 3
Central Intelligence Agency (CIA),
　　23, 64; budget, 109; and Chile, 168;
　　and narcotics, 64, 65; testing of
　　Americans by, 174n. 18
CEOs: compensation, 117; world view
　　of, 27–28. See also bureaucracy;
　　executives
Cerrell Associates, 141
chain of command, 27
Challenger, 24, 25
Chicago, 49, 60; crime in, 40; and
　　environmental racism, 144;
　　unemployment in, 53, 54, 58, 117
Chicanos, 142, 143. See also colonias
child abuse, 78
children, 79; health of, 143. See also
　　accidents; infant mortality; lead
　　poisoning
Chile, 168–69
Chin, Vincent, 92
China, 167

Chrysler, 29
Cigna Insurance, 17, 36
"circle of poison," 137
cirrhosis, 118
Citizens Clearing House for Hazardous Wastes, 142, 146
Civil Rights Movement, 189
class, 13–18, 76; and crime, 49; and dangers to children, 124–25; and domestic violence, 80; and military testing, 157; and pollution, 144–45; and prenatal care, 125; and structural violence, 124–32. *See also* capitalists; command posts; middle class; underclass; working class; working poor
Clean Water Act, 146
Clear, Todd, 67
Cleveland, 58
Clinard, Marshall B., 104
Clinton administration: and General Motors, 139; and OSHA, 111
Clinton, Bill, 5, 31, 35, 85; on King, Jr., 175n. 33; and Native American health, 132; on violence, 1–2
Clinton, Hillary, 36
coal mining, 108, 111
Cohen, Judith, 134
COINTELPRO, 172
Cold War, 152–53, 160, 172. *See also* McCarthyism
Cole, Leonard, 156
Colgate-Palmolive, 115
colonias, 143
command posts, 21–22
community activism, 146–47, 183–89
community structure, 60
Constitution, 108, 179. *See also* Fifteenth Amendment
Contras, 64
Coors, Joseph, 36
corporate crime, 38, 104–5, 135–36. *See also* Gibbs
corporate dumping, 133
corporate investment, 165–66
corporate mergers, 116–17
corporate power, 116–17
corporate recruiting, 23
corporate violence, 104
corporations: and politics, 180. *See also* bureaucracy; military-industrial complex
corporeal punishment, 79
cost-benefit analysis, 138, 141, 146
Council on Economic Development, 36
Council on Economic Priorities, 159
Council on Foreign Relations, 35, 36
Covault, General Marvin L., 172–73
crack, 63, 64–65. *See also* CIA; narcotics
crime: attitudes toward, 38; as economic opportunity, 46; fear of, 45–46; and immigrants, 46; media and, 37–39; and repression, 69–70; social ecology of, 48; and unemployment, 46–47, 54–56, 59, 61; and violence, 63. *See also* corporate crime; street crime
criminal justice system, 49
criminal violence, 6
Crown Heights, 93
Cuba, 168
cultural apparatus, 36–39
culture of poverty, 9. *See also* employment; Quayle; values
cyanide poisoning, 106
cynicism, 182–83

Dalkon Shield, 132–33
Davis, Mike, 57
Davis, Robert, 111
death and work, 107
Decker, Scott, 62
Defense of Marriage Act, 88
deficit, 161
deindustrialization, 53
Denny, Reginald, 93
dental care, 126
Department of Defense, 152; funding, 109
Department of Transportation, 138
Department of War, 152
Depression, 181
deregulation. *See* Reagan administration
Detroit, 58, 92
Deutch, John, 65
diabetes, 128. *See also* Pima
Dingell, John, 34
Dinkins, David, 46

dioxin, 141, 142
discrimination: and employment, 52, 53, 54; and housing, 51–53. *See also* environmental racism; segregation
doctors, 127
Doctors Ought to Care, 34–35
Dole, Robert, 34, 91, 160, 178
domestic violence, 76, 77–82; and attitudes, 74; and guns, 79; stress and, 79–80. *See also* Bobbitt; Simpson
Domhoff, G. William, 35, 36
doublespeak, 29–30. *See also* language: manipulation of
Douglass, Frederick, 180
Dow Chemical Co., 28, 142
"downwinders." *See* atomic testing
Drug Enforcement Agency (DEA), 64
drugs. *See* crack; narcotics
Dudley Street Neighborhood Initiative (DSNI), 184–85
Dukakis, Michael, 47
Duke, David, 91
Dulles, John Foster, 167

Eastern Europe, 182
East Timor, 172
ecology, 141
economic inequality. *See* class; ethnicity/race; gender; income
education, 50; and ethnicity, 20; and income, 20; and prison population, 55
Eichmann, Adolph, 23
El Salvador, 167–68
elderly abuse, 78, 79
Elders, Joyce, 69
electronics industry, 114
Ellsberg, Daniel, 25
employment: attitudes toward, 57–59, 180; opportunities, 57–58. *See also* unemployment
entertainment, 46
environmental activism, 29. *See also* environmental racism; Gibbs; WATCHDOG
Environmental Protection Agency (EPA), 34, 113, 141, 145; and environmental racism, 144; funding cuts, 146

environmental racism, 142–45; protests against, 146–47
Environmental Research Foundation, 146
Environmental Working Group, 141
ethnic/racial inequality, 18; and attitudes, 19; education, 20; income, 19; political, 20. *See also* environmental racism; race; racial violence; whites
ethnicity and gender, 21
ethnoviolence, 89. *See also* bias crimes; racial violence
executives, 14, 16–17. *See also* CEOs

Fairness and Accuracy in Reporting (FAIR), 37
Fagan, Jeffrey, 47
Fair Housing Act, 52
family violence, 78. *See also* domestic violence
Family Violence Research Program, 83
Federal Bureau of Investigation (FBI), 62, 92, 172
federal government: and housing segregation, 51–52
Federal Housing Administration (FHA), 51
female headed households, 59
Ferguson, Colin, 1, 136, 163
fetal mortality, 125
Fifteenth Amendment, 50
Film Recovery Systems, Inc., 106
fire deaths, 124
firings, 28. *See also* doublespeak
Florida, 145
Fontanarosa, Phil, 2
Food and Drug Administration (FDA), 133, 136
food industry, 30
Ford Foundation, 35
Ford, Gerald, 35
Ford Motors. *See* Pinto
Foreign Intelligence Advisory Board, 170
Foreign Relations Subcommittee on Terrorism, Narcotics, and International Operations, 63
Fowles, Richard, 55
Fox, Robin, 8

Freedom Summer, 189
Freeman, Richard, 59
Fuhrman, Mark, 95

gang rape, 1, 83–84
gangs, 56, 59, 60. See also youth violence
Gary, Indiana, 61
Gates, Darryl, 96
Gay and Lesbian Antiviolence Project, 87
gays. See homophobic violence; homosexuality; Schindler
Gelles, Richard, 78, 80
gender: and ethnicity, 21; and health, 132–35; and income, 21; and occupational health, 113–14; and occupations, 21; and politics, 21
gender inequality, 20–31; and homophobia, 27; and rape, 83
gender roles, 132
General Dynamics, 170
General Electric, 25, 36, 170; and nuclear facilities, 158
General Motors (GM), 27, 29, 58, 119; campaign contributions, 34; pick-up trucks, 138; and safety, 137
Gergen, David, 35
germ warfare. See biological warfare
G.I. Bill, 51
Gibbs, Lois, 142, 145
Gibson, James W., 164
Ginsberg, Ruth Bader, 34
Glazer, Myron and Penina, 26
Golden, Jay, 25
Goodyear, 110, 169
Greider, William, 30
Grenada, 162
Griffith, Michael, 90
Grumann, 170
GTE, 116
"Gulf Syndrome," 155
Gulf War, 154, 161, 162; and sexual assaults, 163. See also Iraq; Kuwait
Gunn, David, 86
guns, 38–39, 62, 164–65; deaths from, 139. See also domestic violence
Gunsite Ranch, 164
Guthrie, Woody, 105

Haiti, 166, 167
Hall, Bob, 114
Harlem, 61, 97–98, 128
Harlins, Latesha, 93
Harlow, Benton, 24–25
Harrison, Bennett, 117
Harvard University, 156. See also atomic testing
Hatch, Orrin, 110
hate crimes. See bias crimes; racial violence
Hattori, Yoshihiro, 38–39
Hawkins, Yusuf, 76, 90
hazardous waste. See toxic waste
HE/14, 24
health. See structural violence
health care, 81; faulty products, 136–37; lobbying on, 31. See also Jackson Hole Group
health insurance, 127. See also Medicaid; Medicare
heart catheters, 136
Helms, Jesse, 91
herbicides, 142
Heritage Foundation, 36
Heuring, Dennis L., 137
higher education, 161
Hispanics. See Latinos
HIV. See AIDS
Hoboken, 92
holidays: and domestic violence, 80
Holliday, George, 95
Home Owners Loan Corporation (HOLC), 52
homicide, 5–6, 55; and Native Americans, 132; women and, 78. See also narcotics; violence
homophobia, 88
homophobic violence, 1, 76, 87–88. See also bias crimes; Jones, Jenny
homosexuality, 77, 181. See also homophobic violence
Hooker Chemical Co., 142
Hoover Institute, 36
Horton, Willie, 47, 91
housing: affordable, 81
Howard Beach, 89–90
Hughes Aircraft, 143
Hyde Amendment, 85
hypertension. See cardiovascular disease

immigrants, 50, 54; rights of, 181.
  See also Irish; Italians; Jews
"imperial alibis," 171–72
Imperial Food Products, 112
incarceration. See prisons
incinerators, 141
income, 13; distribution of, 16; and
  domestic violence, 80; and prison,
  55; and rape, 82; and voting, 182–83.
  See also ethnicity/race; gender;
  Reagan
Indian Health Service, 132
individualism, 181
Indonesia, 166. See also East Timor;
  Nike
industrialization, 50. See also
  deindustrialization
inequality, 13–14; and decision-making,
  56; trends and violence, 77. See also
  class inequality; command posts;
  ethnicity/race; gender
Infant Mortality Rate (IMR), 124–25
Inland Steel Co., 111
inoculations, 126
institutional racism, 96
international comparisons:
  executive salaries, 17; health, 118,
  125; military spending, 159, 171;
  prison populations, 55; rape, 82;
  violence, 7
International Ladies Garment Workers'
  Union (ILGWU), 18
International Telephone & Telegraph
  (ITT), 168
interpersonal violence, 76–77, 180; and
  gender, 77–88. See also domestic
  violence; homophobic violence;
  organized violence; racial violence;
  rape; street crime
intimate violence, 78. See also
  domestic violence
Iowa, 83
Iraq, 161, 173. See also Gulf War
Irish: and crime, 46
Italians: and crime, 46, 50

Jack in the Box, 137
Jackall, Robert, 27
Jackson Hole Group, 36
Jackson State, 172

James, David, 22
Japan, 39
Japanese Americans: internment, 35,
  172
Jersey City, 92
Jews, 93; and crime, 46–47
job creation, 52. See also suburbs
Jones, Jenny, 1
Johnson & Johnson, 17
Johnson, Lyndon, 35

Kennedy administration, 153
Kennedy, Edward, 88
Kennedy, John F., 35
Kent State, 172
Kerr-McGee, 25, 26
Kerry, John, 63
kidney disease, 118
Kiely, Dr. John, 124
King, Martin Luther, Jr., 162
King, Rodney, 93, 96
Kissinger, Henry, 169
Kiston, Harold, Jr., 169
Klanwatch, 92
Koreans, 93
Kozol, Jonathan, 20
Kuwait, 171

labor movement. See unions
Labor Party, 188–89
language: manipulation of, 86; and the
  military, 152, 154. See also
  doublespeak
Latinos: crime fears, 45; income, 19,
  20; and occupational health, 112–13;
  and prison, 55. See also colonias
lead poisoning, 126
Lehman, John F., 169
lesbians. See Gay and Lesbian
  Antiviolence Project; homophobic
  violence; homosexuality
Liam, Paula R., 118
Liam, Ramsey, 118
life expectancy, 128
liver disease, 130
lobbying, 22, 30–32
Lockheed, 170
Long Island Railroad (L.I.R.R.):
  shooting, 1–2. See also Ferguson
Lorillard, Inc., 34

Los Angeles, 56, 59, 69, 82, 95; bias crimes in, 93; and pollution, 144, 145; racial violence in, 92; unemployment in, 57; urban disorders in, 98–99. *See also* WATCHDOG
Los Angeles Police Department (L.A.P.D.), 95–96
Love Canal, 141, 142
LTV Aerospace and Defense, 170
lumpenproletariat, 15

McCarthy, Joseph, 172
McCarthyism, 181
McCloy, John J., 35
McGehee, Ralph, 23
McNamara, Robert, 153
Malcolm X, 65
male bonding: and rape, 83
managed competition, 36
marital rape, 82
Marsh Aviation, 29
Martin Marietta, 25–26, 170
Marx, Karl, 15, 114
masculinity: and domestic violence, 81; and rape, 82, 84; socialization for, 87
Massachusetts Institute of Technology (MIT). *See* atomic testing
Mazzocchi, Tony, 189
Mead, Johnson, 137
media: and corporate crime, 105. *See also* cultural apparatus; individualism
Medicaid, 85, 126–27, 160
medical research: bias in, 135
Medicare, 31, 160
mental illness, 118, 155
Merck, 17
Merva, Mary, 55
Metropolitan Insurance, 36
Mexican immigrants, 54
Metzger, Tom, 94
middle class, 14
Milgram, Stanley, 23
militarism, 151–73; and interpersonal violence, 153–57; and police violence, 97; and sexual violence, 163–64; and structural violence, 154–55, 157–59
military: cultural influence of, 163–65; and inequality, 152; and narcotics, 65; and paramilitary activities, 164; sexual harassment in, 163; spending, 151–52, 154, 170–71. *See also* "imperial alibis"; language manipulation; military-industrial complex; Pentagon; Tailhook
military-industrial complex, 169
military interventions, 162, 167. *See also* "imperial alibis"
militias, 165; and environmentalists, 146
Million Man March, 183
Mills, C. Wright, 22, 36, 183
Milwaukee, 47, 53
Minneapolis, 79
Mokhiber, Russell, 105
Monroe Doctrine, 166
Moore, Joan, 63
Morgan, J. P., 105
Morton Thiokol, 24
Motor Vehicle Safety Act, 166
Moynihan, Daniel Patrick, 35, 162
multinationals, 165–66; and narcotics, 65

Nader, Ralph, 29, 138
"narco-terrorism," 66
narcotics: and business, 66; and crime and violence, 62; and employment/unemployment, 61–62; and the government, 63–66; as social control, 68
National Association of Manufacturers, 110
National Crime Survey, 79
National Guard, 172
National Highway Traffic Safety Administration, 138
National Institute of Justice, 2
National Research Council, 2
National Rifle Association (NRA), 164
National Safety Workplace Institute, 107
National Science Foundation, 2
National Toxic Campaign, 146
National Women's Health Network, 133
Native Americans, 130–32; and the environment, 187; health, 131–32
Nazis, 35
Neo-Mul-Soy. *See* Syntex
Neo-Nazis, 94

nerve gas, 157
neutralization techniques, 28–30
New Jersey, 53, 140. See also Asian Indians; Camden; Newark
New Jersey Council of Churches, 53
New Mexico, 146
New York, 46, 50, 52, 53; employment/unemployment, 58; and police violence, 96; repression in, 172
Newark, 90
Nicaragua, 167, 168
Nike, 166
Nitz, Michael, 92
Nixon, Richard, 35
Noriega, Manuel, 64
North Atlantic Treaty Organization (NATO), 153
North Carolina, 143–44
North Dakota, 83
North, Oliver, 64
nuclear testing. See atomic testing
nutrition, 125, 131

Occidental Petroleum. See Hooker Chemical Co.
occupations, 13–14; and African-Americans, 19; and gender, 21
occupational health, 107, 110
Occupational Safety and Health Act (OSH), 109
Occupational Safety and Health Administration (OSHA), 108–11, 114
O'Connor, Sandra Day, 34
Office of Technology Assessment, 160
Oglala Sioux, 131
Oil, Chemical and Atomic Workers' Union, 26, 188
Oklahoma City, 93
Omnibus Crime Bill, 70, 108
Operation Rescue, 86
Order, The, 94
Oreffice, Paul, 29
organized crime, 65

Paisley, Melvyn R., 169
Panama, 154
paramilitary groups: and abortion, 86. See also militias
Parenti, Michael, 179

Paterson, N.J., 98
PCBs, 143
Pentagon, 154, 171. See also militarism; military intervention; military spending
Pepsico, 17, 36, 105
Perdue, 113
perspectives on violence, 7–10
Pfizer, 17
pharmaceutical industry, 31–32
Pharmaceutical Manufacturers Association, 36
Philadelphia, 53
Philip Morris, 17, 29, 33, 34
Physicians for a National Health Program, 36
Pima, 131
Pinto, 138
plutonium, 156, 157. See also Silkwood
¡PODER!, 183
police: and domestic violence, 77, 78–79, 81; and homophobic violence, 88; and racial violence, 95–99; and racism, 48; and rape, 84
policy formation process, 35–36
Political Action Committees (PACs), 31–32; types of, 33
political campaign contributions, 32–34
politicians, 178
pollution. See air pollution; environmental racism; WATCHDOG; water pollution
pornography, 101n. 29
post-traumatic stress disorder, 154–55. See also "Gulf Syndrome"
poultry processing, 111–14
power, 21–22; and rape, 84; and unemployment, 58. See also bureaucracy; command posts
Pratt and Whitney, 170
pregnancy: and domestic violence, 78
prisoners, 54–55; characteristics of, 55, 67, 68
prisons, 66, 180; as business, 68; cost of, 67; and crime rates, 67; and narcotic crimes, 66; violence in, 66
Procter & Gamble, 110, 116, 145
profit motive: and structural violence, 104–6

profits, 18, 22, 114–15; attitudes toward, 182; and auto safety, 137–38; and environmental pollution, 141; and military contracts, 170; and overseas investments, 166. See also A. H. Robins
Prohibition, 46, 61, 62
Project HIP-HOP, 187–88
Prudential, 36
Puerto Rico, 70, 115
Pymm Thermometer Corporation, 106

Quayle, Dan, 99, 110

race, 18; and abortion, 85; and AIDS, 134–35; and cancer, 128; and child abuse, 80; and crime fears, 45–46; and health, 127–32; and homophobic violence, 87; and income, 20; and military testing, 157; and occupational health and safety, 111–13; and prenatal care, 125; and stress, 129–30; and structural violence, 124–32. See also ethnic/racial inequality
racial violence, 1–2, 76, 85–99; characteristics of, 89. See also Asian Indians; Chin; Griffith; Hawkins
racism, 181. See also Billings; ethnic/racial inequality
radiation, 155–56. See also atomic testing; General Electric; plutonium; Silkwood
Radiation Exposure Compensation, 156
rape, 1, 82, 85; and male bonding, 83; rates, 82. See also "Spur Posse"
Reagan administration, 132, 136–37, 138, 169; and the environment, 142, 146; and OSHA, 110
Reagan–Bush, 151, 169
Reagan, Ronald, 18, 34, 35, 84; and Heritage Foundation, 36; and income inequality, 15; on unemployment, 56–57
redlining. See segregation
regulatory agencies, 106
Reich, Robert, 111
repetitive motion disorders, 114
repression, 172–73. See also police

reproductive choice. See abortion
reproductive problems, 114
Republican Party: and abortion, 84
reservations, 130–31. See also Native Americans; Oglala; Pima
"reserve army of labor," 114
restrictive covenants, 52
Reynolds, R. J., 28, 34
Rockefeller Foundation, 36
Rockwell International, 24, 158, 170
Roe v. Wade, 84, 85
rogue-states, 171
Roosevelt, Franklin D., 35
Rosenberg, Mark, 2
Ryan, William, 179

San Francisco, 60, 183
Sanders, Bernard, 183
Sandinistas, 64. See also Nicaragua
scapegoating, 90–91, 182. See also racial violence
School of the Americas, 168
School of Assassins. See School of the Americas
segregation, 49–54, 181; and power, 56; and violence, 49. See also discrimination; suburbs
Service Employees International Union (SEIU), 188
sexual assault. See military; rape
sharecropping, 50
shelters: and domestic abuse, 81
Shiley, Inc., 136
Shipler, David K., 96
Silkwood, Karen, 25, 26
Simpson, O. J., 77
Sloane, Alfred, 137
Smith-Kline, 136
Smith, Roger, 27
Smith, Susan, 48
social change, 180. See also solutions
social distance, 27
social isolation, 80
social programs: and military spending, 160–62. See also solutions
socialization, 77, 163; and rape, 83. See also King
sociobiology, 9
Socol, Ira, 97
Soldier of Fortune (SOF), 164

solutions: to violence, 56, 145–47, 178–89
Soref, Michael, 22
South Dakota, 131
Southern Poverty Law Center, 92
Soviet Union, 152–53; and Central America, 167–68. See also anticommunism; Cold War; militarism
spatial mismatch hypothesis, 54
sports, 46
spouse abuse. See domestic violence
"Spur Posse," 82
Steinberg, Stephen, 50
stereotypes, 46, 48, 54, 96–97; and gender violence, 82, 84; and homophobia, 87–88; and the police, 96–97; and racial violence, 89–91, 92; and unemployment, 54. See also Horton
Stevens, John Paul, 34
"Stonewall Rebellion," 88
Strategic Defense Initiative (SDI), 169
Straus, Murray A., 78, 80, 83
street crime, 45–74; compared to structural violence, 109
stress: and domestic violence, 79–80; and racism, 129
structural approach: to violence, 4–5, 9–10
structural violence, 6–7, 8, 104–19, 124–47; and consumers, 135–39; and the environment, 139–46; international comparisons, 6–7, 8; and unemployment, 114–19; and workers, 104–17. See also profit motive
Stuart, Charles, 47
Stubbing, Edmund, 97
suburbanization, 53
suburbs, 51, 52–53
suicide, 118, 130, 132
Sullivan, Mercer, 57
Superfund, 142
Supreme Court, 52
surplus labor, 47
Sutherland, Edwin, 105
Swartz, Joel, 106–7
Sweden: and occupational health, 111

Sweeney, John, 188
Syntex Laboratories, 136

Tailhook, 163–64
taxes, 18. See also military-industrial complex; Puerto Rico
Teller, Edward, 169
Terry, Randall, 186
Texaco, 185–86
textile industry, 18
Textron, 170
theories of violence. See perspectives
think tanks. See policy formation process
Three Mile Island, 29
Tiger, Lionel, 8
Times Beach, 141, 142
tobacco, 166
tobacco industry, 33, 34. See also Lorillard, Inc., Philip Morris; Reynolds
Tonry, Michael, 67
Tower, John, 169–70
toxic wastes, 140, 141, 142, 143–44. See also environmental racism
transportation, 51–52
Truman, Harry, 35
Tucson, Arizona, 142

underclass, 14, 15
unemployment, 115, 155; and crime, 46–47, 54–56, 59, 61; and domestic violence, 80; and military spending, 159–60; and overseas investment, 166; and racial violence, 90; and rape, 83; and structural violence, 114–19; and suburbanization, 52. See also crime
unions: and incomes, 17; membership, 17, 18; and occupational health and safety, 109; and racism, 50, 186; and solutions, 188–89; weakness of, 109. See also AFL-CIO; American Clothing and Textile Workers' Union; International Ladies Garment Workers' Union; United Farm Workers
Uniroyal, 110
United Church of Christ, 144
United Farm Workers (UFW), 112

U.S. Chamber of Commerce, 110
Useem, Michael, 105
United States, 6–7; military bases, 153. See also international comparisons
urban rebellions. See Harlem; Los Angeles
urbanization: and rape, 83

Veterans Administration (VA), 51
veterans' hospitals, 127
Vietnam, 181
Vietnam War, 154, 172
violence, 3, 6–7; concern about, 2; defined, 4; female, 8; as public health problem, 2; and quality of life, 2; roots of, 179; trends, 5. See also gender violence; homicide; homophobic violence; interpersonal violence; racial violence; solutions; structural violence
voting, 182–83; and women's rights, 181

Wages, Bob, 188
war: See Gulf War; militarism; military; Vietnam War
"warrior" culture, 151
Warsaw Pact, 153
Washington, D.C., 56
WATCHDOG, 185–86
water contamination, 141
Waters, Maxine, 65
wealth, 13, 15, 16
weapons gap, 153
Webb, Gary, 64–65
welfare, 58; and domestic violence, 81.
See also Aid to Families with Dependent Children
Whirlpool, 116
"whistle-blowers," 25–27
White Aryan Resistance (WAR), 94
white collar crime, 105. See also corporate crime
white males, 77
whites: and child abuse, 80; and employment, 57; fear of crime, 46; racial attitudes of, 47–48, 49
Whitman, Christine Todd, 140
Wichita, 86
Wilson, Bob. See marital rape
Wilson, William J., 117
women: physical abuse of, 80. See also domestic violence; gender; rape
women's movement: and domestic violence, 81; and health, 133; and rape, 84
working class, 14
working conditions, 181. See also occupational health; structural violence
working poor, 14, 15
World Bank, 168
World War II, 152. See also Soviet Union
worldview, 28

Xerox Corporation, 34, 116

Yeager, Peter C., 104
youth: and crime, 47; and violence, 62, 178. See also gangs; ¡PODER!; Project HIP-HOP